CORPORATE
SOCIAL
RESPONSIBILITY

Recent Titles from Quorum Books

Innovation Through Technical and Scientific Information: Government and Industry Cooperation
Science and Public Policy Program, University of Oklahoma: Steven Ballard, Thomas E. James, Jr., Timothy I. Adams, Michael D. Devine, Lani L. Malysa, and Mark Meo

Transformations in French Business: Political, Economic, and Cultural Changes from 1981 to 1987
Judith Frommer and Janice McCormick, editors

Economics and Antitrust Policy
Robert J. Larner and James W. Meehan, Jr., editors

A Legal Guide to EDP Management
Michael C. Gemignani

U.S. Commercial Opportunities in the Soviet Union: Marketing, Production, and Strategic Planning Perspectives
Chris C. Carvounis and Brinda Z. Carvounis

An Analysis of the New Financial Institutions: Changing Technologies, Financial Structures, Distribution Systems, and Deregulation
Alan Gart

The Commercialization of Outer Space: Opportunities and Obstacles for American Business
Jonathan N. Goodrich

Computer Power and Legal Language: The Use of Computational Linguistics, Artificial Intelligence, and Expert Systems in the Law
Charles Walter, editor

Direct Marketing, Direct Selling, and the Mature Customer: A Research Study
James R. Lumpkin, Marjorie J. Caballero, and Lawrence B. Chonko

The Ethics of Organizational Transformation: Mergers, Takeovers, and Corporate Restructuring
W. Michael Hoffman, Robert Frederick, and Edward S. Petry, Jr., editors

Cable TV Advertising: In Search of the Right Formula
Rajeev Batra and Rashi Glazer, editors

The Marketer's Guide to Selling Products Abroad
Robert E. Weber

CORPORATE SOCIAL RESPONSIBILITY

Guidelines for Top Management

Jerry W. Anderson, Jr.

QUORUM BOOKS

New York • Westport, Connecticut • London

Library of Congress Cataloging-in-Publication Data

Anderson, Jerry W.
　　Corporate social responsibility.
　　Includes index.
　　1. Industry—Social aspects.　2. Industry—
Social aspects—History.　I. Title.
　　HD60.A43　1989　　658.4′08　　　88-23952
　　ISBN 0–89930–272–6 (lib. bdg. : alk. paper)

British Library Cataloguing in Publication Data is available.

Library of Congress Catalog Card Number: 88–23952
ISBN: 0–89930–272–6

First published in 1989 by Quorum Books

Greenwood Press, Inc.
88 Post Road West, Westport, Connecticut 06881

Printed in the United States of America

The paper used in this book complies with the
Permanent Paper Standard issued by the National
Information Standards Organization (Z39.48–1984).

10　9　8　7　6　5　4　3　2　1

Copyright Acknowledgment

Chapter 2 of this book originally appeared in *Business Horizons* 29, no. 4 (July/August 1986): 22–27. Reprinted by
permission.

Contents

Figures and Tables

Figures

Tables

Preface

Social responsibility is an area of concern that has existed since the early days of mankind. It is only in the last two decades, however, that great emphasis has emerged in this area. This has resulted in a growing interaction between the government, business, and the stakeholder (society as a whole). In the past, business has had to concern itself primarily with the economic results of its decisions; today, business must also consider and weigh the legal, ethical, moral, and social impact and repercussions of each of its decisions.

This book brings this newly emphasized area of social concern and responsibility into clear focus. The procedure used for the presentation, review, and evaluation of social responsibility will imbue the reader with an excellent understanding about what is involved in this area. The numerous references found at the end of each chapter will permit deeper reading and insight into specific issues and areas should the reader desire to pursue them. The scenarios (or mini-cases) found at the end of Chapters 7 through 13 present challenging problems for discussion on the various areas of social responsibility; each scenario is based on a situation that actually occurred in the business world.

Part I covers the background and presents a macro overview of social responsibility of the corporation. Chapter 1 defines what business, society, and social responsibility are and how they are interrelated to one another; it also presents arguments for and against business becoming deeply involved in social responsibility. Chapter 2 is a macro overview of the total social responsibility issue as it pertains to the legal, ethical-moral, and philanthropic areas of involvement by business; this chapter appeared in the July/August 1986 issue of *Business Horizons* and is reprinted here with their permission.

Part II covers the history and development of social responsibility in business from its earliest days. Much of what is included in today's social responsibility issues evolved from social concern in the distant and not so distant past. Only by thoroughly understanding the past can we understand the present and build for the future. As a result, this history briefly discusses major business and social growth and issues, and government, business, society interaction on these issues, from the time of the early Egyptians and Babylonians up through the social issues and legislation of the present day.

Part III examines the interaction and interrelationships of social responsibilities and all of its facets. Chapters 7 through 11 examine the legal aspect of the social responsibility and interaction process in some detail; Chapters 7 through 10 examine the legal external interaction issues, while Chapter 11 looks at the legal interaction issues. Chapter 12 discusses the moral-ethical interactions and issues. Chapter 13 scrutinizes philanthropic interactions and issues.

In Part IV, Chapter 14 reviews, expands upon, and evaluates the social audit and how it can be used by business to determine how complaint business is in the area of social responsibility. Chapter 15 is the conclusion of the book; it includes evaluations, conclusions and recommendations for future involvement of the government, business, and the stakeholders in social responsibility programs.

An undertaking of this type requires considerable assistance. In this area I would like to give deep thanks to three women in particular: Tina Schulz who helped research, amass, and catalog the several thousand reference articles that were gathered and reviewed for the writing of this book; Margaret Maybury who typed and helped review the manuscript several times before its completion; and, my wife, Joan, who gave me moral and spiritual support throughout the entire undertaking. I would also like to give thanks to Tom Gannon for his help and heartfelt understanding while preparing the manuscript; it was a joy and a pleasure working with him and Quorum Books.

PART I

Background and a Macro Overview of Social Responsibility and the Corporation

1

Background

The view has been gaining widespread acceptance that corporate officials and labor leaders have a "social responsibility" that goes beyond serving the interest of their stockholders or their members.... Few trends could so thoroughly undermine the very foundation of our free society as the acceptance by corporate officials of a social responsibility other than to make as much money for their stockholders as possible. This is a fundamentally subversive doctrine.... The claim that business should contribute to the support of charitable activities.... is an inappropriate use of corporate funds in a free enterprise society.

Milton Friedman[1]

I maintain that business must change its priorities. We are not in business to make maximum profit for our shareholders. We are in business for only one reason—to serve society. Profit is our reward for doing it well. If business does not serve society, society will not tolerate our profits or even our existence.

Kenneth Dayton[2]

These quotes depict the dilemma that many businesses are in today. They are being pushed, pulled, shoved, and criticized (and only occasionally commended) from all sides on what is proper and correct for them to do in the area of social responsibility. Numerous businesses today still have only a minimum awareness of what social responsibility is, what it means, or what they should do (if anything) about it. Many of the smaller and medium-sized businesses (and even a few of the larger businesses) do not have a major or separate functional area within their business enterprise assigned to handle such problems. They find it no simple matter to formulate and implement socially responsible actions and programs. In spite of these problems, all businesses today must become concerned and involved in this area.

After reading the lead-in quotes to this chapter, one might wonder how and why two well-known, sincere men can express two almost diametrically opposed views on how a business should treat the question of social responsibility. These quotes certainly show why there is much confusion and much debate on the subject of what businesses should do about social responsibility; they do not, however, show why this difference of opinion exists or how it has evolved. The remainder of this chapter will attempt to shed some light on this matter by first examining what is meant by business, society, and social responsibility and then showing the relationship between the three areas.

BUSINESS DEFINED

Business is composed of the collection of private, commercially profit-oriented organizations that range in size from the single proprietor (the local TV repair shop, florist) to the corporate giants (Procter & Gamble, IBM, Exxon) and all the small and medium-sized organizations in between the two extremes. When business is defined in this all encompassing manner it is easy to see that businesses of all sizes and in all types of industries are included. However, in spite of this broad coverage of businesses, much of the emphasis on being socially responsible is borne by "big" business and "selected" industries. Big business is highly visible for many reasons (well-known name, national advertising and distribution, multiple products) and is thus more often in the critical eye of the public, which in many instances equates bigness with "power" and "badness." Selected industries such as manufacturing firms and power companies are readily visible because of their air, water, and chemical pollution problems. In the case of the automobile industry, it is quite often in the limelight because of the many dangerous problems (actual and perceived) that have existed with automobiles. Pharmaceutical and other similar companies are very visible because of special problems, such as those associated with Tylenol and Rely tampons. Small and medium-sized businesses, nonnational businesses and businesses such as department stores may not receive as much critical scrutiny because they are not as highly visible, do not manufacture dangerous products, or emit large volumes of pollutants.

Even though much emphasis (and possibly too much emphasis) is being focused on the large businesses, sight cannot be lost of the fact that many of the same problems that exist for large businesses also exist for the small and medium-sized businesses. In many instances the rules and regulations impose hardships upon the smaller businesses because of their limited work force and financial resources; they may, therefore, require and in some instances deserve special consideration in certain situations.

SOCIETY DEFENDED

Society may be defined as a grouping of people having certain common interests, manner of life, activities, purpose, values, traditions, or goals and objectives. A society can thus be composed of individuals, small groups of people such as found in a local PTA, or larger organizations such as found in a local or state government, the federal government, or the country as a whole. These groups or societies can be working for the same or similar goals and objectives, have some overlapping goals and objectives, be in direct opposition to one another, or any combination thereof. Most of these groups serve their own self-interests and their power is widely decentralized (total power is not controlled by any one society such as labor, the military, the government, business, or any combination of societies). This is a pluralistic society that maximizes freedom of expression, action, and responsibility; this in turn results in a widely diversified set of loyalties to many different causes and organizations and minimizes the danger that any one leader of any one organization will be left uncontrolled. All of these advantages and disadvantages, along with its structure and composition, are in part some of the cause for the differences in viewpoint on what social responsibility is, what it should be, what it should encompass, and what it should accomplish.

Since there are so many different societies, more popularly referred to today as "stakeholders" (employees; stockholders; consumers; minorities; womens groups; suppliers; competitors; community neighbors; cultural groups; church organizations; charitable organizations; labor unions; environmental action groups; financial institutions; public interest groups; local state, and federal governments; the press), business is buffeted on all sides to go in different directions as each group or society dictates its wishes and desires. The business is usually driven, or at least tilted, in the direction of the desires of the strongest society. This may be its own governing body in the case of a few powerful or self-owned businesses; the local, state, or federal government; its stockholders; or any number of the other societies.

SOCIAL RESPONSIBILITY DEFINED

The concept of social responsibility, or social responsiveness as some now prefer to call it, is a continually evolving concept and means different things to different people.[3] Numerous studies conducted during the 1970s and 1980s have tried to arrive at a consensus definition of social responsibility but have failed to do so. Much of the research attempts to identify various kinds of socially responsive activities, present the list of these activities to the business manager, and then measure and tabulate the relative frequency of response to which the activities are practiced by those agencies or people being questioned.[4] Since different issues are more or less relevant to different industries, the results from these studies are often confounded and confused. Although this may make it difficult to present a precise definition of social responsibility that will be acceptable to everyone, at least the major components that go into making up what social responsibility is can and should be explained.

The concept of social responsibility has been with us since the beginning of mankind and has slowly evolved to its present state. The first comprehensive approach to modern era social responsibility was ushered in in 1953 with the publication of Howard R. Bowen's book *Social Responsibilities of the Businessman*.[5] Bowen felt that public responsibility, social obligations, and business morality were synonyms for social responsibility and described the term *social responsibilities of businessmen* as: "It refers to the obligation of businessmen to pursue those policies, to make those decisions, or to follow those lines of action which are desirable in terms of objectives and values of our society."[6]

In 1971 the Committee for Economic Development (CED) published a book in which they treated the relationship between business and society as a social contract between the two groups, with business' major obligation being the providing of those goods and services that society needs.[7] Traditionally, these needs have been economic, such as production of goods and services, job opportunities, an improving standard of living, and a higher gross national product (GNP). This traditional contract between business and society has been changing because of the addition of new social value responsibilities placed upon business. Some of these new social value responsibilities include: stricter compliance with local, state, federal, and international laws; social problems; human values; health care; pollution; quality of life; equal employment opportunities; sexual harassment; elimination of poverty; child care and elderly care; support of the arts and universities; and many others. Basically, each of these areas of social value responsibility can be placed in one or more of three broader categories or headings of social responsiveness; these three categories are legal, moral-ethical, and philanthropic.

Many people and groups (the stakeholders) feel that business has a moral obligation to correct the social problems that beset society; at the same time, many of these stakeholders feel that much of the business community has not and is not adequately dealing with many of these social problems of concern.[8] All of these forces place pressure on business to respond to the emerging major social issues of the day.

Many businesses today feel that in order to respond effectively and efficiently to the major social issues and demands of the day, corporate social policy must be integrated into corporate strategy.[9] Corporate executives will have to include social policy guidelines into the strategic plans from which the functional policies and operational plans will be derived; the burden of implementing and achieving the social goals will lie on the shoulders of middle and lower management. As a result of this approach, "several corporations have been extremely effective in translating the concept of responsibility into practice—and increasing profits at the same time."[10] This is definitely the basic approach that some of the larger more efficient and profitable businesses are taking today. Peter Drucker expresses this concept by saying: " 'To do good in order to do well,' that is to convert social needs and problems into profitable business opportunities, is rarely considered by today's advocates of 'social responsibility.' "[11] William Norris (the founder and CEO of Control Data Corporation) feels "that it is the purpose of business to do well by doing good."[12] SmithKline, Johnson and Johnson, and Delta Airlines are other companies that have joined the "do good by doing well" bandwagon.[13]

Margaret Stroup and Ralph Neubert of Monsanto feel that the evolution of social responsibility has been from voluntary ("doing good," at reduced business profits by consuming resources) to mandatory (pressure from stakeholders to force certain desired social responses and actions, again at a cost to the business) to investments in the future (social responsibility becomes an investment that improves the long-term performance of a business) and that as a result of this evolution, "Corporations are beginning to realize that, for their survival and competitive advantage, they must evolve from doing good to doing better. Only slowly is recognition growing that long-term value to the corporation of conducting its business in a socially responsible manner far outweighs short-term costs."[14]

This concept of "doing good by doing well," or progressing from "doing good to doing better," in the area of social responsibility simply means that social responsibility is and should be handled as a corporate investment that will result in a long-run corporate profit and not a corporate expense. Most businesses would probably like to achieve this goal, but for many businesses this may be easier said than done.

Although a very desirable and commendable objective, not all people and businesses feel that the "doing good to doing better" concept is achievable or readily applicable to their business. Not all Canadian, European, or multinational businesses look at and treat social responsibility in the same manner as do strictly U.S. businesses.[15] For U.S. businesses, the concept is not totally new; nor is it free from some dangerous pitfalls or the ultimate solution to all social responsibility problems. It is also probably overly optimistic for application by many companies. Further examination of this side of the social responsibility coin will divulge reasons for these comments.

Most dictionaries define *investment* along the lines of "committing or use of (money, capital, etc.) for the purchase of property, securities, a business project, etc., with the expectation of a profit." Therefore, any investment, by definition, is expected to result in a profit for the company. The question must then be asked, can and should all social responsibility items, no matter how judiciously handled, result in increased profits for the company? Is this the best place to invest the money, or can greater returns be achieved elsewhere? These and other similar questions must be answered when it comes to company growth and survival.

Before the "doing good to doing better" concept can work it must have the complete blessing and support of top management and be inculcated and totally supported all the way down the organizational ladder. Studies have shown that this may take several years to accomplish.[16] It is a long-term educational process. If everyone in the company does not support the concept, it is subject to failure anywhere along the line. If outside stakeholders are not properly educated and do not understand the concept and processes involved—and if they do not agree with it—then the entire program can falter and even fail.

In today's environment, when churches, public unions, individuals, foundations, and takeover artists all own large shares of stocks and speak out, many companies are now focusing their efforts on trimming operations and reallocating assets to improve short-term profits and balanced growth. As Stroup and Neubert point out in their article, the investment concept they propose will "improve the *long-term* performance of the enterprise" (emphasis added) if it can be properly formulated and implemented.[17] However, if, in the short run, the company goes out of business or is taken over, all this effort will go down the drain. Management's emphasis on short-term profit improvement will mean that internal competition for the same funds slated for social responsibility investment will become more intense among the internal managers. Keeping internal company priorities straight and yet having a sense of social responsibility thus becomes a difficult balancing act.

Keeping the company in business in order to keep people employed and still generating a reasonable profit for its stockholders are also primary concerns and top priorities of the company.

According to Edward G. Harkness, past chairman of the board of the Procter & Gamble Company: "There is no charity for charity's sake in our handing out the Company's money or in asking the Company's people to give of their time. Procter & Gamble's support of civic campaigns is now and always will be limited to what we believe represents the enlightened self-interest of business."[18] This is probably how many businesses feel and act.

Large companies, with large planning, policy, and strategy staffs, may be in a better position to make the "doing good to doing better" concept work. On the other hand, medium-sized and smaller companies with limited resources may have serious problems in applying this concept of social responsibility.

Two major obstacles that must be overcome for this concept to work, even to a limited extent, can both be listed under the heading of "education." To accomplish the concepts, goals, and objectives requires developing a company culture tuned to such a concept. Conditioning company culture requires an extensive educational process, which takes time and management commitment.

Of equal importance, however, is educating the stakeholder to understand what is going on in industry and what industry is trying to do. The stakeholder also has a social responsibility to be aware of and understand the socioeconomic process.

According to recent studies, students think that businesses make from 10 to 70 percent profit, with most students placing profit at 35 percent, almost 10 times the actual rate.[19] Studies also have shown that these same students have, at best, only limited legal, ethical, and moral standards presented to them.[20] These future businesspeople and decision makers get their notions and concepts about business primarily from the mass media and from their teachers. Therefore, an informed and educated employee and citizenry are also important and necessary cornerstones of social responsibility.

Most of the literature and most people's understanding places the major obligation for socially responsible actions on business. This is not a true or complete picture; the stakeholders also have certain responsibilities and obligations to business—it is a two-way street. For example, business has certain responsibilities and obligations to its employees and the employees have certain responsibilities and obligations to the business.

RELATIONSHIP BETWEEN BUSINESS, SOCIETY, AND SOCIAL RESPONSIBILITY

All of the major participants and components involved in social responsibility have now been briefly discussed. Social responsibility involves two major participants: business and society (stakeholders). It encompasses three major areas of responsibility: legal (complying with the law), setting—and abiding by—moral and ethical standards, and philanthropic giving. Simply defined, social responsibility is the obligation of both business and society (stakeholders) to take proper legal, moral-ethical, and philanthropic actions that will protect and improve the welfare of both society and business as a whole; all of this must of course be accomplished within the economic structures and capabilities of the parties involved.

ARGUMENTS FOR AND AGAINST SOCIAL RESPONSIBILITY

Now that social responsibility has been defined, it is not unfair to ask the question, "Why should business get involved in it, and what are the advantages and disadvantages of becoming involved in social responsibility?

Why Get Involved in Social Responsibility?

There are many arguments that can be presented to justify why a company should and must get involved in and support social responsibility; however, Thomas Petit probably summarizes the reasons in two short points as well as most people do in a full page of arguments. Petit asserts that even though people such as Elton Mayo, Peter Drucker, and John Maynard Keynes have different views on the subject of social responsibility, they all agree on his two fundamental points: "(1) Industrial society faces serious human and social problems brought on largely by the rise of the large corporation, and (2) managers must conduct the affairs of the corporation in ways to solve or at least ameliorate these problems."[21]

This definition has at least two major implications associated with it: First, many of the social problems that are faced by industry today were brought on by the growth of business itself; second, business must take a leading role in rectifying these problems. It also implies that if industry does not take action on its own, these problems may get worse and business itself may have trouble surviving in the future. Business must either police itself or society in general may alter business conditions through pressure and law changes in a manner that will not permit some businesses to survive.

Major Arguments Supporting Social Responsibility

Today, to a greater extent than ever before, most people support companies becoming involved in social responsibility. For example, over the past 10 years, surveys taken in my graduate business policy and strategy course show that in all instances more than 90 percent of the students (average age of 35 and with an average of 10 years or more business experience) strongly support their company and other companies becoming involved in social responsibility activities. This is a marked increase over the number of similar business students who voted in the affirmative during the 1950s. Many reasons are given for these positive positions being held today. The quote by Kenneth Dayton at the beginning of this chapter reflects the reasoning of many companies for becoming involved in social responsibility projects. Some other major popular arguments for business supporting social responsibility activities are:

1. It is in the best long-run interest of the business to become intimately involved in and to promote and improve the communities in which it does its business.

2. It can and should improve the corporate and local image of the company.

3. It is in the stockholders best interest. By making communities a better place to live, it can entice superior and happier workers to the company who in turn will put out better products and increase profits.

4. Social actions can be profitable to the company if handled with care and forethought.
5. It increases the visibility of the business firm and the business system and places them in a more favorable light and makes them a more viable institution with the general public.
6. It will help prevent possible unpalatable and even destructive government regulations.
7. Business is partially responsible for getting themselves in the mess they are in so they should help to get themselves out of it.
8. Ethical-moral and sociocultural norms require it.
9. It will help maintain and gain customers.
10. Investors prefer to invest in socially responsible firms.
11. Governmental agencies have miserably failed to solve many of the existing social problems. Business has the necessary talent, money, and know-how to solve these problems so they should be encouraged to do so.
12. It is better to prevent the problems from occurring in the first place.
13. It is better to take some positive action than to take no action at all.

Major Arguments against Social Responsibility

The major prevalant view held against business actively participating in social responsibility activities is expressed in Milton Friedman's quote at the beginning of this chapter. Even Friedman stipulates that a company may participate in social responsibility activities if the marginal gains exceed the marginal costs. Some other popular major arguments against a company becoming involved in social responsibility activities are:

1. Society would be better off if it asked businesses only to maximize their efficiencies and thus lower costs.
2. It violates the policy of profit maximization, and as a result stockholders will suffer.
3. It will increase the price of the end item, and as a result all purchasers of the end item will suffer.
4. Most corporate executives lack the knowledge, perception, skills, and patience to deal with and solve society's problems.
5. Social actions cannot be measured, so why participate in them?
6. The trade balance against America will suffer. Higher priced domestic goods will cause purchasers to buy foreign goods and U.S. money will leave the country.
7. Businesses already have too much power. Increased activity in the social arena will only increase its power to remold society to their way of thinking.
8. Business is not directly accountable to the public; therefore, the public would have little or no control over where and how deeply a company became involved.
9. It decreases short-run profitability.
10. Stockholders are unhappy for numerous reasons.
11. Governments should pass the laws they want obeyed and enforce them and not expect business to go beyond the law in solving the problems of society.

12. If the government wants businesses to support social activities, it should give them adequate incentives to do so.

Conclusions about Businesses Performing Social Responsibility Activities

The question is not really whether a company should become involved in social responsibility activity, but rather how deeply a company should become involved in social responsibility activity. Every company most certainly must obey all social responsibility–oriented laws and requirements. They must also have a minimum code of morals and ethics to which all of their employees must agree and adhere; otherwise, each employee will establish and operate under his or her own standards to the possible detriment of the company and society as a whole.

Finally, in the area of philanthropy, each company must examine its physical capabilities, desires, and economic resources to determine just how far they want to go and can go in this area.

NOTES

1. Milton Friedman, *Capitalism and Freedom* (Chicago: University of Chicago Press, 1962), pp. 133, 135.

2. Kenneth Dayton, chairman, Dayton Hudson Corporation, "Seegal-Macy Lecture," delivered at the University of Michigan, Ann Arbor, October 30, 1975.

3. Peter Arlow and Martin J. Gannon, "Social Responsiveness, Corporate Structure, and Economic Performance," *Academy of Management Review* 7, no. 2 (1982): 235–241.

4. Vernon M. Buehler and Y. K. Shetty, "Managerial Response to Social Responsibility Challenge," *Academy of Management Journal* 19, no. 1 (March 1976): 66–78; Jules Cohn, "Is Business Meeting the Challenge of Urban Affairs?" *Harvard Business Review* 48, no. 2 (March–April 1970); John J. Corson and George A. Steiner, *Measuring Business's Social Performance: The Corporate Social Audit* (New York: Committee for Economic Development, 1974); Henry Eilbirt and Robert Parket, "The Current Status of Corporate Social Responsibility," *Business Horizons* 16, no. 4 (August 1973): 5–14; Robert Ford and Frank McLaughlin, "Defining Corporate Social Responsibility: A Three Group Survey," *Review of Business & Economic Research* 17, no. 1 (1981): 72–77; Robert Ford and Frank McLaughlin, "Perceptions of Socially Responsible Activities and Attitudes: A Comparison of Business School Deans and Corporate Chief Executives," *Academy of Management Journal* 27 no. 3 (1984): 666–674; Eugene G. Gomolka, "An Analysis of Social Responsibility Activities Undertaken by Small Companies," *Proceedings of the Academy of Management* (1975): 336–338; Louis Harris, "The Public Credibility of American Business," *The Conference Board Record* (March 1973): 33–38; Arthur M. Louis, "The View from the Pinnacle: What Business Thinks," *Fortune* (September 1969): 92–95; Milt Moskowitz, "Defining Corporate Social Responsibility: A Three Group Survey," *Business & Society Review* no. 45 (1983): 23–24.; Harlan C. Van Over and Sam Barone, "An Empirical Study of Responses of Executive Officers

of Large Corporations Regarding Corporate Social Responsibility," *Proceedings of the Academy of Management*, (1975): 339–341.

5. Howard R. Bowen, *Social Responsibilities of the Businessman* (New York, Harper & Brothers, 1953).

6. Ibid., p. 6.

7. Committee for Economic Development, *Social Responsibilities of Business Corporations* (Washington, D.C.: U.S. Government Printing Office, 1971).

8. Ralph Nader and Kenneth R. Andrews, "Reforming Corporate Governance/ Difficulties in Overseeing Ethical Policy," *California Management Review* 26, no. 4 (1984): 126–137; David Vogel, "Trends in Shareholder Activism: 1970–1982," *California Management Review* 25, no. 3 (1983): 68–87.

9. Archie B. Carroll and Frank Hoy, "Integrating Corporate Social Policy into Strategic Management," *Journal of Business Strategy* 4, no. 3 (1984) 48–57; Gregory A. Daneke and David J. Lemak, "Integrating Strategic Management and Social Responsibility," *Business Forum* 10, no. 2 (1985): 20–25.

10. Daneke and Lemak, "Integrating Strategic Management and Social Responsibility," p. 21.

11. Peter Drucker, "The New Meaning of Corporate Social Responsibility," *California Management Review* 26, no. 2 (1984): 53–63.

12. Ibid., p. 59.

13. John E. Fleming, "Whatever Happened to Social Responsibility?" *New Management* 2, no. 2 (1984): 44–49.

14. Margaret A. Stroup and Ralph L. Neubert, "Doing Good, Doing Better: Two Views of Social Responsibility—The Evolution of Social Responsibility," *Business Horizons* 30, no. 2 (1987): 23.

15. George Bicherstaffe, "What Companies Are Doing to Make Themselves Good Neighbors," *International Management UK* 36, no. 5 (1981): pp. 30–32, 35: Vassilios Filios, "Assessment of Attitude Toward Corporate Social Accountability in Britain," *Journal of Business Ethics* (Netherlands) 4, no. 3 (1985): 155–173; Allen R. Taylor, "Business and the Community," *Vital Speeches* 51, no. 5 (1984): 154–157.

16. Robert W. Ackerman, *The Social Challenge in Business* (Cambridge, Mass.: Harvard University Press, 1975); John W. Collins and Chris G. Ganotis, "Is Social Responsibility Sabotaged by the Rank and File?" *Business and Society Review/Innovation* 4, no. 3 (Autumn 1973): 82–88; Edwin A. Murray, "The Social Response Process in Commercial Banks: An Empirical Investigation," *Academy of Management Review* 1, no. 3 (July 1976): 5–15.

17. Stroup and Neubert, "Doing Good, Doing Better," p. 25.

18. See "Views on Corporate Responsibility," excerpts from the Procter & Gamble year-end annual meeting report, December 8, 1977, pp. 14–15.

19. Gerald J. DeBrunner, "Students, Teachers Need to Understand How Economy Works," *Cincinnati Business Courier*, December 22–28, 1986, p. 7.

20. Red M. Christenson, "Teaching Morality in Schools," *Cincinnati Enquirer*, December 16, 1986, p. A–10.

21. Thomas A. Petit, *The Moral Crisis in Management* (New York: McGraw-Hill, 1967), p. 58.

2

Social Responsibility and the Corporation

A company's social responsibility program has three major areas: complying with laws, setting—and abiding by—moral and ethical standards, and philanthropic giving. How can firms evaluate their strengths in each of these areas?

Social responsibility is a major subject of concern and action for all but the smallest or least aware of companies. Today it is generally accepted that business firms have social responsibilities that extend well beyond what in the past was commonly referred to simply as the "business economic function." In earlier times managers, in most cases, had only to concern themselves with the economic results of their decisions. Today managers must also consider and weigh the legal, ethical, moral, and social impact and repercussions of each of their decisions.

In many company organizations, however, this area of social responsibility is often not identified as a major or separate functional area. Quite often the responsibility for actions in this area is vested in an individual or small staff, frequently within the human resources management area. Personnel assigned to this area, then, have responsibility for social issues in three major areas:

1. Total compliance with international, federal, state, and local legislative laws and acts
2. Moral and ethical standards and procedures under which the firm will operate
3. Philanthropic giving

Most companies find it no simple matter to formulate and implement socially responsible actions and programs. However, all companies must become concerned and involved in this area. To operate without major disruptions, a company must at all times be in compliance with legal requirements—international, federal, state, and local. It must develop, establish, implement, and police a code of ethical and moral conduct for all members of its organization. In the area of philanthropic activity, where there is considerably more latitude of operations in how, when, where, and even *if* the company or division wants to contribute money or other resources to "worthy causes," the firm must deliberate about and resolve many questions prior to establishing fair and workable guidelines.

Gone are the "public be damned" attitudes once held by some companies. With a more active government and populace, company social responsibility in each of the three major areas has continued to gain greater concern and prominence over the past several decades. Social responsibility will continue to take more time, money, consideration, and concern in all future management decisions and actions. Diverse managerial skills, ranging from simple to highly complex, are required in all of these areas of social responsibility.

UNIQUE PROBLEMS AND CONFLICTING DEMANDS

Social responsibility is complex because decisions must be made in a wide variety of areas.[1] Among the factors that must be considered are:

—Unique laws and codes of ethics in each country

—Taxes, price fixing, and bribery

—Joint ventures as differentiated from full ownership of foreign operations

—Training of foreign nationals

—Control of air, water, solid waste, radiation, noise, land, and chemical pollution

—Safety standards

—Health care

—Education

—Equal opportunity regardless of race, sex, age, handicap, religion, or creed

—Unemployment

—Inadequate transportation

—Product safety, packaging, and quality

—Pricing

—Support of the arts

—Other areas of community enrichment

When evaluating these conflicting demands and their impact upon the revenue and profitability of the company, management must maintain a degree of detachment. Professional decisions must be relatively free of hypocrisy or self-deception. This is no easy task, as reflected by the pragmatic view of one observer: "Few corporations engage in philanthropy because others need money, as though a corporation were a well-heeled uncle who should spread his good fortune around the family. For the most part, corporations give because it serves their own interests—or appears to."[2]

Each of the three major decision areas of legal compliance, moral and ethical standards, and philanthropic giving represents unique problems as well as some overlapping points of concern.

LEGAL COMPLIANCE

Corporate policy should state clearly, "Illegal actions in any form will not be condoned or tolerated by the company." Stringent enforcement of such a policy must develop at the highest levels and be supported all the way down the organization. Internal enforcement action should be immediate, not simply a reaction to external discovery and prosecution.

Even though such policies are found in most firms, they are not uniformly enforced. *Fortune* listed 117 companies that were prosecuted by the federal government during the 1970s for violation of a major U.S. law or statute.[3] The federal government is now going after defense procurement frauds, bank scams, money laundering, and insider trading.[4]

MORAL AND ETHICAL STANDARDS

Closely related to legal compliance are moral and ethical standards. Political contributions, bribery, and other acts of conduct illegal in this country may not be illegal in other parts of the world. They fall into this category, as do areas such as proprietary information, product misrepresentation, disparagement, premature disclosures, acquiring or divulging confidential information, certain gifts and entertainment, and conflicts of interest. One example of the border between legal and ethical-moral boundaries is Steven Jobs' leaving Apple Computer with some other employees to found another company.[5]

To deal with areas that may be considered technically legal but, in the eyes of American Management, improper or unethical, companies must develop and disseminate explicit policies that are rigidly and expeditiously enforced if broken. A typical set of the clearly delineated policies generated by large companies is a small booklet handed out to IBM employees.[6]

Developing a code of morals and ethics is not always simple. The frame of reference is large and sometimes complex. Consideration must be given to existing and proposed laws, Judeo-Christian values, family norms, society and industry as a whole, the firm, and the background and desires of owners, managers, and other employees.

In spite of these complexities, a recent survey (condensed in Table 1)

Table 1

Percentage of Companies (Overall and by Size) Reporting Various Practices Related to Corporate Codes of Conduct

Question	Overall Response	Size Categories*									
		1	2	3	4	5	6	7	8	9	10
Does your company have a code of conduct?	(N = 611)										
Yes	77%	40	57	74	75	72	90	85	87	92	97
Who receives a copy?	(N = 486)										
Officers/key employees	97%	83	97	94	98	100	100	98	96	100	100
Other employees	55%	46	60	35	54	58	42	60	46	70	68
Who signs it periodically?	(N = 481)										
Officers/key employees	85%	75	62	80	87	80	85	91	86	91	90
Other employees	(N = 451) 27%	23	27	12	17	30	25	23	31	47	39
Are procedures specified for handling violations of the code's provisions?	(N = 478)										
Yes	63%	41	46	38	54	58	55	66	75	85	83
Have procedures been enforced in the last several years?	(N = 463)										
Yes	62%	42	43	30	48	48	64	63	77	83	91

Source: Bernard J. White and B. Ruth Montgomery, "Corporate Codes of Conduct," *California Management Review* 23 (Winter 1980): 82.

*The overall sample of 673 was broken into deciles by size. Category 1 is $0–60 million; category 2 is $60–132 million; category 3 is $132–207 million; category 4 is $201–300 million; category 5 is $300–467 million; category 6 is $467–717 million; category 7 is $717–1,150 million; category 8 is $1,150–1,900 million; category 9 is $1,900–4,000 million; category 10 is $4,000 million and above. The overlap in categories 3 and 4 exists in the original table.

shows that most large and many smaller firms have codes of conduct that are distributed to offices and employees, who periodically must sign a statement that they have read the code. Further, these firms have specific procedures for enforcing the code and handling violations.

PHILANTHROPIC GIVING

Under the changes in the 1982 federal tax laws, a company may allocate up to 10 percent of taxable income to philanthropic causes. Prior to the tax changes, the upper limit had been set at 5 percent. Quite a few companies give 5 percent of their taxable income. However, in recent years company contributions have averaged only a little more than 1 percent.[7]

One of the basic problems in philanthropic giving is to first determine whether the company wants to give any money at all to social causes and, if so, how much. After a decision to give has been made, questions remain. Which internal and external agencies should receive money and how much? Should the money be distributed equally between all contributing subsidiaries or should it be spent primarily in a few selected high payoff areas? Should other companies be pushed to give the maximum allowable amount? What strings, if any, should be attached to the funds? Who should be involved in determining the answer to these questions?

The answer to these questions must take into account the views and reactions of the company owners, the stockholders, the potential recipients, the competition, and society as a whole. In making decisions on giving, emotions and feelings sometimes run high. They may vary from an absolute "No," to a "Yes, under certain conditions," to a very emphatic "Yes."

On the "No" side of giving, Howard Johnson, when interviewed by management consultant Chester Burger, said, "My job is to make a profit. I give my taxes to Uncle Sam, and he spends it to improve social conditions."[8] Milton Friedman basically agrees with this philosophy. He states, "Corporations have no money to give to anyone. It belongs to their workers, their employees, or their shareholders."[9]

Moving slightly away from the "Absolutely no" position, Friedman does, however, make two exceptions. First, he feels that closely held corporations, in which the managers are the owners, should be permitted to contribute directly to charity to decrease the tax bite. Second, he approves of contributions to local institutions and arts (such as hospitals, universities, parks, and museums) when they provide marginal returns to the company greater than the marginal cost. Friedman does not consider this second category true philanthropy, however. He considers it a business expense. Friedman is opposed to real philanthropy: "Real philanthropy is that which will cost the company more than it will add to its value in the short term or in the future."[10]

Some individual stockholders do not believe that companies should contribute their income to charitable, educational, or similar organizations that do not further the business interest of the corporation. They feel that this money could better help society by improving or expanding facilities and creating more jobs.

One such person is Evelyn Y. Davis, who has twice submitted a proposal (in 1972 and again in 1979) to the board of directors of the Procter & Gamble Company asking that stockholders vote on her proposal at the annual meeting. The proposal would have the company give no corporate funds to any charitable, educational, or other organizations, except for the purposes of directly furthering the business interests of the corporation. In 1972 more than 97 percent of the shares voted against Mrs. Davis' proposal. At the 1979 shareholders' meeting the proposal received only 1.2 percent of the vote.[11]

Today, more and more companies and their chief executive officers believe very strongly in corporate charitable giving and sit on the "Yes" side of the fence. Dayton-Hudson Corporation has given 5 percent of its taxable income to philanthropic agencies since 1945 and pushes other corporations to do so as well.[12]

At one annual meeting when an angry stockholder assailed the company's hefty donation to charity, Xerox's C. Peter McCollough replied, "You can sell your stock or try to throw us out, but we aren't going to change."[13]

The Berkshire Hathaway Company has tried to solve some of these problems by letting the shareholders designate, on the basis of shares owned, to what recognized charities they want to send money.[14] With proper precautions, people can make charitable donations without subjecting the money to double taxation: once as company profits and a second time as taxpayer dividends, which would occur if the company first sent the stockholders the money in the form of dividends and then the stockholders sent the money to their favorite charities. In essence, the Berkshire Hathaway plan permits the stockholders to have a choice in where the money goes and the ability to contribute up to twice as much tax-free money through the company as they would on an individual contributor basis. This idea has not been widely accepted by most major companies, who think it would be too costly. The IRS has serious reservations about this and other similar procedures.[15]

ESTABLISHING AND IMPLEMENTING A SOCIAL RESPONSIBILITY PROGRAM

The choices of avenues in which to participate are quite limited in the legal arena. They are a little broader in the moral and ethical area, and there is considerable latitude in the philanthropic area.

Alternatives should be chosen in light of the personal values and support of the manager and retention of the inner coherence and health of the organization. The depth and breadth of involvement in any area will depend on the company's available resources. Once involvement is determined, it must have the complete backing and support of all levels of management if it is to be satisfactorily complemented and enforced. This need for continuous top management and other levels of management participation and support in such programs is reinforced by four separate studies on establishing and implementing social responsibility programs.

The four studies indicate that establishing and implementing a program is not a simple process and requires continued top management involvement. Although these studies looked at only a small number of companies, they pointed out several areas that must be considered in establishing and implementing social responsibility programs within a company.

According to Robert Ackerman's studies, successful implementation of these programs takes place in three overlapping phases and can take up to eight years from inception to completion.[16]

—Phase I is the commitment phase. Top management acknowledges the corporation's responsibility in a certain area or on a certain issue, and a policy statement is generated.

—Phase II is the learning phase. Pertinent data are collected, analyzed, and evaluated by top and middle management.

—Phase III is the institutionalization phase. Responsibility for the program is transferred from the staff to the line organization. Resources are committed, performance and expectations are communicated, and evaluation is instituted.

Edwin Murray's study identified the same three-phase responses as did the Ackerman studies but defined two subphases within Phase II: technical learning and administrative learning, with administrative learning the more time consuming of the two.[17]

The principal purpose of the study by John Collins and Christ Ganotis was to determine if there was any gap between the attitudes of top, middle, and lower management in implementing corporate social involvement.[18] The study indicated a definite difference in the attitudes toward social issues and the perceived ability to influence the implementation and corporate response to such issues.

As these four studies demonstrate, for the proper implementation and participation in the areas of social responsibility, top management must continuously be active in all phases of the program.

After the broad objectives of social responsibility have been determined, then the more detailed objectives in the three major areas—legal, moral and ethical, and philanthropic—must be established.

Legality

In the legal area the objective should be simply to obey the law. If the company considers the law unfair, then it should make efforts to get the law modified or repealed, or it should attempt to get relief from certain sections

Table 2
Typical Strengths and Weaknesses in Planning, Organizing, Directing, and Controlling Social Responsibility

	Strengths	Weaknesses
PLANNING	A committee or organization studies, evaluates, and prepares legal interpretations, practices, and codes of moral and ethical conduct to be adhered to by company employees.	No formal legal, moral, or ethical standards planning exists within the company.
	A committee studies, evaluates, and recommends: • Recipients of company philanthropic aid, and • Company people and money amounts to be allocated to such endeavors.	The only remedial action taken against legal, moral, or ethical problems is a reaction to a serious problem that has arisen in one or more of these areas. There is no consistent plan for philanthropic giving.
ORGANIZING	There is a clearly defined firm written policy against any illegal acts.	There is no written policy about moral or ethical standards or it is poorly or loosely worded.
	There is a clearly defined written policy on moral and ethical conduct.	Unwritten or loosely worded, vague standards are poorly communicated.
	A social responsibility committee within the company ensures a consistent policy of giving and screens potential recipients.	There is little or no consistent or organized policy of charitable giving with respect to quantity, organization, or location.

22

DIRECTING	The president and all management levels firmly support direct adherence to legal, moral, and ethical standards.	Little or no direction or support is given with respect to conduct, penalties, or punishments to be taken by management and/or employees in the areas of legal, moral, or ethical standards.
	All charitable giving is reviewed by the president and key management personnel to make certain that it is distributed where it will be of the most help to the company and to society.	Little or no direction, guidance, or support is given with respect to what the company will do about choosing or giving to charitable organizations.
CONTROLLING	All company personnel are required periodically to read, agree to, and sign a code of legal, moral, and ethical practices.	There is poor or little or no control over legal, moral, or ethical conduct.
	Immediate remedial action is taken against violation of legal, moral, and ethical standards.	Each person performs according to his or her understanding and standard of legal, moral, and ethical conduct.
	Monitoring, feedback, and evaluation are required on results achieved as a result of each area of charitable giving.	Money is given and/or people are loaned to charitable organizations without regard to efficiency, standards, or quality of work undertaken by the organization.
		Little or no control exists over the consistency of giving.

of the law. If none of these options is available and the law is too restrictive, then the company must evaluate the possibility of changing its way of doing business or of moving to a new location where the law does not exist.

Moral and Ethical Standards

Because many people perceive right and wrong from different angles, the objective of the company in the area of ethical and moral standards must be to establish what it will and will not tolerate. Once the level of integrity has been established, then the areas of vulnerability must be examined and limits established in each of these areas. Since not detecting or overlooking violations weakens the fear of punishment, a system of inspection must be implemented and strict levels of punishment enforced for violation of the code. Great care must be exercised in all of these areas. Expenses for implementation and control cannot get out of hand, and policing and enforcement cannot be done in a way that adversely affects the attitudes or the creativity of the employees.

Philanthropic Giving

The objectives of the company in the area of philanthropic giving should be as clearly defined and explicit as are those in economic policy and strategy. The company should be as firm about what it intends to be and do in this area as it is about the business in which it wants to be involved and the type of people it wants to attract to its organization.

COMPANY EVALUATION

To help evaluate how well as company is doing in the areas of social responsibility, Table 2 has been developed as a preliminary guide. This table can assist in determining the strength of the company in the various social responsibility areas. Based on the results of this basic evaluation, the company can then see what and where improvements can be implemented.

Complying or not complying with a law is fairly straightforward; however, great care must be exercised in assessing and evaluating the correctness or incorrectness of moral and ethical codes and philanthropic giving. Extensive value judgments and the personal desires of top management enter into these decisions.

NOTES

1. Dan R. Dalton and Richard A. Cosier, "The Four Faces of Social Responsibility," *Business Horizons* 25, no. 3 (1982): 19–27.

2. Lee Smith, "The Unsentimental Corporate Giver," *Fortune* 104, no. 6 (September 21, 1981): 121.

3. Irwin Ross, "How Lawless Are Big Companies?" *Fortune* 102, no. 11 (December 1, 1980): 56.

4. Carol J. Loomis, "The Limited War on White-Collar Crimes," *Fortune* 112, no. 2 (July 22, 1985): 91.

5. "When a Key Worker Leaves With Secrets," *U.S. News & World Report* 99, no. 15 (October 7, 1985): 67; and Bro Uttal, "The Adventures of Steve Jobs," *Fortune* 112, no. 8 (October 14, 1985): 119.

6. *Business Conduct Guidelines* (Armonk, N.Y.: IBM Corporation, 1983).

7. Smith, "The Unsentimental Corporate Giver," p. 122.

8. Chester Burger, "What It Takes to Run a Business Today—An Expert's Advice," *U.S. News & World Report* 75, no. 2 (July 10, 1978): 81.

9. Smith, "The Unsentimental Corporate Giver," p. 123.

10. Ibid., p. 124.

11. See the Proctor & Gamble Company, Notice of Annual Meeting and Proxy Statement, Annual Meeting of Shareholders, September 4, 1979, Cincinnati, Ohio, p. 10, and Report to the Shareholders of the Proctor & Gamble Company Annual Meeting of Shareholders, October 19, 1977, p. 11.

12. According to C. Roland Christensen et al., *Business Policy: Text and Cases*, 5th ed. (Homewood, Ill.: Irwin, 1982), p. 510.

13. Richard A. Shaffer, "Xerox Faces Problems in Trying to Duplicate Its Own Past Success," *Wall Street Journal*, February 16, 1978, p. 1.

14. Lee Smith, "Shareholders Get to Vote on Charity," *Fortune* 110, no. 10 (November 30, 1984): 169.

15. See Ibid., p. 170.

16. Robert W. Ackerman, *The Social Challenge to Business* (Cambridge, Mass.: Harvard University Press, 1975) and, by the same author, "How Companies Respond to Social Demands," *Harvard Business Review* 51, no. 4 (July–August 1973): 88–98.

17. Edwin A. Murray, "The Social Response Process in Commercial Banks: An Empirical Investigation," *Academy of Management Review* 1, no. 3 (July 1976): 5–15.

18. John W. Collins and Christ G. Ganotis, "Is Social Responsibility Sabotaged by the Rank and File?" *Business and Society Review/Innovation* (Autumn 1973): 82–88.

PART II

History and Development of Social Responsibility in Business

3

Premedieval Period (5000B.C.–550A.D.) and Medieval Period (550A.D.– 1450A.D.)

Much of our present day thinking and action in the area of social responsibility is a product of our past. No matter how rapidly social attitudes change, they still have their roots in past history and are influenced by it to a greater or lesser extent. Whether we look at the present as part of a historical development from what has happened in the past or a rejection of it, the past still has an influence on the present. It is therefore imperative, if we are to understand current values and what the future may hold for us, to at least have a brief knowledge of the path we have followed to get where we are today. This reflection on the past is necessary in order to see what our foundation was, how effective it was and what we can learn from it to help us today and in the future.

Today, in the highly industrialized societies, people are questioning their behavior (good or bad) more than in the past, less rapidly moving times. This is occurring for several reasons. The higher level of formal education, even though considered by studies conducted today to be lacking in historical perspective and quality compared with education of earlier days, encourages these people to be more questioning of past and existing values. Second, there is a feeling among many that the traditional values of the past are not adequate for today's rapidly changing dynamic society. Third, the perceived and/or actual rights of the stakeholders and business are more often in conflict today than in the past. The fourth reason is that the increased number of choices that people now face in the modern industrial society—greater ease of moving around, choosing a career, choice of lifestyle, whether to marry, whether to have children—gives them a wider choice of options upon which to base their decisions.

This chapter and the next three chapters will briefly examine the historical development of present day business operations and practices and social responsibility from the time of a primarily rural, agriculturally predominant society to today's primarily city-oriented, industrial society.

Although all business operations and practices were not socially motivated they did result in an eventual change and move toward social awareness and increased social responsiveness as it is seen today. It is therefore necessary also to examine some of those business practices and thoughts over time along with the direct change in social responsiveness over the same period.

Figure 1 depicts the various major periods along with the associated dates for each period. In addition, two other things are shown on the figure: (1) the relationship between historical period and the chapter where the discussion on the period can be found and (2) the areas of the world that had the most influence and impact on the thinking, formulation, and implementation of the business and social thinking of the day, as it applies to the United States for each period.

PREMEDIEVAL TIMES (5000B.C.–550A.D.)

Although the premedieval times did not have social responsiveness as it is understood today, they did have management, economic, philosophical, religious, and work concepts that are heavily reflected in today's social responsiveness.

Egypt

The building of the pyramids in ancient Egypt (5000B.C. to 500B.C.) is mute testimony to the management and organizational capabilities of the ancient Egyptians. Where the stones were to be quarried, what size they should be, how they were to be transported, how much labor was to be used, and when and where the labor was to be used, all required what would be classified today as long-range planning. Efficiency, waste, and economy were, however, probably not prime considerations in the labor area since there existed an abundant supply of peasants, slaves, and mercenaries.

Egyptian writings also show concepts and thoughts used in present day business. The book of instructions of Pitah-hotep (advice from father to son), written about 2,000B.C., was used in Egyptian schools.[1] Typical of the advice given in the book is:

If thou art a leader commanding the affairs of the multitude, seek out for thyself every beneficial deed, until the business be free from wrong. Maat [translated as order or

Figure 1
**Historical Period/Chapter Relationship for the Development of Social
Responsibility in Business**

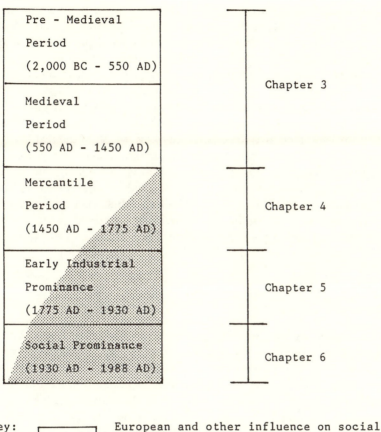

Key: European and other influence on social
responsibility formulation and implementation

American influence on social responsibility
formulation and implementation in North
America and the U.S.A.

truth] is great and its effectiveness is lasting.... Wrongdoing has never brought its
undertaking to port. [Honesty and truth are always the best policy.][2] [Emphasis added.]

In another Egyptian manuscript (again from father to son) it points out that
the Egyptians were well aware of honesty in dealing with other people, a
need for planning, and the use of staff and staff advice by managers.[3]

Babylonia

During Babylonia's early period of prominence (2000B.C.–1700B.C.) its transactions were highly documented on stone; this gave them a system of uniformity of laws and a control system. Laws were developed in areas such as sales, loans, agreements, partnerships, contracts, and promissory notes. During this period the Code of Hammurabi was developed. It presents one of the first views of management and worker responsibilities to their fellow man.[4]

Babylonia's period of greatest power and influence occurred beginning in approximately 600B.C. under the reign of Nebuchadnezzer. Examples of production control and incentive wage payments were found in the textile mills and graneries of this time. Each week, different colored tags were placed on the yarn going through the mill so that production flow could be monitored and controlled. Colored reeds were placed in the jars containing harvested and stored grain so that the year of entry into the storehouse would be known. Women engaged in spinning and weaving were paid in the form of food, the amount of food paid each woman was a function of the woman's production output.[5]

China

China has been long known for its beautiful art and for its "ancient wisdom." As early as 1100B.C. there were writings of "wisdom" that showed they were aware of principles and concepts concerning organizing, planning, directing, and controlling. Much of this work is contained in the Constitution of Chow.[6]

About 500B.C. another writer, Mencius, wrote about the need for system, methodology, and models in effective management.[7] He also wrote about specialization since each of the crafts in China in those days was hereditary and the craftsman was committed to his trade for life.[8] They were located and trained away from the masses so that they could learn better. These concepts were similar to those used by the Greeks and artisans of other countries and were the forerunner of what were later to become guilds and unions.

Approximately 500 years later (100B.C.) Chinese Prime Minister Kung-Sun Hung established a system of examinations for those who worked for the government; those who obtained the highest scores were given the government jobs. Later the system was expanded to classify the positions into nine different grade levels. This might be considered as a forerunner of our modern day bureaucracy and our civil service exams required of most federal, state, county, and local government employees.

Greece

Greek economic, philosophical, religious, legal, business, social, and other problem areas and proposed solutions are found in their legal codes and in their religious and philosophic writings. The Socratic philosophers and military are the chief sources of the economic, business, and social thought of that day; their writings are intertwined with philosophy, ethics, and politics.

The thinking and writings of the Greeks had a profound influence on the civilization of their time and have influenced thought and action down through history. A number of Plato's and Aristotle's thoughts and ideas are felt by many to be socialistic and communistic in leaning, with some of their basic ideas being drawn upon by Karl Marx. The Greek Orthodox and Russian Orthodox churches adopted some of Plato's ideas while the Roman Catholic church followed a number of Aristotle's teachings, with St. Thomas Aquinas later modifying them and expanding upon them in a number of cases. In the teachings of the Greek civilization is also found the foundation of many early present day management practices, such as the scientific method of management; the research and objective inquiry point of view; consultation and consultive supervision; specialization of labor; maximization of output through the use of uniform methods, standard motions, and work tempos— many of them set in harmony with music; and numerous other concepts and practices. It will be shown later how these ideas and concepts had a deep influence on the scientific management groups of people (Frederick W. Taylor, Henri Fayol, Lillian and Frank Gilbreth, Morris R. Cooke, and Harrington Emerson).

To obtain a better feel for precisely what impact these early writers and thinkers had on present day management and ethical, moral, and social practices, two of these Greek writers will be examined. First, the writings of Plato (427 B.C.–347 B.C.) and then Aristotle (384 B.C.–322 B.C.) will be examined. The scope of Plato's and Aristotle's writings was wide and represented the general thinking and beliefs of the Greek philosophers of that time; they delved into the economic and social system in its parts, how it should work, and how it should be used to achieve the desired goals and objectives.

Plato, as did the other Greeks of his time, believed that the citizen existed for the state. He said, "And is not a state larger than an individual?"[9] Plato and other Greek philosophers also believed that the philosopher would rule and that work and commerce were demeaning to the Greek citizen; at the very least, Plato felt that it was a task that one might become involved in only for the purpose of survival.[10]

Plato also proposed abolishing all private property and family, with the state teaching the smartest children. The population in the state was to be built up with different classes of people: the landowners (the only one that would have any leisure), slaves (slavery was acceptable and permissible), workers (those of lower education and intellect), and merchants (those who were too weak in body to do the menial tasks of labor but were strong enough and smart enough to serve as middleman between the seller and the buyer). The merchants served a very necessary and useful purpose in Plato's scheme of things because of his belief in the division of labor and the specialization of labor.[11]

The state that Plato envisioned was a happy state and a moderate state. Everything was fine as long as it stayed this way; however, if the people started wanting too many goods or luxuries, and the fixed amount of land would not produce it, then expansion would become necessary; the need for expansion would eventually and inevitably lead to war.

Aristotle, one of Plato's best-known students, covered many of the same areas as did Plato. In addition, he added his own touches to Plato's ideas and went on to cover a wider area of topics. These topics covered all areas of politics and economic and business aspects of the questions of exchange, division of labor, money, interest, usury, private property, and a just price. On the subject of work for instance, Aristotle agreed with Plato's revulsion of it but was even harsher in his criticism of the subject than was Plato: "... The citizens must not lead the life of mechanic or tradesmen, for such a life is ignoble, and inimical to virtue. Neither must they be husbandman, since leisure is necessary both for the development of virtue and the performance of political duties."[12]

He agreed with Plato that the state is superior to the individual. Aristotle said, "Thus the state is by nature clearly prior to the family and to the individual, since the whole is of necessity prior to the part."[13] He also believed that man is a political animal endowed with the gift of speech and man needed society to live in, otherwise he is an animal or a god and not a part of the state.[14]

Continuing on in his writings from "Politics," Aristotle discusses two types of business and trade activity, the distinction of which is at the root of a major business and social problem that causes much mental anguish and soul searching among present day businessmen: the difference between careful management of household (or business) goods and what may seem to many to be merely a selfish profit orientation. He approves of the first but not the latter. In the management of the household (or business) he approved of the fair exchange of one commodity for that of another commodity (barter) or the selling of a commodity for money in order to purchase another commodity. On the other hand, he did not approve of the use of one's skill or goods to make an excess profit. He described this as the use of money to purchase a commodity and then turn around and sell it at a large profit or to take money and use it to make more money and on into infinity (what he termed "usury").[15]

Aristotle also felt that all people were not equal. He believed that there were a more intelligent master or ruling element and a ruled element or slave. Among slaves and barbarians he believed that the female and the male were equal and occupied the same lowly position; whereas, in the ruling class the female was higher than the slave but was below the male and served primarily as his mate.[16]

Hebrew and Christian

Even though the early Greek and other cultures have had a profound influence on today's business activity and social responsiveness, they run a far second to the impact that the Hebrew and Christian religions have had on total work, ethics, morals, and social responsiveness. In many areas the Hebrew and Christian approaches to the ethical, moral, business, human, and social problems were considerably different from that of the Greeks and other cultures.

Whereas the Greeks had slaves and detested work, the Hebrew had work as part of his culture and everyday life. Even though work might be considered by the Hebrew to be a hardship, it was necessary and dated back to the original sin of Adam and Eve in the Garden of Eden.[17] This gave reason, meaning, and strength to a work ethic that was abhored by most other cultures and that eventually developed into what later became known as the "Protestant work ethic." The God of the Hebrews was very close to his people and showed them doing, for all others to see, various types of labor, such as work in precious metals,[18] stone,[19] animal pelts,[20] fine linens and silk,[21] pottery,[22] and vineyards.[23] No legitimate work was excluded; however, acts that were considered sinful were prohibited and prescribed punishment was given. The books of Exodus, Leviticus, and Numbers in the Old Testament (or Pentateuch) list and discuss many of these work methods and laws and rules of ethical and moral conduct and the consequences of not obeying them, with advice that if you do deviate from them, " ... be sure your sin will find you out."[24] These laws and rules for living and of ethical and moral conduct are based on the Ten Commandments, which are summarized in Table 3. The laws and rules cover every aspect of life, including such business topics as merchandise, goods, barter, trading, merchants, neglect of duty, business engagements, diligence, fidelity, honesty, just weights, industry, integrity, vices, extortion, fraud, unjust gain, slothfulness, borrowing, lending, credits and debts, pledges, usury, contracts, real estate transactions, wages, employee considerations, threats, just dealings, and labor and labor problems.

With regard to work, trade, commerce, ethics, morals, and social responsibility, Christianity endorsed the Hebrew beliefs and built upon them. Jesus and the Apostles were themselves all working men. Before Jesus started his ministry he was a carpenter,[25] Paul was a tentmaker,[26] and most of the Apostles came from the ranks of fishermen. To the Christian, work is a serious business and responsibility;[27] on the other hand, the Christian is also warned that he must not turn his entire concern to work and other problems of the world.[28]

Table 3
The Ten Commandments and the "Golden Rule"

TEN COMMANDMENTS

—Thou shalt have no other Gods besides me

—Thou shalt not make or worship any graven image

—Thou shalt not take the name of the Lord thy God in vain

—Remember the sabbath day, to keep it holy

—Honor thy father and thy mother

—Thou shalt not kill

—Thou shalt not commit adultery

—Thou shalt not steal

—Thou shalt not bear false witness

—Thou shalt not covet anything that is thy neighbor's

"GOLDEN RULE"

—Do unto others as you would have them do unto you

Note: The Ten Commandments are condensed from Exodus, Chapter 20. The
        "Golden Rule" is adopted from St. Matthew, Chapter 19, verse 19; St.
        Matthew, Chapter 22, verse 39; and St. Mark, Chapter 12, verse 31.

The feelings of the early Christians on the subject of work is perhaps best summed up in the short verse by Paul, " . . . if any would not work, neither should he eat."[29]

The positive attitude toward work is not, however, the only contribution or necessarily the most important or unique contribution of Christianity to everyday living, work, ethics, morals, and social responsiveness; it is its total concept of love and hope and promise. In addition to its positive attitude toward work, Christianity also shows in word and deed that the value of work and all other things is done out of love, charity, and compassion for one's fellow being: " . . . Thou shalt love thy neighbor as thyself."[30] (This is commonly referred to today as the "Golden Rule.") It informs us not only to love one another but to share our good fortunes by helping one another:

But a certain Samaritan, as he journeyed, came where he was: and when he saw him, he had compassion on him, and bound up his wounds, pouring in oil and wine, and set him on his own beast, and brought him to an inn, and took care of him. And on the morrow when he departed, he took out two pence, and gave them to the host, and said unto him, Take care of him; and whatsoever thou spendest more, when I come again, I will repay thee.[31]

Christianity completely accepts and endorses the Ten Commandments,[32] which treats male, female, nobleman, and slave all as equals: "There is neither Jew nor Greek, there is neither bond nor free, there is neither male nor female: for ye are all one in Jesus Christ."[33] For those who believe in Jesus Christ and believe in and abide in his teachings He is Lord and Savior and everlasting life.

In the early centuries after the death of Christ, the Hebrews and Christians continued to spread their influence throughout the world. The Hebrews generated the Talmud, which is a written compilation of what was previously the Jewish oral law (the Old Testament, or Pentateuch, of the Bible is written law). Covered in the Talmud are in depth discussions of most business, ethical, and moral problems.

The Talmud presents a very favorable attitude toward business and is filled with various levels of business, ethical, and moral behavior and advice. The Talmud presents detailed rules, laws and discussions on almost any imaginable subject from purely religious matters through secular matters such as real estate, inheritance, property, commerce, marriage, divorce, damage and compensation, business problems, and the ethics of the Jewish elders. Although the Talmud is an old document, it addresses many of the problems that we have today. This is particularly true of ethical and moral behavior.

It appears that many people and some companies have a difficult time in today's world in establishing and abiding by a set of firm ethical and moral standards. The hard and difficult lessons learned by the Hebrew people over hundreds of years and listed and discussed in the Old Testament and the Talmud can prove, and in many instances have proven, most adaptable and applicable to the so-called modern age. The Talmud uses a variety of different approaches to resolving problems at what it considers different levels of ethical behavior; these levels of ethical behavior extend from the level where the individual is just barely inside the borderline of the law at its lowest level to the way of the pious or "altruistic" (a person would not take advantage of another's problems even if it meant giving up some of their own time and/ or money; that is, the person's acts are purely altruistic but not obligatory) at its highest level.

In the meantime, Christianity was spreading throughout much of the Roman empire, with Augustine of Hippo (354A.D.–430A.D.), one of the early Latin church bishops, being one of the more influential spokesmen of that time. He preached the basic Christian beliefs and in the business arena was in favor of farming, commerce on a small scale, selling at a "just price," and handicrafts; he opposed asking interest on money and felt that it was an immoral act. In accordance with Christian teachings, he felt that those whom God had blessed and entrusted with wealth should take care of their own modest needs and then share the remainder with the poor and needy. He also felt that work was an obligation to which all monks should adhere; the Benedictine monasteries soon picked up this requirement and developed a very strong work ethic for which they are credited by some as possibly being "the original founders of capitalism."[34]

MEDIEVAL PERIOD (550A.D.–1450A.D.)

With the collapse of the Roman Empire, the early and mid-period saw the growth of the feudal system, the growth and increasing power of the Catholic church, and the teachings of its foremost spokesman: Saint Thomas Aquinas. The later part of the period saw the revival of trade, particularly in Venice.

The Feudal System

The feudal system existed in the latter days of the Roman Empire in a scattered form and grew rapidly during the Dark Ages as a means of self-preservation and protection for many of the poorer people. In order to secure protection from murder, robbery, and violence, many of the people sold themselves into a level of subservience, including the loss of their individual freedom, to the people who were more powerful than they were and who could offer them some form of protection.

The feudal system form of organization continued on and dominated Europe for several centuries. The feudal system was basically a scalar organization with the king on top and then going in pyramid form to the bottom where the workers were found. Again, as in the Roman system devised by Diocletian, there was a centralized control and authority and a decentralized operation and delegated semicontrol for those fiefs and serfdoms under the control of those whom the king trusted. This delegation of authority to run the fiefs and serfdoms was not an abdication of authority, because as in today's business system the authority that is delegated can be forfeited and/or the lower level leader replaced.

The Catholic Church

During this same period the Catholic church, itself a great landholder like the feudal lords, was a dominant power all over Europe because it was a unified body while the landholding feudal lords were temporal and acted independently. The church's canon law influenced almost all of the business, trade and economic activities of the day. The church canonists tried to develop ways to regulate evils that they felt could not entirely be stopped. Some of these evils they considered were monopoly, trade for selfish advantage, moneylending, and interest on money. With trade increasing in the latter part of this period they also started to look at other areas of business concern, such as a just price, a just wage, extent and legitimacy of interest and profit, taxation, value, and distribution. In examining these problems the canonists were greatly influenced by the teachings of Aristotle.

Saint Thomas Aquinas (1225A.D.–1274A.D.)

The most influential thinker and writer of this time was Saint Thomas Aquinas, who in his "Summa Theologica" attempted to harmonize Christianity with the philosophy of Aristotle. His writings and teachings were broad and covered all aspects of economics, politics, church, private property, common goods, trade, interest, usury, ethics and morals, business practices, and social responsibility. More specifically, some of the things he believed and taught were that private property is the best, not because of any natural law, but because it has proven best; commerce and trade are morally lawful only if pursued for a lawful end, such as seeking a modest gain for a livelihood; charging interest on loans is morally wrong because payment is exacted for use that is inseparable from the thing used—money; a person is entitled to an income only because he labors or because he risks something; the needy have a "natural right" to superfluous income; citizens should participate in their government; the state exists for the individual; woman should be dominated by man; slavery is acceptable; cheating is not permissible; excess profit or loss must be compensated; defective merchandise cannot be sold; and usury is not permitted.[35] Saint Thomas' views were still endorsed as late as 1879 by Pope Leo XIII.

Venice

In the later part of this same period trade started to flourish again, with Venice being one of the more prominent areas. This was the period when the concepts of partnership, joint ventures, joint ownership, agency, and commission agents were used and refined to fairly standard practices. It was also the early days of development and building of some of the large shipping and trade organizations that would follow.

NOTES

1. Adolf Erman, *The Literature of the Ancient Egyptians*, trans. Aylward M. Blackman (New York: E. P. Dutton, 1917), pp. 55–60.

2. John A. Wilson, *The Culture of Ancient Egypt* (Chicago: University of Chicago Press, 1951), p. 84.

3. Erman, pp. 59, 76, 195, 242.

4. Robert F. Harper, *The Code of Hammurabi, King of Babylon* (Chicago: University of Chicago Press, 1904), pp. 126, 130, 157.

5. L. P. Alford, *Laws of Management* (New York: Ronald Press, 1928) p. 37.

6. Kuo-Cheng Wu, *Ancient Chinese Political Theories* (Shanghai: Commercial Press Ltd., 1928), pp. 40–41.

7. Ibid., p. 226.

8. Chen Huan-Chang, *The Economic Principles of Confucius and His School*, vols. 1 and 2 (New York: Columbia University, 1911).

9. Plato, "The Republic," in *Dialogues of Plato*, ed. J. D. Kaplan (New York: Pocket Books, 1950), p. 240.

10. Plato, *The Laws of Plato*, trans. A. E. Taylor (London: Dent, 1934), p. 235.

11. Plato, "The Republic," pp. 242, 243.

12. Aristotle, "Politics," in *Basic Works of Aristotle*, ed. Richard McKeon, (New York: Random House, 1941) p. 1141.

13. Aristotle, "Politics," in *The Politics of Aristotle*, ed. and trans., Ernest Barker (New York: Oxford University Press, 1962), p. 6.

14. Ibib., p. 6

15. Ibid., p. 29.

16. Ibid., p. 3.

17. Gen. 3. Unless otherwise specified all Bible quotes will be from the original King James Version of the Bible.

18. Exod. 25: 36.

19. Exod. 28: 11.

20. Num. 31: 20.

21. Ezek. 16: 13.

22. Gen. 2: 10.

23. Matt. 21: 28.

24. Num. 32: 23.

25. Mark 6: 3.

26. Acts 18: 3.

27. Luke 12: 41–48.

28. Matt. 6: 24–34.

29. 2 Thess. 3: 10.

30. Matt. 22: 39; Mark 12: 31; Matt. 19: 19.

31. Luke 10: 33–35.

32. Matt. 19: 17; I John 5: 3.

33. Gal. 3: 28.

34. Adrians Tilgher, "Work Through the Ages," in Nosow and Form, *Man, Work and Society* (New York: Basic Books, 1962), p. 13.

35. St. Thomas Aquinas, *Summa Theologica* (New York: McGraw Hill, 1964).

4

The Mercantile Period (1450–1775)

The mercantile period was one of sharp reawakening on the European continent in the areas of new thoughts and writings and in the expansion of trade, colonization, and business activity. On most of the European continent agriculture held sway well into the end of the period, whereas in England the industrial revolution was starting to take hold by the end of this period. All European countries were deeply involved in colonization and world trade by the end of the period.

In Europe, the early part of the period was influenced by such men as Sir Thomas More, Niccolò Machiavelli, Martin Luther, and John Calvin. The middle and latter parts of this period were heavily influenced by John Locke, Jean Jacques Rousseau, and the economic mercantilists, physiocrats, and those who in philosophy fell in between the mercantilists and physiocrats. This "in between" group was referred to by some as the forerunners of economic liberalism. In reviewing these people and groups it should be noted that as movement is made into the latter part of the period and into the study of the views, philosophies, and writings of some of the economists, other than for the physiocrats, there is a marked decrease in emphasis placed on the equality of mankind and the helping of one's fellow man, while increased emphasis is placed on the making of money and building up a large store of wealth. In many ways the worker and his family are again relegated to the level of the slave and given only sufficient food and wages to maintain him and his family at the subsistence level. Decreasing thought and emphasis is given to God, reference to moral and ethical values are left out of many of the discussions, and little or no social responsibility is discussed. The solution to many of the problems seems to be that if someone does not agree with you, go to war—after all, in their words, war is inevitable.

Meanwhile, in the fledgling world of colonial America, many of the immigrants and their early generation followers were risking their lives and their fortunes for freedom in the new world, escape from oppression in Europe, and the ability to worship God and practice Christianity free from man-made control. The early part of the period in America is considerably influenced by the Puritan work ethic and the establishment of colonies along much of the East Coast by various trading companies. The mid and latter part of the period is covered by the growth of the country and by the work and efforts of the colonial founding fathers of this country.

EUROPEAN INFLUENCE

During the mercantile period the writers and thinkers of Europe held the positions of predominant influence in the world. Writers and thinkers such as More, Machiavelli, Luther, Calvin, Locke, and Rousseau were considered as free thinkers and independent of any special school or group of thought. On the other hand, many of the economic writers of the middle and later part of the period were grouped into schools of economic thought, based on the feeling that many of their presentations were similar to one another or built upon one another's ideas.

The economic thinkers, writers, and spokesmen came from many different disciplines (philosophy, law, medicine, sociology), and even though economics was not a separate profession at this time the various writers were in many instances best noted for their work in this new area. Rather than discuss the contributions of each writer in the three major schools of economic thought (mercantilists, physiocrats, and forerunners of economic liberalism), since each writer within a given school does express similar main theme ideas, only the main context of each school of thought will be discussed along with any important deviations or special contributions made by a given writer.

Sir Thomas More (1478–1535)

Sir Thomas More is perhaps best known for his book *Utopia*, written in two volumes.[1] He was born in London in 1478 and was beheaded by King Henry VIII in 1535 when he would not take an oath to impugn the pope's authority over the church in England when King Henry VIII insisted on divorcing Catherine of Aragon and marrying Anne Boleyn.

More was considered a moralistic economist and humanist who blamed the economic ills of England on management by the nobelmen and ruling class of England, whom he claimed were nonproductive parasites preying on the labors of the people working for them. The middle managers who surrounded the ruling class were also considered unproductive and excess baggage who neither truly learned a trade or earned their keep. This unproductive activity, along with the pleasures and diversions of both the rich and the poor, caused most of the economic troubles in England according to More.

More's book is to a great extent a caustic attack and reprimand of the business practices of the ruling class of England at that time. In his ideal society he calls for communal dining halls, mass production, specialization of labor, and a system of government by elected officials. Aside from a few chosen people who would spend the major portion of their life in scholarship, all other people of both sexes would be required to learn a trade, preferably one handed down from their parents, and work at this trade for the remainder of their lives. Needless to say, these views expressed by More did not sit too well with the English ruling class who showed very little if any desire to do much with the social problems of the working class.

Niccolò Machiavelli (1469–1527)

Across the continent in Italy was another influential writer of this time. Niccolò Machiavelli differed in philosophy from More in that he was a shrewd observer of the affairs of state and tried to present them in a manner he considered practical realism. In 1512 he lost his position in the Florentine government when the powerful Medici family was restored to power. This period of idleness gave him a chance to turn to writing when he wrote perhaps his best known works, *The Prince* and *The Discourse*.[2]

The Prince did not cover a subject area that had not been covered previously; however, it did differ from earlier writings in that it discarded much of the theology, metaphysics, and pious handling of traditional writings in the areas of leaders and rulers. What he did was to lay bare the innermost workings and power structure behind the operation of the city-state. It is basically a discourse on the principles of leadership and power as they existed then and in many respects exist even today. From a business and management standpoint, there are several broad concepts that might be considered relevant for today's business: (1) reliance on mass consent (the continued existence of any organization depends on the support of the masses), (2) cohesiveness (retain a firm hold on your friends and let the people know what they can expect from you as well as what you expect from them; this is the principle of cleancut responsibility; in addition, the people should be advised of what rewards and punishments will be awarded for good and bad behavior), (3) leadership (the leader, whether a natural born leader or a trained leader, should set an example for his followers and should try to raise their spirits at all times), and (4) the will to survive (one of the primary concerns of any organization is to survive. Machiavelli felt that any disorder should be caught and stamped out as early as possible, since survival is the key desire and goal, all pretense of virtue and good faith may be dropped in order to divest the organization of the disruptive force within or external to the organization.)

Martin Luther (1483–1546)

Martin Luther helped break the yoke of power of the Catholic church and its canon law over the people and helped Protestantism usher in capitalism and the "Protestant work ethic." Luther was distressed by the high living of some of the popes and local merchants and princes and, in some cases, the overriding of pure Christian teachings by the canon law or the rule of the local priests. This sharp contrast between ideal Christianity and what he saw going on around him forced him to push for reforms and to take actions that would remedy the situation; this reformation movement resulted in his removal from the Catholic church.

In addition to calling for a return to pure Christianity, Luther also called for a return to a simple, hard-working peasant life where a person could make a decent living without making an excessive profit. Luther believed that idleness was unnatural and charity should be given only to those who were not able to work; he felt that a number of the religious institutions of that day were encouraging idleness and supporting many who could be and should be working. He also emphasized that the best way to serve God was to do the work of one's profession to the best of one's ability, as long as it was in obedience to God's word, and to perform service that was beneficial to one's fellow man. Under these conditions all work was honorable and of equal value to God. He was careful, however, to point out that even though work approved by and pleasing to God was necessary that it by itself would not obtain a person's salvation; according to Luther and Christian teachings, salvation is achieved through faith in God and not by works alone,

Knowing that a man is not justified by the works of the law, but by faith of Jesus Christ, even we have believed in Jesus Christ, that we might be justified by the faith of Christ, and not by the works of the law; for by the works of the law shall the flesh be justified.[3]

Luther, by his undertaking, rectified many of the ills and wrongs that existed in the church body at that time. Unfortunately, however, for those who were more unscrupulous he also made it easier for them to deviate more openly from the teachings of the scriptures and establish their own ethical and moral norms now that they could separate themselves from the influence of the scripture and the church.

John Calvin (1509–1564)

John Calvin was a French Protestant reformer and had one of the more important influences on the Protestant work ethic. Calvin, as did Luther, set out to reform what he felt were many of the ills that existed in the church body at that time. Calvin's central theological theme, which helped distinguish him from Luther and Catholicism, was "predestination." Calvin felt that since God is infinite, absolute and supreme, and there is no way to completely understand the total workings of God, He has in His infinite power and wisdom determined for us, for His glory, which small number of men and women should be saved. Since God has predetermined who will be saved, there is nothing one can do to change it; however, since a person lives to glorify God, if a person bends all of his or her talent to work and is successful at it this might be an indication that God is looking favorably upon that person. On the other hand, if a person disliked work or was unsuccessful or a failure, this was probably a sign that the individual was not among the saved.

Based on this main theme of Calvin's, he went on to teach that everyone must work and continue to work all of his or her life; any profits that were made were to be reinvested in new works and were not to be hoarded. Investment and any resulting profit and wealth were therefore encouraged. Additionally, Calvin deviated from the teachings of Luther and the Catholic leaders in that he did not continue to condemn interest and business trade. Everything anyone did was, however, to be done to glorify God. Adriano Tilgher summarized this by saying, "With the new creed comes a new man, strong willed, active, austere, hard working from religious conviction. Idleness, luxury, prodigability, everything which softens the soul is shunned as a deadly sin."[4]

The teachings of Luther and Calvin in themselves did not produce a piece of paper or a listing of what the Protestant work ethic was; however, their business area teachings did evolve into this. Basically then, the Protestant work ethic that evolved and was so prominently quoted in years past urged hard work, self-reliance, self-control and sobriety, perseverance, saving and planning ahead, honesty and integrity, helping one's fellow man, and obedience to God and His word.

John Locke (1632–1704)

The teachings and philosophy of John Locke, an Oxford-educated English philosopher, had a considerable influence on the early leaders of America and on the American Constitution. He was deeply involved in natural rights, with his major concern, and some feel overemphasis, on the right to private property. He felt that people had a right to self-preservation and the right to the means to meet this end. Private property filled this requirement by supplying food and clothing to the hard-working people who worked the land. In a country like America where so much land was available he felt that any one who would settle on the land and work it deserved title to the land—a person's hard labor transferred title of the land to that person. He did put limitations on this philosophy, however, in that he believed that people should not have more than they could use; this excess belonged to others and should be shared with others.

Jean-Jacques Rousseau (1712–1778)

Jean-Jacques Rousseau and John Locke combined had a large influence on the French Revolution and the reform moves that were to take place in France after the revolution. Rousseau saw the original state of man to be free; however, under the existing unjust society dominated by the rich and by civil and church authorities he saw mankind everywhere bound in chains. He also felt that even though man must be free that some form of society was necessary and this society would in turn provide the freedom, reverence, and family life needed to keep balance. This freedom was to rest on some general consensus of the people, for it could not be expected that people would feel duty bound to compliantly obey on the pure basis of the power of those in authority.[5]

Rousseau departed from Locke in his views on private property. Rousseau was of the opinion that private property was a departure from primitive simplicity and this departure would lead to a number of evils and injustices such as domination, selfishness, and servitude. He also believed in no taxes on property that was needed to modestly support man and his family, but for anything above and beyond that a sharply increased tax should be imposed on the property.

The Mercantilists (1571–1770)

The best known and most influential in the mercantilist group were Thomas Mun of England (1571–1641), Philip Wilhelm Von Hornik of Austria (1638–1712), Edward Misselden (1608–1654), and Sir James Stuart of England (1712–1780). These mercantile writers not only had an impact on the world of their day but the world today.

The scope of the mercantilist writers was broad and covered the areas of trade, politics, farmers, cost, price, demand, interest, gold, and many other subjects. Although they did not totally agree on all of the details of how their concepts were to be accomplished, they did agree in general on the broad concepts of what should be done.

The group agreed on the aggrandizement of national power where the state is superior. A large population was desired and even required so that wages could be kept low in order that the cost of export goods could be kept low, and to supply men for armies since they felt war was inevitable. A favorable balance of trade and high production was needed to increase the national wealth. Trade was to be regulated and controlled through all levels from the highest to the lowest through the firm establishment of national power. The colonies existed only for the purpose of enrichment of the mother country. They also encouraged farming and a plentiful money supply. They discouraged hoarding, pushed for full employment, and understood the relationship between interest rates and money.

The Physiocrats (1694–1770)

The second group of economic thinkers and writers of this time period were the physiocrats, who were mostly from France. Their view in many areas were different from those of the mercantilists. Best known and most influential among the physiocrats was François Quesnay of France (1694–1774), Pierre-Paul Mercier De La Riviere of France (1720–1793), and Anne-Robert-Jacques Turgot of France (1727–1781).

The physiocrats attempted to grasp economics as a whole and developed the first consistent body of economic thought. All of this was based on moral philosophy and a social point of view—what was theoretically best for society as a whole. Their major emphasis was in the area of support for a strong agricultural economy and for support of a laissez-faire policy.

The physiocrats placed the source of all wealth on the farmer and agriculture, in contrast to the mercantilists' emphasis on the merchant and money; the physiocrats felt that land owners were the most important and man working side by side with nature and his fellow man was the most important thing because money was only a medium of exchange. Only the nobility was to be taxed because the wages of the working classes were already held down to the subsistence level, and to tax these people would remove capital needed to cultivate the land—as a result the entire nation would suffer. In addition, they advocated free trade, reduction in court luxuries, improvement of the transportation system, nonintervention by the state, and the right to own private property. Finally, they felt that there was no conflict between self-interest and public good; mankind was guided solely by self-interest and an overwhelming desire for maximum profit; and the iron law of wages predominated—wages always fluctuated around the subsistence level.

The Forerunners of Economic Liberalism (1623–1770)

The seventeenth and eighteenth centuries were periods of transition; therefore, it is not unreasonable to find writers who combined elements of both the mercantilists and the physiocrats in their writings. Best known and most influential among these writers were Sir Dudley North of England (1641–1691), Richard Cantillion of Ireland (1680–1734), and David Hume of England (1711–1776).

The scope of their thinking and teaching again was broad and covered the pertinent subjects of the day, such as trade, government restrictions, agriculture, money, unemployment, taxation, rent, and production.

As a group, most of them felt that the mercantilists put a straightjacket on agriculture, whereas the physiocrats put an overemphasis on it; they thought that in reality equal emphasis should be placed on both agriculture and trade since they were the breasts of the economy. On taxes they were in favor of them falling on profit from earnings and not on other things. Most of them were in favor of worldwide free trade, with Sir Dudley North being the prime advocate of this. Some of them doubted that the favorable balance of trade proposed by the mercantilists was valid at all times under all conditions or that all the restrictions proposed by the mercantilists were a good idea. North based his concept of this idea on the fact that prices in trade must and will make themselves and as a result there will be times when there is a glut and times when there will be a scarcity in the market.[6]

EARLY AMERICA

The early immigrants came to the New World to a land of what many felt was unlimited resources and freedom from oppression. The work was hard but rewarding and there was freedom to worship God and practice Christianity without hierarchical control. The development and founding of much of early America was also a business venture of several chartered trading companies.

Four colonies subsequently part of the United States—not to mention others in Canada and the West Indies—were, in part at least, the work of large trading corporations: Virginia, founded in 1607 by the Virginia Company of London; New Netherlands, planted by the Dutch at Fort Nassau in 1614; Massachusetts, established by the Massachusetts Bay Company in 1630; and Delaware, begun by a Swedish commercial company in 1638.[7]

The charters and ordinances, which allocated certain parcels of land to the recipients, were handed down by the heads and leaders of the respective trading company's mother country. Those charters and ordinances basically carried several typical provisions in each charter: access to specified areas of land and permission to subdivide it for purposes of establishing colonies and for development, but only if the land "be not actually possessed or inhabited by any other Christian Prince or Estate,"[8] the charters were established "in the name of God," with the additional provisions for the people to "earnestly pray" and to promote God and Christianity among the colonies and its people.

... Bend their Care and Endeavors to assist the said Governor, first and principally in the Advancement of the Honour and Service of God, and the Enlargement of His Kingdom among the Heathen people.[9]

We greatly commending and graciously accepting of, their Desires for the Furtherance of so noble a Work, which may, by the Providence of Almighty God, hereafter tend to the Glory of his Divine Majesty, in propagating of *Christian* Religion to such People as yet live in Darkness and miserable Ignorance of the true Knowledge and Worship of God.[10]

Local governments were established that were responsible to both the people and mother country with provisions that the mother country could abolish the local government if it got out of hand and the gold, silver, lumber, and other needed raw materials resources of the new country were to be sent back to the mother country, usually in an amount not less than 20 percent of that gathered.

This combination of a God-fearing, Christian-worshipping country, along with a business and work-oriented foundation, made for the founding of a Christian nation whose people had two major callings: a specific calling to serve God and Jesus Christ and be obedient to their teachings and a calling to work hard and do well in one's business. As was pointed out under the discussion on Luther, both of these callings are essential to the salvation of the Christian—man is not saved by work alone but by both faith in Jesus Christ and the carrying out of His work. Thus, the foundation was established in America for a strong Judeo-Christian based, ethical-moral work ethic along with the need to put forth one's best work effort in order to support the family and to please God. This, coupled with business activity established by the large trading companies, got America off to a running start.

As more people poured into the country and the lands along the East Coast became more crowded many of the people, in the form of hunters, traders, ranchers, and farmers, poured westward in an attempt to conquer what appeared to be unlimited land and resources. There was much risk involved, but there was also tremendous reward for the fortunate ones; if one did fail there was still plenty of room, land, and opportunity to start over again. This move westward helped to keep alive the strong God/Christ-oriented values of the people along with their strong work ethic.

In the beginning the colonies were busy with farming, fishing, hunting or trading; however, manufacturing was by no means neglected. Every principal industry in the United States had its beginnings before the American Revolution. Flax, hemp, and wool were grown in abundance in this country and much of it, through the use of simple machines, was turned into cloth goods to be used within the colonies. By the early 1700s the domestic industries became so active and important and made such high-quality goods that many British merchants became alarmed. These British merchants in turn complained to the British Government. The British Government in turn eventually imposed certain duties and restrictions on the use of domestic goods and the import and export of domestic and foreign goods. All of this, along with other problems eventually led to the American Revolution. In the meantime the Spanish were moving up from Central and South America into Florida and Louisiana, and the French were moving into Canada and into central North America into territory also claimed by the English.

The Puritans (1620–1770)

The early Puritans adopted much of the theology preached by John Calvin. The businessman, realizing the positive implications of this Puritan work ethic, supported the preachers and an understanding relationship developed between the preacher and the businessman.

These early Puritans were devout Christian and God-fearing people who were dedicated to their Lord and hard work and service in order to please Him, for according to Calvin work and service were the most effective ways to please and give glory to God. John Cotton (1584–1652), one of the early Puritan preachers, presented this hard work and service ethic of the early Puritan by saying, "when he serves man, he serves the Lord; he doth the work set before him and he doth it sincerely and faithfully so as he may give account for it."[11]

During the next two generations this Puritan or Protestant work ethic continued in full force. Cotton Mather (1663–1728), the grandson of John Cotton, was quoted as saying that

A Christian had two callings: (1) a general calling "to serve the Lord Jesus Christ," and (2) a particular calling which was his work or his business. Both of these callings are essential if the Christian is to achieve salvation. The Puritan divine says, "Contemplation of the good means nothing without accomplishment of the good. A man must not only be pious; he must be useful."[12]

Benjamin Franklin (1706–1780)

Benjamin Franklin believed in God and accepted the work values of the Puritans and other hard-working early Americans; however, through his many writings for public consumption much of the emphasis on these work values was removed from its religious foundation over into a secular foundation for the people reading his writings. In his much read and influential *Poor Richard's Almanac* he pronounced short, incisive, and easy to remember secularly founded remarks that he later gathered together and in 1758 published as an essay "The Way to Wealth."

God helps them that help themselves. . . . Diligence is the mother of good luck. . . . Be ashamed to catch yourself idle. . . . ' Tis true that much is to be done, and perhaps you are weak handed, but stick to it steadily, and you will see great effects, for constant dropping wears away stones...and little strokes fell great oaks....A man, may, if he knows not how to save as he gets, keeps his nose all his life to the grindstone.[13]

Franklin's works were best sellers in his day and far past the time of his death. These works had a tremendous influence on America at that time and still do even today. For those people who were not totally religiously oriented it now gave them a way to support the Puritan (or Protestant) work ethic from a secular viewpoint, for here was a man expounding the same work ethic in secular terms as were the ministers in religious terms.

Thomas Jefferson (1743–1826)

Thomas Jefferson, who drafted the "Declaration of Independence" and was the third President of the United States, believed in the hard-working individualistic ideals for the American worker. His feelings in this area were more closely in tune with the physiocrats of France than with the mercantilists of England. He believed that the virtues and happiness of the American people could best be continued and cultivated in an agricultural economy (which at that time contained more than 80 percent of the American work force) than in an industrial society. He did not like what he classified as the undesirable changes manufacturing eventually fostered and brought into the country. He felt that manufacturing brought with it urbanization, landless workers, banking, additional costs, bureaucracy, and eventual government regulation. In simple terms Jefferson felt "That government is best which governs least."

Jefferson was very careful in his reference to the expression "That government is best which governs least" to explain that he did not mean no government, for no government leads to no law and anarchy. Anarchy in the past had usually been corrected by a strong leader who imposed complete rule over the people; this then resulted in tyranny over the people through a monarchy, autocracy, plutocracy, aristocracy, oligarchy, emperor, or a military dictatorship. Historically, Jefferson and other founding fathers (such as James Madison, Benjamin Franklin, Samuel Adams, John Quincy Adams, John Jay, Alexander Hamilton, George Wythe, and James Wilson) were well aware of this problem and knew that in the past 99 percent of the human race had to live out their lives under some form of control where all power was in the hands of the rulers. Jefferson and the others despised tyranny but considered "mobocracy" or anarchy even worse. They were looking for what they called the median point where there must be sufficient government to ensure order and justice but not so much government that it could and would abuse the people.

Jefferson, in his search for the median point, found a possible solution in two ancient examples. He found that ancient Israel was the first nation in history to have a system of representative government; he then discovered that approximately 1,500 years later the Anglo-Saxons were living under an almost identical system. It was from these sources that many of the ideas and the pattern which eventually evolved into the Constitution of the United States and supplied the United States with what is sometimes referred to as the "people's law"—a form of government where the pendulum oscillates around the midpoint of too much and too little government, or as Jefferson stated, "We are now vibrating between too much and too little government, and the pendulum will rest finally in the middle."[14]

George Washington supported Jefferson and his fellow founders in the balanced government they were seeking. He also was well aware of the patterns of the two extremes of too much government control (tyranny) and no law or government control (anarchy). He not only refused the honor of becoming King George I of America but he also pleaded with the military to be patient with Congress until the political leaders had worked out all the knots, bumps, and problems in the system.

Everyone can be thankful for the integrity, sincerity, and hard work of all of the founding fathers for hammering out a Constitution and a form of government where the people elected their public officials and had extensive freedoms to do what they wanted to do as long as it did not hurt or impinge on the rights and welfare of their neighbors. As the country became more highly industrialized and more heavily and densely populated in later years, the pendulum has, as Jefferson feared, swung farther and farther over to the side of "big government" control—almost always under the guise of protecting the rights and welfare of the people.

SUMMATION

The period thus comes to a close with philosophers, religious leaders, and economists in Europe expounding differing views on the problems of the world and how their countries and the rest of the world should meet these problems; the firm establishment of merchant trading companies in many countries and their expansion into America where they were chartered to develop colonies loyal to the crown and to return the resources of America to the mother country; the breaking of Catholic and canon law power in Europe and the building of a strong Protestant work ethic based on the Bible scriptures; the movement of large numbers of people from Europe to America where they could have freedom of worship and be involved in the development of a continent with almost unlimited resources; the founding of the Industrial Revolution in England and its beginning development in America; the founding of a new country (the United States) based on a "people's law"–oriented form of government; and a weakening and drifting away from a solid Judeo-Christian oriented, moral-ethical culture and work ethic to a beginning shift by some in the direction of a secular-oriented, moral/ethical culture and work ethic.

NOTES

1. Sir Thomas More, *Utopia*, ed. Edward Surtz (New Haven, Conn.: Yale University Press, 1964).

2. Niccolò Machiavelli, *The Prince and the Discourse* (New York: Random House, 1950).

3. Gal. 2:16.

4. Adrians Tilgher, "Work Through the Ages," in Nosow and Form, *Man, Work and Society*, (New York: Basic Books, 1962), p. 19.

5. Jean-Jacques Rousseau, *The Social Contract and Discourse on the Origin and Formulation of Inequality among Mankind* (New York: Washington Square Press, 1967).

6. Sir Dudley North, *Discourses upon Trade* (E. Ardsley, England: S & R Publishers, 1970).

7. Harry J. Carman and Harold C. Syrett, *A History of the American People*, vol. 1 (New York: Alfred A. Knopf, 1957), p. 24.

8. "The Third Charter of Virginia, March 12, 1612," in *Documents of American History*, 9th ed., ed Henry Steele Commager (Englewood Cliffs, N.J.: Prentice-Hall, 1973), p. 12.

9. Ibid., p. 13.

10. Ibid., p. 8.

11. John Cotton in Perry Miller, *The American Puritans* (Garden City, N.Y.: Doubleday, 1956), p. 176.

12. A. Whitney Griswold, "Two Puritans on Prosperity," in *Benjamin Franklin and the American Character*, ed. Charles L. Sanford (Boston: D. C. Heath, 1955), p. 41.

13. Benjamin Franklin, *The Autobiography and Other Writings* (New York: New American Library, 1961), pp. 190, 192.

14. Paul Leicester Ford, ed. *The Writings of Thomas Jefferson*, 10 vols. (New York: G. P. Putnam's Sons, 1892–1899), vol. 5, p. 3.

5

Early Industrial Prominence (1775–1930)

The period of 1775–1930 was one of rapid growth, change, and industrialization in both Europe and America. In America it involved becoming a separate nation under its own rule and destiny; escape from dominance by Europe but with retention of many business and trade ties; continued but decreasing influence from European writers and thinkers; rapid industrialization and continued expansion westward; growth and power in the world; emergence of its own thinkers, writers, and business leaders; the beginning of unions; and a slow continued drift away from God and Judeo-Christian ethical and moral values to an increasingly secular, humanistic, pragmatic, and even atheistic influenced way of thinking and acting.

INDUSTRIAL DEVELOPMENT

There are a number of different approaches to the form that industry took in developing. Rather than get into a cumbersome detailed discussion of all the minute periods of development, an examination of the macro evolution of industry will suffice.

At the beginning of this period, approximately 200 years ago, 85 percent of the people in the world were needed to produce enough food to keep the people fed. Today in America, fewer than 4 percent of the people are producing food; at this production level the food supply is in surplus for the basic needs of the country. This then gives a rough idea of how rapidly the economy in America turned from a farm economy to an industrial economy, accompanied with most of the problems that Jefferson feared.

The period between 1700 and 1785 highlights the period of the Industrial Revolution in England. This was a short period for the transition from a rural economy to an industrial economy. England was the first country to successfully make the shift from the rural agrarian–dominated society to the industrial and commercial–dominated society. This change to an industrial society then moved to other European countries and to the United States.

Moving from an agriculturally dominated economy to a industrially oriented economy required new concepts and ideas and a move into a production organization mode of operation. In the macro sense this took place in several major steps: (1) the individual made enough to supply his own needs; (2) specialization developed and individuals now made more goods than they needed so that they could trade them or sell them for other needed goods; (3) cottage industries and rural fairs developed where contracts were made with families, by brokers who served as middlemen, to buy the families' entire output at a fixed price for future sale by the broker (this also meant that the manufacturing family now had to contract with other suppliers for raw materials and possibly develop efficient tools of high quantity production); (4) the factory system of high-speed mass production and its associated material supply and finished goods distribution system; and (5) the development and growth of merchants to sell the products.

During this time period, writers, thinkers, and practitioners on both the European continent and in America continued to generate ideas, concepts, innovations, and applications to direct and control how they felt the industrial economy should be developed. A brief review of some of the major contributions made by these European and American men during this time of industrial growth will be beneficial in seeing how the different views helped mold this period and the time up through today.

EUROPEAN INFLUENCE

As indicated in Figure 1, the influence by European thinkers and writers on the thinking and operation of the United States was still considerable; however, the United States, with its new-found freedoms from direct European control, was beginning to generate its own ideas and concepts on how to run its own rapidly growing and expanding industry.

Although the number of prominent European writers, thinkers, tradesmen, and industrialists abound, only a top few who had influential contributions to the changing world in American business growth, moral and ethical thinking and action, and social awareness and responsibility will be discussed at this time.

Adam Smith (1723–1790)

It was while on the European continent that he wrote much of his best known work, *The Wealth of Nations*, which was published in 1776.[1] He was a strong supporter of the laissez-faire doctrine of the physiocrats and felt that government should only get involved in the national defense, home defense, and public works where necessary and no more. To Smith it is the labor of a nation that supplies its needs; it is the aggregate labor that creates all useful goods and services, and it is labor that is the real measure of the exchange of value.

As did Thomas Jefferson, Smith felt that government governs best that governs least, and that the sum of individual interests equaled the national interest. He felt that it is not altruism but self-interest that moves the world and individuals often aid society without intending to do so; this concept arose from his discussion of the "invisible hand" for which he is possibly best known:

He generally, indeed neither intends to promote the public interest, nor knows how much he is promoting it. By preferring the support of domestic to that of foreign industry, he intends only his own security; and by directing that industry in such a manner as its produce may be of greatest value, he intends only his own gain, and he is in this, as in many other causes, led by an invisible hand to promote an end which was not part of his invention.[2]

Smith also advocated payback computations for machine application, division of labor, and specialization of labor.[3]

Jeremy Bentham (1748–1832)

Bentham was classified in England as utilitarian with the application of hedonism on the social level; that is, happiness is the end of all human existence. He based his social reform on what he considered right and wrong, which in turn was developed from his definition of utility. Utility was measured on a pain-happiness relationship, which was reduced to a common denominator: money. This reduction to the common factor of money was necessary because different people have different utility for the same item.[4]

Although his ideas were considered controversial at the time, they were later accepted by many, as can be seen in a recent study conducted by the American Council on Education of more than 200,000 students. The survey showed that more than three quarters of college freshmen now think that getting rich is what will make them happy and what life is all about. Twenty years ago, only 39 percent indicated that affluence was an essential goal; at that time, a "meaningful philosophy of life" was what mattered—a goal that now motivates only a minority of students.[5]

Matthew Boulton (1728–1809)

The employees' physical well-being was of utmost consideration to Boulton. His concepts were felt to be radical by many people of that time, but a century or more later became commonplace. He built homes for the workers and part of their wages served as rent for these homes. At Christmas time he gave gifts to the employees and their families. He also provided special entertainment for employees to improve their morale, paid overtime wages after a certain number of hours per day, and made the in-plant working environment as pleasant as possible.[6]

Thomas Robert Malthus (1766–1834)

Malthus was horrified and deeply concerned with the living conditions of the working class in England and other European countries. After completing his schooling for the ministry and accepting his first parish post, he anonymously published his famous "Essay on the principle of population as it affects the future improvement of society." He opposed the conception of that day that there would be continuing social improvement and emphasized the theory that the procreative powers of the human race were sufficient to inundate the earth if the population was not held in check by "misery and vice." This became known as the Malthusian population theory, for which Malthus is best remembered. He based his theory on the belief that population increased geometrically while the food supply only increased arithmetically; therefore, an excessive population would reduce the subsistence level since land availability for increasing the food supply was limited and the people would live in worse and worse misery.

Malthus felt that population could be controlled by what he termed as powerful positive and/or negative checks. These checks are summarized as moral restraint, vice, and misery. The positive checks of Malthus were the cruel aspects of life; he included in this category such things as overwork, insufficient food, poor habitation, overcrowded urban areas, unwholesome foods and medicines, sickness and disease, and war. While Malthus wrote of negative checks, he confined his recommendations to continence and delayed marriage as the only acceptable to preventative checks.[7]

As a result of his theories, economics for a while was classified by many as the "dismal science." To help combat this dark image cast upon economics, Malthus' concept has been criticized primarily from two aspects. The first was that Malthus believed incorrectly that society could not effectively help the poor through charity and other means since they would simply lose all incentive to work productively or to limit births; as a result they would produce more poor, have more people with whom to divide the scarce food supplies, and become even more distressed. Second, he is charged with ignoring the fact and anticipating the tremendous increase in the rising productivity of cultivated land.[8]

Malthus was severely criticized by Marx as being a liability to the human race and that his proposal was a capitalistic plot to exterminate the working class of people.

Charles Babbage (1792–1871)

Charles Babbage, in writing his book in England *On the Economy of Machinery and Manufactures*, contributed considerably to the founding of the scientific school of management and predated Frederick Taylor in this country by many years.[9]

Babbage emphasized the division of labor, the use of time study, the observation of the work process so that it could be divided into mental and physical work, and the payment of a bonus in proportion to the workers' efficiency and the success of the business. He also issued specific directives on the principle of optimum size of the manufacturing unit for each type of product and brought forth the importance of balance in the various processes used.

Georg Wilhelm Friedrich Hegel (1770–1831)

Georg Wilhelm Friedrich Hegel was a German philosopher. His ideas and concepts changed with time and were confusing and hard to understand by many. The central assumption of his philosophical system is, however, that the real is the rational of the world so that all things are logically related to one another and anything short of the absolute totality or perfection is a distortion of reality. It maintains that dialectic reasoning, a process whereby thought passes repeatedly in ascending stages from thesis to antithesis to synthesis can unravel the necessary order of development in which human consciousness and reality participate. Basically, everything is in a constant stage of change, always moving toward a higher and improved state over that previously existing. This philosophy became known as "Hegelism."

If Hegel's philosophy is reduced to its simplest concept as it applies to religion, business, ethics, morals, social responsibility, or any subject area, there is no "black or white," there are no absolutes, there is only gray, because everything is in a constant state of flux that is always moving in the direction that Hegel considers an improvement over the past. This so-called improvement, however, is based on one's thought process and values and starts from what exists in one's surroundings or what one thinks is one's surroundings and then moves on to what one thinks or feels is an improvement. It is based on what is going on or appears to be going on in the world rather than what should be going on: Everything is relative to one's own thought process.

Hegel's influence was short lived in Germany, his home country, where his philosophy was being replaced by the rising influence of the new-found psychology. It did, however, have considerable impact and influence in England and other parts of the world. Karl Marx used Hegel's dialectic and added materialism to it to form the core of his economic and social philosophy. John Dewey, who taught thousands of students at the University of Chicago from 1894 to 1904 and at Columbia Teachers College from 1904 to 1930, was also considerably influenced by Hegel and passed many of Hegel's philosophies and ideas on to the future teachers of America and the world.

Karl Heinrich Marx (1818–1883)

Karl Marx was born in Germany and studied at the universities of Bonn and Berlin, where he joined the "Young Hegelians" and became a student of Hegel's ideas; this radical connection prevented him from obtaining a college teaching post he had desired.

Marx took an entirely different approach from his predecessors to the formulation of economic and social thought. Many of his ideas are revolutionary and have been adopted by the communist party. His works were a revolt against the classical school of economists (Smith, Say, Bentham, Malthus, and others). Marx explored and presented his ideas in his *Das Kapital*, which was published in several volumes.

In addition to his complete departure from the more conventional approach to economics, business, ethics, morals, and social responsibility, Marx used words such as "exploitation," "alienation," "imperialism," and "revolution" in his writings; these words jarred the minds of many people, especially the businessmen, merchants, and capitalists at whom they were aimed. This almost immediately turned most of the industrial and merchant-controlled economies against him and his works.

Marx covered many areas and issues and examined and wrote on them from a different viewpoint from most writers of the past. His writings were centered on several major points that have had considerable impact on many people.

He wove his writings and major points around his main thesis, which used the concept and term *dialectic materialism*—an atheistic view of the world—as his first line of attack. He combined two very old ideas: (1) dialectics (taken from Hegel)—everything in the universe, whether a tree or a human being or society itself, its constantly changing and (2) materialism—that God does not exist and the world is composed only of "living" matter. Therefore, man is walking dust, and carries no spark or image of his divine creator.

Marx said that constant and bitter struggle is not all bad. In order to achieve progress, mankind has always been in conflict, with each conflict ending in an improvement, with the end conflict being the perfection of communism. Distorting the philosophy of Hegel somewhat, Marx explained this constant struggle between the different classes of people (which he claims has always existed) through a formula, commonly called the "Thesis-antithesis-synthesis" dialectic plus atheism.

In simplistic terms, the way that Marx depicted this formula working can best be shown with an example. For example, a certain economic class of society exists (a *thesis*). This class is the prevailing power in society and controls the means of production, what clothes will be worn, where and how one will live, and so forth (the slave-owning class, for instance). Soon an opposing class with different ideals, motives, and ambitions arises (an *antithesis*) that wants to overthrow the first class (rivals who want to abolish slavery). The two classes of people struggle and a new class (*synthesis*) comes forth (feudalism), and again the world is off in a new struggle.

Each succeeding struggle is supposed to produce a higher stage of civilization. The feudal society that evolved out of early slavery was, for instance, a dominant force in the past but it also developed and was attacked by the "antithesis" forces from within—its own body. This struggle lasted for hundreds of years and ended in a new "synthesis" called "capitalism"—again representing the best features of both classes and an improvement over feudalism.

Marx felt that the capitalist class has already developed its own "antithesis"; this class Marx named the "proletariat" or working class. According to Marx, the new "synthesis" that will evolve from this latest struggle will be communism. At this point, according to Marx, struggle will cease because the apex has been reached. Other than to say that it was a fact, Marx never did adequately explain or support why in his theory communism had to be the apex. This new world would be perfect and the final society; it would be stateless, classless, godless, and where all property used in production would be held in common. At this point his "thesis-antithesis-synthesis" dialectic would no longer be necessary and would cease to exist.

Marx was a keen observer of the times and shrewd and cunning in his use of words and phrases, which he used to catch hold of those in particular who were greedy, ambitious, discontented, or down trodden in any way. According to Marx, the struggle was between the "imperialistic capitalists" (those who owned all the tools of production, made all the money, and had all the privileges) and the "proletariat" (the "wage earners," the "property-less," the "exploited," the "alienated," and the "downtrodden"). If necessary, there was nothing wrong in reaching this new apex of communism through revolution between these two classes, such as occurred in Russia in 1917.

Herbert Spencer (1820–1903)

Herbert Spencer, the son of a schoolmaster, was basically a self-taught Englishman. His mother's and father's background familiarized him with the doctrines of the Quakers and the Methodists. His close friendship with Thomas Huxley and Charles Darwin deeply influenced him in the theory of evolution. He felt that the universe had evolved through mechanical forces from relative simplicity to relative complexity.

He applied to society as a whole the same evolutionary concepts and principles that Darwin had applied to biological life; as a result, Spencer's philosophy is referred to by some as "social Darwinism." It was not based upon a simple social progression theory, however, but on the harsh realities of the times that Spencer saw surrounding him and the workplace. He applied his concept to what he saw and believed the world condition to be and arrived at what has become known as the harsh "survival of the fittest" philosophy. His basic thesis here was that since the bright, healthy, and able people contribute most to society they should be encouraged and rewarded by living or surviving; while on the other hand, the poor, the weak, the tired, the sickly, and the handicapped demand more out of society than they contribute and therefore should not be supported but instead permitted to die a natural death. To Spencer this was reality that should not be tampered with through welfare and social programs. If "natural" principles were followed and let take their own course, evolution would follow and the survival of the fittest in the survival of human life would take place. He did not apply this to a particular ethnic group, race or color of people but felt that it applied to all people as a whole—his thesis was culture-free. According to Spencer, society improves by the "survival of the fittest":

The poverty of the incapable, the distresses that come upon the imprudent, the starvation of the idle, and those sholderings aside of the weak by the strong, which leave so many "in shallows and in miseries," are the decrees of a large, farseeing benevolence.... Under the natural order of things society is constantly excreting its unhealthy, imbecile, slow, vacillating, fatherless members.[10]

Spencer's philosophy was much more popular in America than it was in his native England. It fit in with the thinking and times in America where emphasis was still on hard work, rugged individualism, and optimism for the growth of self and the country. His philosophy provided a rationale and justification for the attitude and feelings that already existed in the minds of many of the people. Spencer was an influential leader of thought and a hero to many in the United States during the last third of the nineteenth century and well into the first quarter to the third of the twentieth century.

William Stanley Jevons (1835–1882)

William Stanley Jevons was born in Liverpool and educated at University College. His economic and business concepts and writings had a definite hedonistic philosophy that rested upon pleasure and pain, a similar but slightly different approach from Bentham's. He felt that the use or value of an item to a person was based on two things: the amount of pleasure or pain the item brought and how much of the item was available, with each additional unit of possession of the item rendering a declining amount of use or value to the holder of the item.

Jevons also contributed much to management thought and the improvement thereof. Again, Jevons' ideas were similar to those expressed by Taylor but predated Taylor's work by a considerable amount of time. He advocated cooperation between labor and management as did Taylor; however, he went further than Taylor in that when he presented industrial partnerships, he also advocated the inclusion of profit sharing and ownership of stock in the company by the employees. He was also interested in the maximizing output through the use of proper tools and equipment. Jevons also predated the Gilbreths in his reference to time study and rest periods.[11]

Vilfredo Pareto (1848–1923)

Vilfredo Pareto's most notable contribution to social economics and social responsibility was in the area of his theory of "Pareto optimality" or what some people call perfect bliss or constrained bliss. C. E. Ferguson defines Pareto optimality as "any organization (point) is said to be Pareto optimal or Pareto efficient when every reorganization that augments the value of one variable necessarily reduces the value of another."[12]

The Pareto optimality concept is used and has had tremendous impact and influence on the inputs, outputs, and distribution of social welfare and any of the problems that are connected with attempting to resolve equitably a problem involving two sides to an issue, such as the pollution issue.

Max Weber (1864–1920)

Max Weber was a combination philosopher, sociologist, and economist and was considered by many to be one of Germany's greatest writers and thinkers. He concerned himself with the relationship between capitalism and specific economic conditions.

Weber defined capitalism in general as any system of rationally conducted exchange for a profit. He felt that one of modern capitalism's outstanding features is "bureaucratic organization" dedicated to the precuniary ends and the disciplined organization of the labor force; bureaucracy, however, was not limited to capitalism alone. Influenced by the Prussian Army school of thought, Weber felt that a bureaucracy could be an ideal, international, rational, and very efficient form of organization founded on the principles of logic, order, and legitimate authority.

In further analysis of business ideology, Weber makes some other interesting observations. In examining Luther and Calvin and the Protestant work ethic he notes that the teachings therein demanded sobriety, self-discipline, diligence, and, above all, planning ahead and saving. He also noted that counter to the tendency that had been observed at all previous times, there was a smaller participation of Catholics in the modern business life; the Catholics showed a stronger propensity to remain in their crafts, whereas the Protestant was attracted to the factories in order to fill the upper ranks of skilled labor and administrative positions. He attributed the explanation of this to the intrinsic character of their religious beliefs and the new Protestant work ethic.[13] If a recent survey, conducted by *Forbes* magazine, of the leaders of the nation's 100 largest corporations is correct, it appears that this trend still continues today, at least in the leadership positions.[14]

John Atkinson Hobson (1858–1940)

John Hobson expounded his theories on the importance and welfare of the worker. He expressed the belief that the cost of and to the human being had to be considered along with the monetary costs in any economic analysis. For instance, he postulated that fatigue and monotony were just as important costs to humanity on the whole as were raw materials, labor, and profit to the entrepreneur.[15]

Arthur Cecil Pigou (1877–1959)

Arthur Pigou was successor to the chair of economics at Cambridge University when Alfred Marshal stepped down. Pigou's best known follower and member of the so-called Cambridge school was John Maynard Keynes. Both Pigou and Keynes used the guiding principle of the desirability of maximizing social and economic welfare. With this concept in mind Pigou went on to set up important categories of welfare.[16]

Pigou defined his concept of welfare to refer to satisfactions, not goodness, thus leaving it possible that in certain circumstances a government ought to foster a situation embodying less welfare (but more goodness) in preference to one embodying more welfare.

Although Pigou involved himself in discussions of all types of welfare, he did extensive work on the subject of the welfare of externalities and his work in this area is often referred to when this subject arises. An externality, as referred to here, involves the effects upon those external to, or not associated with, specified purchases or activities of the generating source. A simple example is air pollution. Who should pay for the abatement of the smoke or make up the difference in the reduced value of the property as a result of the smoke?

Henri Fayol (1841–1925)

Henri Fayol was a French engineer who dealt with the principle of general management. His major works, *Administration Industrielle et Generale* was published in France in 1916, was available in England in English in 1929, and finally published in America in 1949.

He divided the functions of management into the five major areas of planning, organizing, commanding, coordinating, and controlling. He divided all industrial activities into six major categories: (1) technical (or production), (2) commercial (buying, selling, and exchange), (3) financial (how to best use capital), (4) accounting (keeping track of use of money, including statistical analysis), (5) security (protection of personnel and property), and (6) management (use of the five functions of management listed earlier).

Fayol felt that the first five areas of industrial activity were fairly well known and had been quite extensively explored; therefore, he concentrated his efforts on the managerial aspects of business. In doing this he came up with a list and discussion of 14 major areas he felt would improve the practice of general management: (1) division of work, (2) authority and responsibility, (3) discipline, (4) unity of command, (5) unity of direction, (6) subordination of the individual to the general interest, (6) renumeration, (7) centralization, (8) scalar chain of command, (9) order, (10) equity, (11) stability of tenure, (12) initiative, and (13) esprit de corps.

Fayol's work was the first full-scale undertaking where the major emphasis was on the management function of the business and how it should be conducted. Although slow to circulate throughout the world, the impact of his writings had considerable impact upon the worldwide business community and its operations.

AMERICAN INFLUENCE

While European writers, thinkers, and practitioners were continuing with their work and influence throughout the world, America was starting to take increasing control of its own destiny; it was producing its own leaders, inventors, thinkers, writers, practitioners, and laws and controls. Again, to mention them all would be to fill volumes; therefore, only a few of those who have made major contributions to the founding formulation, implementation, or changing philosophy of business operations, moral and ethical standards, and social awareness and responsibility will be discussed.

Frederick Taylor (1856–1915)

Taylor, even though predated in many areas of his work by contemporaries in England, is considered to be the father of scientific management. Starting out as an engineer, Taylor developed his concept of management: The maximum good for all society can be best achieved through the cooperation of management and labor and the application of scientific methods to the operation of the business.

Taylor's concepts and goals were to be implemented and achieved in a number of ways. If maximum production and profits were to be achieved and more cooperation from employees obtained, a shift from the "whip" philosophy of management would have to take place. A more comprehensive view of planning, organizing, directing, and controlling would have to be implemented. His plan for doing this was to: (1) have management use a scientific approach rather than a "whip," a "seat of the pants," or a "rule of thumb" approach to management problems, (2) assign the appropriate man to each operation in order to achieve the most harmonious operation, (3) establish the best means of economic production, (4) implementation of equally good supervision of the employee and labor and management, (5) specialization of labor with the goal being an increase in the efficiency of production, and (6) working of both management and labor for improved prosperity for both.[17]

Henry L. Gantt (1861–1919)

Henry Gantt, a contemporary and protégé of Taylor, is best known in business circles for his contribution to humanistic management concepts, planning and scheduling, and his wages and bonus system. He was the developer and popularizer of what today is known as the Gantt chart, or more popularly know as the simple time and activity bar chart. This chart displays in bar (or picture) form the tasks to be performed, the sequence in which they are to be performed, and the time of start and completion of the task.

His bonus system was based upon a person being given a specified salary for producing a given quantity of items. If the individual produced more than the specified quantity he would receive a bonus; however, if the individual produced less than the specified quantity, he was not penalized. This plan permitted the worker to earn a living while he also learned to increase his efficiency. With the introduction of this system, it was not uncommon for production to more than double.

Although a contemporary of Taylor's, Gantt placed much more emphasis on the humanistic consideration of the employee. He had great compassion for the underprivileged and the worker. He felt that management had a responsibility to work with and train the employee to be more skilled, efficient, reliable, and form better work habits. He was well ahead of his time in what some call the application of the "psychology of human relations" to the workplace. He carried his concept of emphasis on the humanistic side even further when he pleaded with management to orient their first concern on service and quality rather than on profit. His concern and emphasis in this area went far in introducing the concept of industrial and social responsibility into industry.

Frank (1868–1924) and Lilian (1878–1972) Gilbreth

Both Frank and Lilian Gilbreth are noted and remembered for their work and perfection in the area of time and motion studies. Their work and life were portrayed in the motion picture "Cheaper by the Dozen." A major portion of their work was done in the area of micromotion study in an attempt to determine the least tiring and fastest way to accomplish a task.

After Frank Gilbreth's death, his wife continued on with his work and was as well known as her husband. The work and influence of these two people were very extensive and helped industry to establish standard times and improve efficiency in most work processes. The unions became very concerned with these procedures and felt that in many cases the companies were overworking the employee for maximization of company profits. The unions therefore started conducting their own time study programs and began to refute some of the figures generated by industry. These studies and their time and motion results became part of negotiations between management and labor during contract negotiations.

James D. Mooney (1884–1957)

James Mooney used a very strict engineering approach in presenting his system of superior-subordinate relationship arranged in a hierarchical fashion, which he classified as a scalar principle. He considered neither the human nor the sociological aspects or impact of such a system.

Mooney arrived at his scalar principle by studying the past history of organizations and leaders such as found in Alexander the Great, Caesar, the Catholic church, and other bodies. What he found was that throughout history all strong organizations were founded on the system of a superior-subordinate relationship arranged in a hierarchical fashion. Mooney therefore adopted this system and presented it to the modern world of his time as the scalar principle. Lyndall Urwick, later in his blending of the ideas of many writers, added his own work on the span of control to Mooney's scalar principle to arrive at what today is known as the formal pyramidal organization chart that governs the relationships and interrelationships of all the people within a given business organization.

John Dewey (1859–1952)

John Dewey was a philosopher by degree and training. He was appointed chair of the department of philosophy, psychology, and education at the University of Chicago in 1894. While at Chicago he founded the Dewey School laboratory where he tested and developed his psychological and pedagogic hypothesis. During his stay in Chicago, Dewey also participated in the Hull House, where he mixed with workers, union organizers, and political radicals of all sorts.

In 1904 he left the University of Chicago because of increasing friction with the university administration concerning the laboratory school and joined the education department at Columbia, where he remained until his retirement in 1930.

Dewey very rapidly gained international prominence through the Columbia Teachers College, which was a training center for teachers from countries all over the world. As a result of this powerful position, Dewey's educational

philosophy permeated the American school system and spread throughout
the world. Not only did he spread his philosophy to almost every school
system in the world from his teaching position at Columbia but he was also
a prolific writer and gifted speaker. He wrote numerous books, wrote articles,
or had articles about him appear in almost every volume of *The Journal of
Philosophy* from the time of its founding in 1930 until his death in 1952. He
lectured at Tokyo, Peking, and Nanking from 1919 to 1921 and conducted
educational surveys of Turkey, Mexico, and Russia.

His general philosophy was sympathetic to that of Hegel. In keeping with
Hegel's concept that there were no absolutes but only constant change from
one state to another, Dewey felt the world must move from what he classified
the older individualism, through a transition period, to a new and improved
individualism.

The old individualism that must be replaced, as discussed by Dewey, was
that the American people clung to antiquated religious ideas, principles,
concepts, morals, and beliefs of the past, which held them down, rather than
believing in what he felt were the more modern scientific proofs. These old
antiquated ideas had to be eliminated if there was to be meaningful progress.[18]

One of the main difficulties in understanding the present and apprehending its pos-
sibilities is the persistence of stereotypes of spiritual life which was formed in old
and alien cultures.... Nowhere in the world today at any time has religion been so
thoroughly respectable as with us, and so nearly totally disconnected from life....[19]

On the subject of morals and standards he is just as definite that they are
also antiquated and must be changed. The new standards are to be set by
sociologists, psychologists, novelists, dramatists and poets.

Our moral culture, along with our ideology, is...still saturated with ideal values of
an individualism derived from the prescientific, pretechnical age.... It is the work of
sociologists, psychologists, novelists, dramatists, and poets to exhibit the consequence
of our present economic regime upon taste, desire, satisfaction and standards of
value.[20]

According to Dewey we are, for better or worse, living in a corporate age
and must get into this new age of new individualism through a period of
transition from the old individualism. The people must free themselves from
the old traditions and move on to the new. The new would not be solid and
rigid but would be a function of that which imagination and emotion from
the individual's mind could attach itself.

The problem is seen to be essentially that of creation of a new individualism as
significant for modern conditions as the old individualism at its best was for its day
and place.... Individuals might in consequence find themselves in possession of objects to which imagination and emotion would stably attach themselves.[21]

When the old individualism and its associated religiously founded ideals, standards, and morals are destroyed, with what are they to be replaced? Dewey wants to have the new individualism founded and based on a constantly changing science to which will be applied a new psychology and morals. It is assumed that the new psychology and morals will always be changing as science changes. "The 'given' which science calls us to accept is not fixed; it is in process.... How shall the individual refind himself in an unprecedentedly new social situation, and what qualities will the new individualism exhibit? ...It is one of forming a new psychological and moral type...."[22]

Dewey goes on to explain that forming new people, culture, and how people think would be through the educational process. The graduates, after their new enlightenment, must go out and help change the thinking of the rest of the world.

Schools ... are the formal agencies for producing those mental attitudes, those modes of feeling and thinking which are the essence of a distinctive culture.... The effective education, that which really leaves a stamp on character and thought, is obtained when graduates come to take their part in the activities of an adult society....[23]

According to Dewey, these graduates are the core nucleus of enlightened individuals whose job it will be to spread the word that the roots and foundations that have bound the people together in the past are archaic and no longer valid and must be replaced by new updated ideas of the times. This will be done with emphasis for the new individualism based on everything that Dewey believes science has shown to be true and that he feels will continue to generate new concepts and ideas. Dewey feels that science is all encompassing and is a good potential foundation upon which to build.

Science is a potential tool of such liberating spiritualization; the arts, including that of social control are its fruition.... Such a society would meet the demand for science that is humanistic, and not just physical and technical.... Individuality will again become integral and vital when it creates a frame for itself by attention to the scene in which it must perforce exist and develop.[24]

Dewey's teachings have had a profound impact, not only on the business community but every aspect of life. Hundreds of thousands of teachers who studied and trained under him have gone out into the world, thoroughly trained in his beliefs, to train other teachers and teach hundreds of thousands of school students throughout the world. His philosophy of disposing of the so-called antiquated stable religious beliefs and morals and replacing them with the new concepts, ideas, psychology, emotions, and morals that each individual feels are found everywhere today throughout society.

As Dewey said, new psychology and morals based on science will have to be established by educators, sociologists, psychologists, novelists, dramatists, and poets. Dewey accomplished much of what he proposed. Today, many in each of these groups are expounding the Dewey philosophy (even though they may not call it that), the schools and universities are filled with Dewey-trained teachers or their successors, industry is being strongly influenced by behavioral management specialists (usually with a psychology, philosophy, sociology, or behavioral management degree that reflects many of Dewey's ideas), and ethical and moral conduct throughout industry (and elsewhere) is in a constant state of flux and has very little consistence, varying from person to person and situation to situation as one's own conscience and imagination dictates.

The Robber Barons

The United States entered the nineteenth century with a primarily farm society of 5 million people; by the end of the century the population had grown to more than 75 million people who were producing twice the output of England and equal to the combined economies of France and Germany. By 1914, the production of goods and services in the United States was equal to more than one-third of the world's industrial output. The city population grew from 6 percent of the total population in 1800 to roughly 33 percent by 1900.

This rapid industrial growth in the United States was attributed to the favorable social and political environment established by the founding fathers, plentiful natural resources throughout the country, rapid urbanization and population growth (both from large American families and from the influx of foreigners), the transportation revolution with expansion of the railroads throughout the country, the improvement and expansion of the communication industry primarily through the spread of the telegraph and the telephone, the rapid spread of the use of electricity and its application to all types of machinery, and the aggressive use and application of all of these available tools to molding and forming large businesses and trusts by a few dynamic and innovative people—better known today as the "robber barons."

Much of the rapid growth of industry and capitalism during the 1800s was constructed around the rugged individualism and enlightened self-interest of a few—the robber barons. While a few prospered, the vast majority of working-class people were often hurt by the practices of the robber barons. Huge fortunes were amassed by these people before much social legislation was enacted and applied.

A number of these people came into prominence during and after the Civil War. John D. Rockefeller, J. Pierpont Morgan, and Jay Gould started out their early careers by sending substitutes into the Civil War to fight for them. This was based on the permissible practice of the time and the advice given by Judge Thomas Mellon to his son.[25]

All of these men started out at an early age. By 1861 on the East Coast and in the Midwest were found such notables as John D. Rockefeller, Andrew Carnegie, J. Gould, J. Pierpont Morgan, and Edward Harriman (none of them were more than 26 years old and all held responsible positions); in the West were found equally as prominent figures, such as Collis Huntington, Mark Hopkins, Charles Crocker, and Leland Stanford (all part of the western portion of the Union Pacific transcontinental railroad building group). Most of these men had left home by the age of 16 to make their way in the world, and only two of them, Morgan and Stanford, had any college training.

With a minimum of laws and no meaningful social legislation in place, many of the methods and tactics used by these robber barons would be classified as unethical, immoral, and, in many cases, illegal today.

Stories abound on John D. Rockefeller's climb to his position as monopolist in the oil industry. Some of his more infamous tactics to gain this monopolistic control of the oil industry included such actions as offering to buy out a competitor at roughly 40 percent of asset value; bankrupt noncooperating companies by such tactics as selling his own products at below cost, refusing to sell Standard Oil–controlled raw materials to the competing company at any price; and recommending that railroads not handle their products or at least charge double or even quadruple the normal rate. Rockefeller, although probably the most successful in applying the above and other related techniques, was in no way the only one to employ them. Most of the trusts founded in this period also made ample use of questionable acquisition and growth techniques at that time.

The trust was in actuality a monopoly or a pooling arrangement of a large number of similar product producing companies working together for a unified cause. In the 1870s and 1880s there was much price cutting and other similar disruptive tactics going on between companies selling similar products. In response to trying to eliminate this undesirable impediment to profit maximization the companies gathered together in a pooling arrangement; that is, rival firms joined together and agreed on common prices for their various products, establishment of output quotas, and a division of the market into prescribed territories. Voting power in the pool was allocated on the basis of market power, with the stronger companies having the most votes. If anyone deviated from the rules of the pool they were assessed a fine. Price cutting was hard to detect in many instances and fines hard to collect even when price cutting was detected.

The best solution to the continued price cutting was to have the pooling competitors join into one organization called a "trust." The most successful model trust was established by Rockefeller in 1879. In this trust the stockholders of 40 companies joined together and turned over their stock certificates and voting rights to a central committee (the "trustees") who then became the directors of the Standard Oil Company. Whenever a new company was added to the trust it too came under its umbrella and protection. Several other large trusts were assembled in salt, sugar, whiskey, tobacco, leather, gas, cottonseed oil, gun powder, and many others.

Because of these pools, trusts, and other forms of monopolistic business practices, it became evident by the 1880s that a substantial monopolization had occurred in many industries and the competitive marketplace was not a self-sustaining entity. The fifty-first Congress, which convened in 1889, was convinced that something had to be done to control these abuses and the behavior of business. Although much confusion was associated with Congress' venture into this new legislative territory, it finally produced the Sherman Antitrust Act of 1890. The broad purpose of the law was to encourage the growth of competition through the removal of significant impediments to the competitive process, to make certain types of business combinations and efforts to monopolize unlawful, and to specify penalties for violation of the law.

Initially, not too much action was taken by the federal government in invoking the Sherman Antitrust Act; however, in 1907 the federal government successfully brought suit against DuPont for violation of the act. The suit, which was resolved in 1911, divided DuPont into three companies: DuPont, Atlas Powder, and Hercules Powder. In 1911, cases against Standard Oil and American Tobacco were also completed and the companies were required to break up into smaller companies. In these two cases, however, the Supreme Court also concluded that Congress had meant to outlaw only unreasonable restraint of trade.[26] This resulted in what is now referred to as the "rule of reason": The Court, when examining a case, would also inquire into motive and conduct—an important but vague principle and interpretation of the law.

In spite of all the horror stories told about the robber barons, these wealthy individuals used much of their fortunes to help and benefit the public. Andrew Carnegie built libraries all around the country; Rockefeller funded and built the University of Chicago; and Collis Huntington built an excellent rapid transit system for the city of Los Angeles. These men and others also established various charitable foundations.

The Sherman Antitrust law was only the beginning of much federal legislation to follow in the regulation and control of business and its activities. The days of wide open "do as you want and can" operations were at an end. Federal legislation and court rulings involving industry and society started out slowly but have multiplied rapidly since the 1930s.

The Entrepreneurs and Builders (1800–1930)

In order not to give the wrong impression that the United States during this period was developed only by people of robber baron qualities, some of the other leading lights and incidents of the period should be briefly examined.

The founding and growth of the transportation and communication industries opened up the country to continued expansion and growth. In transportation there was the development of the local, regional, and transcontinental railroads; the development of the steamboat and shipping on the waterways; the early development of the road system and cars and trucks; and the early beginnings of air travel and shipping. In the communications area growth came through the pony express, the telephone, the telegraph, the movies, the radio, and the high-speed printing press, followed in the next period by the addition of television, copiers, computers, and satellite communications.

The entrepreneurs and early businessman saw commercial opportunities where others did not and had the determination to pursue these opportunities long after employees and experts had given up on the projects. Thomas Edison developed the first research and development laboratory and thereby pointed the way to making development of inventions a conscious effort. When told he had made hundreds of mistakes, he took issue with the comment and responded that these were not mistakes but were positive progress in that they had found out hundreds of things that would not work—they were not mistakes.

King Gillette worked for six years in developing a process to replace the straight edge razor with a disposable model. He developed a new process for hardening steel that was necessary before he could develop his disposable razor blade. Cyrus McCormick increased productivity in the farm sector with his invention of the reaping machine. Gustavus Swift refined the new technology of the refrigerated railway car and developed a comprehensive distribution and marketing strategy for bringing western beef to eastern markets.

As the country grew, both slavery and agriculture decreased as manufacturing continued to grow. In the early 1800s the first true factories in this country were developed. Samuel Slater of Providence, Rhode Island, and Francis Cabot Lowell of Waltham, Massachusetts, were two of the leaders in this area. Lowell brought both spinning and weaving together under one roof and laid the groundwork for organizing people into work groups. His plants served as models for other manufacturing plants in the early part of the century.

At the beginning of the period transportation throughout the country was slow and difficult. DeWitt Clinton built the Erie Canal with other canals to follow. Canals, lakes, and rivers accounted for much of the early traffic; with the major drawback being that they froze over in the winter. Henry Wells and William Fargo developed an integrated system of overland transportation to carry both goods and passengers. The railway system was developed and spread throughout the nation. Henry Ford developed the assembly line and brought an inexpensive automobile to the public. Alfred Sloan, through General Motors, improved automobile technology and gave the public a choice of colors and styles. Henry J. Kaiser changed the lives of many with the highways, bridges, and dams he constructed. During World War II he built many of the wartime ships on the West Coast. After the war he developed large aluminum mills, produced automobiles for awhile, and developed one of the less expensive comprehensive company health plans in the country.

Lydia Pinkham developed profitable patent medicines through target and market advertising. Montgomery Ward and Sears, Roebuck catalogue sales took inexpensive retail goods into the homes of all Americans. William Procter, of Procter & Gamble, promoted 99.44 percent pure Ivory soap and other soaps through advertising and direct distribution. R. H. Macy of New York sold dry goods and other specialty goods to the mass market at standard prices through the department store; John Wanamaker did the same thing in Philadelphia with stress on money-back guarantees; and Marshall Field built similar stores in Chicago and dominated the retail trade in that city.

This may not be the best list of "shakers and movers" of this time period, and it certainly is far from complete, but it does give some examples of the many things that transpired during this period and helped develop the social responsibility that exists today.

Unions (1800–1930)

With the abuses that big business was inflicting upon working-class people, the solution for the people appeared to be to band together into unions. Unions grew very slowly during this period and were rebuffed at almost every turn by both big business and by the judiciary. The unions fared much better between 1932 and World War II under the New Deal era of President Franklin D. Roosevelt; in fact, during this period, labor was encouraged in many favorable ways. Since World War II, the law has been in an ambivalent state and can be and has been interpreted as being pro labor or pro management, depending on which sections of the law one chooses to read out of context with the rest of the law and which political administration happens to be in charge of interpreting and administering the law.

Until the 1930s labor law for the most part was shaped by the judiciary through the common law, equity proceedings, and constitutional interpretations. Since the banding together of people in a union to act with one accord against the company was considered a conspiracy by both management and the judiciary, it was placed under the common law doctrine of conspiracy.

The first criminal conspiracy trial in the United States, which is credited as being the beginning of the history of the unions and American labor law, was the 1806 conspiracy trial of the Philadelphia cordwinders. Between 1806 and 1842, at least 17 trials for conspiracy were tried. In many instances the penalties were mild and in the later part of the period, from 1829 to 1842, acquittals occurred about as often as convictions.[27]

As indicated above, there was no true consistency in the courts' interpretation of the conspiracy doctrine, and by the 1880s criminal conspiracy charges began to lose their momentum as a legal doctrine. With more cases going to jury trial, they could last for extended periods of time, with the juries not always returning a guilty charge. Management, therefore, began to change its tactics and bring the labor injunctions into play. This proved to be a much more effective legal tool with which to harass labor organizations.

Following the Civil War the unions used various tactics to try to thwart the conspiracy doctrine. They used strikes, picket lines, and primary and secondary boycotts in an attempt to pressure employers into conceding to the unions what the unions wanted.

Labor unions continued to grow in size and power and when conflicts occurred between labor and management they were no longer local fights between a dozen or so workers and a boss, but between management in general and large organized bodies of workers who were no longer obsessed by the middle-class dream. The laborers were beginning to see their fortunes, good or bad, dependent on whatever wage concessions they could obtain from their employer, either peacefully or, if necessary, through some combination of strike, boycott, or picketing.

Management chose the injunction as the weapon to fight against labors new tactics. The injunction was first used against labor as early as the 1880s; however, its full power was not demonstrated until the 1984 Pullman strike, when an injunction issued by a federal court was instrumental in breaking the strike by the American Railway Union. The injunction continued to be used thereafter by management with more frequency.

The unions continued to fight on to obtain their basic objectives, which have been to win recognition from the employer and to obtain wage and other concessions from him through negotiations. In 1919 Samuel Gompers, sometimes referred to as the father of the trade unions in this country, stated it this way:

The primary essential in our mission has been the protection of the wage-worker, now; to increase his wages; to cut off the long workday, which is killing him; to improve the safety and the sanitary conditions of the workshop; to free him from the tyrannies, petty or otherwise, which seemed to make his existence a slavery. These, in the nature of things, I repeat, were and are the primary objectives of trade unions.[28]

Alarmed by many setbacks and the hostility of the courts, the American Federation of Labor, in 1906, submitted a "bill of grievances" to the president and Congress, requesting that unions be exempted from Sherman Antitrust prosecution and for relief from court injunctions. Little response was forthcoming from the federal government until in 1914, under a more liberal Congress during the Wilson administration, Congress enacted the Clayton Act. Most of the law consisted of provisions that supplemented the Sherman Antitrust Act. Sections 6 and 20 of the new Clayton Act did, however, deal specifically with the complaints of labor. It permitted them to form unions;

unions were given freedom from being classified as illegal combinations, and it permitted relief on restraining orders.

The first major case tried under the Clayton Act was in 1921 in the case of *Duplex* v. *Deering*.[29] The International Association of Machinists tried through strike and secondary pressures to get the employees of the Duplex Printing Press Company, a nonunion company, to join the union. In this case the Supreme Court ruled against the union. The majority opinion in this case indicated that the Court was unwilling to concede that labor organizations had any legitimate interest in the conditions of employment in nonunionized companies.

In this brief examination of labor union–management confrontations, it can be seen that up to 1930 early labor law developed in three broad ways: (1) as a result of labor disputes, state and federal courts had many opportunities to rule upon the legality of various union tactics and actions; (2) judicial interpretations of the Sherman Antitrust Act developed a line of law concerning the relationship of that law to the actions and activities of labor unions; and (3) a small amount of new statutory law was generated but it was almost immediately torn to shreds by the courts.

Western Electric Hawthorne Studies

The Western Electric Company has always been a company that showed concern for the welfare of its employees. It has provided good physical working conditions, good wages, and good hours for its employees. As a result of these concerns for the worker there have always been good relationships between management and the worker.

In the late 1920s and early 1930s Western Electric wanted to test out the theory that work output was directly related to working conditions. To test this theory Western Electric arranged with Elton Mayo (a psychologist) and his associates at the Harvard Graduate School of Business Administration to conduct experiments on light intensity versus work output.[30] Two groups of workers were set up with one group (the control group) working under a constant light intensity while the intensity of the light was varied for the other group. All other work conditions were held as identical as possible for the two groups. Precise records of output were also kept on the two groups.

In the test group, work output did differ as the light intensity changed; however, it did not change in the anticipated manner. As light bulbs were changed the light intensity was increased, decreased, or kept at the same level. The workers commented favorably on the improved lighting under all light intensity changes (whether increased or decreased) and work output increased. Since all other variables were held constant in the two groups the conclusion of the experimenters was that the changes in work output were from psychological causes and not real causes—people reacted to the light intensity changes in the manner they thought management expected them to change rather than to the actual changes. Other similar experiments were made with the results best explained as a psychological reaction rather than a physiological reaction.

These results intrigued and puzzled the investigators. A new test was developed in an attempt to eliminate the psychological factors from the experiment and to possibly answer work-related questions in the areas of worker fatigue, desirability, and need for rest periods; optimum length of the working day; worker attitude toward their work and the company; effect of changing type of working equipment; and why production normally fell in the afternoon. All of this was done because management had a sincere interest in knowing more about its workers.

In April 1927 six women were selected from a large shop department at Western Electric's Hawthorne plant to participate in what came to be known as the "relay assembly test room" experiment. The six women were considered to be average workers whose work consisted of assembling telephone relays. Five of the women were to do the actual assembly of the relays while the sixth woman supplied the parts.

The test room was separated from the main assembly area with the work bench and assembly equipment identical to that in the shop area except for one thing: To the right of each woman was placed a slot in the bench into which she dropped the completed relay. When the relay was dropped into the slot it opened a gate that closed an electrical circuit that in turn punched a hole in a constant speed moving tape. This arrangement then recorded a permanent record of relay production output at all times of the working day.

From earlier experience in the light intensity experiment they were aware that many factors could enter into the work output speed. As a result, the experimenters also recorded a number of other items over the five-year test period. Other than for a "test room observer" who helped collect and maintain the records there was no supervision of the women in the normal factory operation sense.

When the test was ready to start, the women were called in for an interview and the nature of the test was explained to them in detail. They all consented to participate in the test. Each time a change in the experiment was to take place the women were again called into the office and the contemplated changes explained to them.

There were 12 major periods to the test in which different factors were changed. None of the results were truly what was expected. No matter what changes were made, the daily output in each test period increased over the daily output rate in the previous test period. If changes in output were truly directly related to the physical conditions of work, as had previously been supposed, the experimenters felt that then certainly there should have been a similarity in output rates in certain similar periods. Still somewhat puzzled they repeated several periods. Again, somewhat to their surprise, the daily output rate was higher in each succeeding period. Now they were certain that, as in the previous illumination studies, something was happening that could not fully be explained by the experimentally controlled work experiments that were conducted.

Test room experiments continued to the end of 1933 with continuing rise in output until a high plateau was reached. This high plateau was maintained until near the end of the tests when it declined slightly as a time of discouragement and deepened economic woes set in as a result of the depression. Statistical analysis of the data, conducted by T. N. Whitehead of Harvard University, showed that there was no simple correlation between work output and any of the other physical factors of change involved in the tests.

On the basis of these unexpected and interesting results the women were interviewed to see what reasons they might give for the continued increase in output regardless of the test conditions. Several reasons were given by the women, the most important being

1. The women thought it was fun and liked to work in the test room.
2. The absence of old supervisory control permitted them to work freely without anxiety. For example, if one of the women had a good reason for being tired the others would "carry" her.
3. The women knew they were taking part in an interesting experiment whose outcome would help them and the other workers at Western Electric. They knew that management was watching them and was interested in them.
4. Each contemplated change was explained to them and discussed with them by a high ranking company official. Their views were solicited and in some cases they were given veto power over what had been proposed. They were considered to be intelligent, thinking human beings.
5. A social group developed as well as a working group; on birthdays they were permitted to bring in cake and soft drinks and have a short celebration. They also went together socially after hours.
6. They developed and picked their own leader from among the members of the test team.
7. They developed and had a common purpose to increase the output rate without trying to make a race out of it. According to company reports, there was only one predominant item that showed a continuous relationship with the improved work output: the positive mental attitude of the test room operators.

Based on the early results of the relay assembly test room experiment a third phase to the program was developed. This was an interview program where all 40,000 employees were scheduled to be interviewed for a period of approximately one and one-half hours each. The employees endorsed the interview program with enthusiasm. Not only did the employees release their pent up feelings, views, and attitudes about the company and fellow workers (some well founded, some irrational, and some emotional) but in return had their own thoughts and views clarified. The interviews started in September

Table 4
Business Leader Attitudinal Changes from the Pre- to Post-Hawthorne Studies Period

Pre-1930 Period Taylor Philosophy	←—1930—→	Post-1930 Period Hawthorne Finding
1. Worker was economically motivated (prime concern for working was money)		1. Worker was economically motivated but was also socially motivated
2. There was a linear relationship between working conditions and output (work output went up in direct proportion with physical conditions of work area-lighting, heating, ventilation)		2. The relationship between working conditions and output was nonlinear
3. The worker was simple (easy to understand, manipulate, control)		3. The worker was quite complex
4. The workers' attitude was rational (They ran on a smooth path towards prescribed goals)		4. The workers' attitude was socially determined
5. The workers were indifferent to type of work they did (type of job workers had did not matter so long as they had a job)		5. The workers were not indifferent to the type of job they had
6. The workers' intelligence level determined output (the greater the intelligence, the greater the output)		6. There was no direct correlation between intelligence and worker output
7. Improve workers' efficiency by management improving processes		7. Worker involvement in process improvement also helps efficiency
8. What is good for the Company is good for the worker		8. Workers must be considered when making company changes
9. There was no place for unions		9. There was a place for unions

1928, a year and a half after the beginning of the relay assembly test room experiments started, and were completed in early 1929.

The interviews, in conjunction with the relay assembly test room experiment, revealed that many problems existed within the company and that informal organizations existed within the company for the purpose of rate setting (determining what was a fair day's work of the group) and for responding to technical questions (how the operation worked and what was being done). Normally a different informal leader was picked to head up each of the two areas of concern. A third test was set up to test out these findings. This was called the bank wiring observation room test, which ran for seven months from November 1931 to May 1932. Both earlier findings were verified.

The result of all of these findings electrified industry as a whole and changed the attitude of many business leaders. Perhaps what the union had been saying wasn't all wrong. No longer was the laborer a simple-minded economic creature who had no thinking capacity of his or her own but instead was a social person with deep feelings who was complex and intelligent. Table 4 summarizes the differences in how business leaders pictured workers being prior to the Hawthorne studies and after the Hawthorne studies.

These studies, along with Dewey's work and writing, placed the early opening in the doors of industry for increased involvement by psychologists, sociologists, philosophers, and behavioral management specialists to enter into industry and advise (and sometimes even direct) upper management how best to operate their business.

SUMMARY

This chapter reviews some of the leading European and American writers, thinkers, and practitioners from the time of the American Revolution up to 1930. It discusses and shows how they influenced the operational and social awareness changes in industry during this period. It historically discusses the growth of America from a rural farm–dominated economy to a predominantly industrial economy. Industry formation, growth, and operation are reviewed from the early "robber baron" formative years through the taming of this monopolistic growth pattern by the implementation of new laws and judiciary restraint as the federal government grew in power. The growth and battles with management and judicial personnel that the workers go through in their early union-forming days are reviewed as are the early Hawthorne studies that show that workers are not simple indifferent persons as management depicted them but are complex social persons as the union was trying to say.

NOTES

1. Adam Smith, *An Inquiry into the Nature and Causes of the Wealth of Nations* (Oxford: Clarendon Press, 1976).

2. Ibid., book 4, ch. 2.

3. Adam Smith, *An Inquiry into the Nature and Causes of the Wealth of Nations* (Oxford: Clarendon Press, 1976), vol. 1, pp. 7–8.

4. Jeremy Bentham, "Introduction to the Principles and Morals of Legislation," in Bowring's edition of *Bentham's Works* (Oxford: Clarendon Press, 1879).

5. "Greed Gains Ground," *U.S. News & World Report* 104, no. 3 (January 25, 1988): 10.

6. Erick Roll, *An Early Experiment in Industrial Organization* (London: Longmans, Green, 1930).

7. Thomas Robert Malthus, *Population: The First Essay* (Ann Arbor: University of Michigan Press, 1939), p. 38.

8. Thomas J. Hailstones, Bernard L. Martin, and Frank V. Mastrianna, "Contemporary Economic Problems and Issues," 2d ed. (Cincinnati: South Western Publishing, 1970), pp. 474–508.

9. Charles Babbage, *On the Economy of Machinery and Manufacturers* (London: Charles Knight, 1832).

10. Herbert Spencer, *Social Statics* (London: Appleton, 1850), pp. 323–326.

11. W. S. Jevons, *The Theory of Political Economy* (New York: Macmillan and Company, 1888), p. 204.

12. C. E. Ferguson, *Microeconomic Theory* (Homewood, Ill.: Richard D. Irwin, 1969), p. 455.

13. Max Weber, *The Protestant Ethic and the Spirit of Capitalism*, trans. Tolcott Parsons (New York: Scribner's, 1958).

14. Barbara Kallen, "Praying for Guidance," *Forbes* 19, no. 4 (December 1, 1986): 220–221.

15. John A. Hobson, *Work and Wealth: A Human Valuation* (New York: Macmillan, 1914).

16. A. C. Pigou, *The Economics off Welfare*, 4th ed. (London: Macmillan, 1932).

17. Frederick W. Taylor, *The Principles of Scientific Management* (New York: Harper and Brothers, 1911).

18. John Dewey, *Individualism Old and New* (Capricorn Books, 1962), pp. 14, 15, 29, 93, 98, 149.

19. Ibid., pp. 14, 149.

20. Ibid., pp. 74, 131.

21. Ibid., pp. 33, 70, 71.

22. Ibid., pp. 83, 187.

23. Ibid., pp. 122, 129.

24. Ibid., pp. 138, 146.

25. Quoted in Matthew Josephson, *The Robber Barons* (New York: Harcourt Brace Jovanovich, 1962), p. 50.

26. 211 U.S. 1; 211 U.S. 106.

27. John R. Commons and Associates, *Documentary History of American Industrial Society* (Cleveland: Arthur H. Clark Co., 1910), vols. 3, 4.

28. Samuel Gompers, *Labor and the Common Welfare* (New York: Doulton, 1919), pp. 7–8.

29. 254 U.S. 443 (1921).

30. Elton Mayo, *The Human Problems of an Industrial Civilization* (New York: Macmillan, 1933).

6

Social Prominence
(1930–1988)

The 1930s signaled a transition from a primarily laissez-faire economy with industrial power and might in control to a more mixed economy with unions and government taking a more activist role. The Western Electric Company Hawthorne studies alerted both industry and labor to the fact that workers were not just simple-minded people whose only concern in life was economic, but rather that the worker was intelligent and was a socially oriented human being with feelings and desires beyond a weekly paycheck. The Great Depression of the 1930s weakened business' hold on labor and the economy as a whole and showed that business did not have all the answers. The New Deal under President Franklin D. Roosevelt ushered in several factors that changed the entire atmosphere of the country:

1. The passage of the Wagner Act in 1935 swung the pendulum in the direction of favoring labor over industry.

2. The conversion and/or replacement of conservative, business-oriented Supreme Court judges with more socially oriented pro-labor judges gave the federal government and labor more active power than they had ever previously had or exercised.

3. The implementation of numerous federally sponsored socially oriented programs to help out the deplorable economic condition of the country made people more socially minded.

4. The adoption of Keynesian welfare-oriented economics permitted the federal government to try to speed the country into recovery through large deficit spending and implementation of numerous welfare programs.

5. The U.S. entrance into World War II where business recovered, employment sky-rocketed and women entered the work force in large numbers.

During the 1930s, 1940s, and into the 1950s business' social responsibilities grew with emphasis placed on employee welfare (pension funds, insurance plans, and a few profit-sharing plans), medical care, retirement programs, safety programs, and vacation, sick leave, and special situation time off. Competition and in some instances government regulations, and growing social concern and responsibility for the employee helped bring about these changes in industry behavior.

The period from the mid and late 1950s on through the present time have brought about the most dramatic changes in social awareness and responsibility in this country. Social responsibility and social awareness have changed both in scope and in the broadening of the meaning. Humanistic, psychological, socially, and behaviorally minded educators and leaders have continued to conduct research beyond the Hawthorne studies and have written about and implemented the results wherever possible into the educational system for training and guiding business leaders. Local, state, and the federal governments have continued to enact and enforce increased numbers of more in-depth legislation that is favorable to social responsibility and social conduct by business. This action has taken place through such legislation as the Civil Rights Act of 1960, the National Environmental Policy Act of 1969, Fair Packaging and Labeling Act of 1966, the Truth in Lending Act of 1969; the Privacy Act of 1974, and many others. Industry is also more deeply involved in social awareness and self-generation of social programs. This is shown in their attempted compliance with all new government legislation as well as the increased efforts on their part to increase company initiated and sponsored programs such as stock purchase, profit sharing, child care, maternity leave, and a variety of other programs. The enactment of the Taft-Hartley Act and the Landrum-Griffin Act have swung the pendulum back nearer the center in an attempt to stabilize and balance power between labor and management. The welfare economics proposed by Keynes are still being employed even though they have been somewhat modified in recent administrations.

In another area, judicial action has removed active access to and dissemination of much of the Judeo-Christian teachings that were the foundation for most of the moral and ethical direction of early business and government. In 1963 the Supreme Court banned prayer and other Bible recitation in schools, in 1980 the display of the Ten Commandments in public schools was banned, and in 1987 a state law requiring balanced treatment of creation and scientific evolution was ruled unconstitutional.

In the meantime in the moral-ethical area, more emphasis is being placed on psychology and the philosophies of Hegel, Spencer, and Dewey (everything is relative; nothing is absolute; everything is constantly changing, so set your own morals and ethics based on the times); the existentialism of Jean-

Paul Sartre (a philosophy of nihilism and pessimism); Jevon's pain-pleasure principle and Bentham's pain-happiness principle (if it feels good, do it); Maslow's psychology that self-actualization is the peak of satisfaction and fulfillment (the "I am number one" philosophy); and Malthus' concepts of positive and negative population control (zero population growth, abortion on demand, planned parenthood, and even euthanasia in some instances).

Broad issue orientation has given way to sharper focus not only on issues but on social awareness, social responsiveness, and on social responsibility implementation of these issues.

Other than for the period of the Depression, this was a period of rapid growth, particularly during and following World War II. In the early part of the period, farm employment continued to decrease and industrial growth was rapid. Today the service industry is the most rapid growth sector in the economy. The civilian labor force has grown from 60.6 million in 1948 to almost 112 million in 1983. Over the same period men in the labor force have increased from 43.3 million to 63.0 million while women have increased from 17.3 million to 48.5 million.

European influence continued to decrease with time and the United States became more powerful in setting its own destiny. Perhaps the strongest European influence of this period came from English-born John Maynard Keynes, with lesser influence from French philosopher Jean-Paul Sartre. The major changes in American business and service industry growth came about through worldwide trade expansion and increased output efficiencies, new governmental laws and judicial decisions, the large influx of women into the business area, and the goals, objectives, desires, and aspirations of the administration in power.

EUROPEAN INFLUENCE

Even though the thinking and writing of the European classicists (Adam Smith and David Ricardo) and their neoclassical followers (Alfred Marshall and Arthur Cecil Pigou) still had some influence on the American continent as well as in Europe, it was very quickly replaced in the mid–1930s with the economics of John Maynard Keynes, who had tremendous influence on the economic policy of America during the early and mid-part of this period. Of lesser but still of significant influence on the thinking of America were the teachings of French philosopher, novelist, and dramatist Jean-Paul Sartre. Most of his influence permeated this country and its educational systems following World War II.

John Maynard Keynes (1883–1946)

Keynes was born in Cambridge, the son of an economics professor. His book *The General Theory of Employment, Interest and Money* hit the market at an appropriate time: The world was in the middle of a chaotic depression.[1]

It was Keynes' position that the full employment equilibrium of the classical economists was not the one and only equilibrium but only one of many that the economy could settle at; that is, the classical equilibrium was not a general equilibrium but only a special case. Whereas the classical economists held the position that equilibrium was at full employment and any drift below this level would automatically put into motion forces that would tend to drive the economy back to full employment, Keynes held that equilibrium point below full employment would be just as stable as one at full employment.

More than any other economist, Keynes was able to shift the emphasis in economics from micro economics (the study of individual economic men and business) to macro economics (the study of groups and measurable aggregates). In addition, he shifted the emphasis in economic inquiry to the central problem of what factors influence and control the employment level in an economy. By taking output as a variable, Keynes demonstrated that equilibrium could be reached at a level less than full employment.

When considering the economy as a whole, if for any reason society decides to save more without a corresponding increase in investment, effective demand will fall, output will fall along with it, and eventually employment will fall; therefore, the level of employment is determined by the demand for goods, which in turn is dependent on the rate of consumption at the time. Thus, the willingness to invest will help decide the level of output. This willingness to invest is in turn dependent upon the rate of return on the invested capital over cost and the rate of interest.

Keynes recommended a reduction in bank interest rates to stimulate investment. He also favored progressive income taxation that would make income distribution more equal and thus create a higher aggregate capacity to consume. The contribution for which he is probably best noted and remembered by is his advocacy of government investment, through public works and other means, as a means of "pump priming": to get the economy moving again when private investment falls off.

It is not difficult to see why these concepts of Keynes' were quickly adopted in an attempt to pull the country out of the Depression. In 1932 gross private domestic investment was less than $1 billion down from $16 billion in 1929 prior to the crash. New construction was down from a level of $7.8 billion in 1929 to $1.7 billion in 1932 and $1.1 billion in 1933. Producers' durable equipment had slipped from a level of $6.4 billion in 1929 to approximately $1.8 billion in 1932 and 1933. Business inventories went from a positive level of $1.6 billion in 1932 to a disinvestment level of $2.6 billion in 1932 and $1.6 billion in 1933. This, then, was an almost total collapse on investment; construction was down 85 percent, private domestic investment was down 90 percent, durable equipment was down 70 percent, and inventories had slipped into the negative column. Because of this, 25 percent of the work force was unemployed by 1933 and many of those still working had their wages reduced by 60 percent.

Jean-Paul Sartre (1905–1980)

Sartre espoused the philosophy of existentialism. This was a movement in philosophy, with roots in nineteenth-century Germany that developed from the thoughts of Kierkegaard and Nietzsche. The chief exponents of the philosophy in Germany have been Martin Heidegger and Karl Jaspers with Sartre being the chief expounder of the philosophy in France. Following World War II a cult of nihilism and pessimism developed in France based on the doctrines of Sartre and other existentialist writers. Some of the aspects of this cult and philosophy are that it involves (1) a doctrine that denies existence; (2) a doctrine that denies any basis for knowledge or truth; (3) a total denial of all traditional and existing principles, values, and institutions; (4) a doctrine that the world and life are essentially evil; (5) the theory that the existing universe is the worst possible world; and (6) a disposition to take a gloomy or cynical view of affairs and situations with little hope for a happy ending.

This philosophy and thinking moved from France into the writings and educational systems of America in the 1950s, 1960s, and 1970s. Many public school systems and schools of higher learning made the reading of existentialist writers required reading material. This had a very negative impact on the students of that time because of the extreme nihilistic and pessimistic leanings of many of the writings. Much of this teaching still haunts many of these people today and leaves them with flexible moral/ethical attitudes and in some cases pessimistic and even fatalistic feelings and emotions.

AMERICAN INFLUENCE

During this time period, other than for Keynes and worldwide depression, the United States was almost totally under its own influence. To discuss all areas of influence would be insurmountable; therefore, in keeping with the previous format, only a few major areas will be discussed in this historical development of business and social responsibility. The major areas that will be briefly discussed for background purposes to show their impact and influence on this period's business growth and social responsibility are the various presidential administrations, writers and thinkers of the time, the rapid increase and proliferation of new laws, new business ventures and growth of old ones, and the influence and impact of unions under new-found freedoms.

Presidential Administrations

This period opened in the middle of a deep and severe depression. Big business appeared helpless to lift the economy out of its slump and the local, state, and federal government was not in too much better shape to help. However, with no other place to turn, many of the people did ask the federal government to help out. This gave each new administration an opportunity to make many promises and then try to solve the multitude of problems as they saw them, in a manner they thought best. Each administration had its own approach and introduced many changes into a country that was ready to experiment and change and was ready for big government.

With World War I and the era of prosperity from 1923 through 1929, social reform and business reform were relatively dormant during this period that President Warren Harding had termed as a return to "normalcy." The stock market crash of late 1929, the failure of business to bring the economy out of the Depression, and the findings of bank and stock market manipulation, fraud, and corruption by the Senate Committee on Banking and Currency in 1933 left the public with little or no confidence in any business activity and left them open for the reform programs of the New Deal under the Franklin D. Roosevelt administration.

The New Deal

Franklin D. Roosevelt was sworn into office as president on March 14, 1933. He immediately blamed the bankers for most of the problems confronting the country: a poor economy, 25 percent of the work force unemployed, wages of the remainder lowered by as much as 60 percent, and the farmers suffering because of low commodity prices. Two days after his inauguration the president went on the air with the first of his many "fireside chats." He assured the country that the banks would be reopened (they had been closed several days earlier to prevent mass withdrawals) and that they had already started working on things to aid the ailing country.

President Roosevelt immediately organized a "brain trust" of economic advisers to help him draft legislative programs to help with social reform for the country. The National Industrial Recovery Act (NIRA) was enacted in 1933 and was quickly found unconstitutional by the Supreme Court. The Supreme Court continued to be a thorn in President Roosevelt's side during his first administration. The Court was divided into basically three camps: four justices were totally out of sympathy with the philosophy of the New Deal legislation; three judges, while not necessarily enthusiastic with the New Deal legislation, believed basically that the Constitution imposed no barriers against Congress to enact New Deal reform and recovery measures; the third group, or swing group, was made up of two judges who in most instances voted with the first group of four conservative, pro-business judges. This Court philosophy became an issue in the 1936 presidential election and it became quite apparent that with his landslide return to office, President Roosevelt would immediately take the offensive on this issue. The method of attack he chose was to "pack" the federal courts by appointing additional judges when incumbents over 70 years of age refused to retire. This caused sufficient political excitement that it caused the two swing votes on the Supreme Court to swing over and start voting in support of more social causes.

President Roosevelt also learned during his first term that he could not solve the problems of the country by putting his major emphasis on labor. He started working closer with all three sections of the economy—labor, business, and the farm sector. Regulatory controls were issued over banks, issuers of securities, public utility holding companies, motor carriers, and securities exchanges. Numerous job relief programs were initiated for the needy and unemployed, electrical power was provided to farmers and the countryside, public housing was erected and other public works programs were initiated, expanded natural resources conservation was undertaken, low-interest loans were provided to various individuals and institutions, and the national security program was formally introduced.

With all of its programs the country was still in deep problems. At the start of his second term the president for a short period tried to balance the budget but quickly went to his Keynesian economic policies, deficit spending, and "pump priming" in an attempt to keep the floundering economy moving. His antitrust head, Thurman W. Arnold, aggressively prosecuted collusive agreements between businesses and in 1940 alone 87 cases were prosecuted; this was more than were prosecuted in the entire administration of Theodore Roosevelt who was known as the great "trust buster."[2]

With continued pump priming, deficit spending, the outbreak of World War II in Europe and the United States starting to supply some goods to the allied forces in Europe, the U.S. economy continued to improve. With his third term and the entry of the United States into World War II, the economy improved with government and business once again working closely together. Midway through the war, President Roosevelt died and the country emerged from the war under President Harry S. Truman.

The Fair Deal

President Truman served for two terms during and following World War II. He continued many of the policies of the previous administration and guided the country through the postwar period of capital goods shortages, price controls, wage controls, rent controls and many other government controls. The term *fair deal* came from his 1949 State of the Union address in which he stated, "Every segment of our population and every individual has a right to expect from his government a fair deal."[3]

The "fair deal" administration suffered through a not too active Eightieth and Eighty-first Congress. In fact, they were noted at the time as being the "do-nothing" Eightieth Congress of 1947–1948 and the "ho-hum" Eighty-first Congress of 1949–1950. In spite of a not too active Congress, this was the time period of passage of the Employment Act of 1946 wherein a three-member Council of Economic Advisers was established; the Council's role included assisting the president in formulating economic policy and also publishing an annual economic report. Also passed in this time period was the Taft-Hartley Act of 1947 (see the section on Unions in this chapter for details on the Act), extension of the idea of the Tennessee Valley Authority to other river basins, and improvements in social security, medical insurance, and public housing.

Business and unions were not to be outdone by the federal government in their response to social welfare and social responsibility. In 1948 General Motors gave the United Auto Workers an "escalator clause" in their contracts; this clause automatically adjusted the pay level according to changes in the consumer price index. This was the beginning of many concessions by management to labor over the following years.

The Eisenhower Years

The Eisenhower years from 1953 to 1960 were relatively stable years of a good economy and relatively low inflation. His administration followed a middle-of-the-road domestic policy while trying to maintain a balanced budget under a Democratic Congress. Although a Republican, he worked well with the Democratic Congress and was able to generate respectable achievements in air and water pollution control, civil rights, social security, aid to education, highway construction, agricultural support, and major river basin projects. He also undertook government reorganization and was able to create a Department of Health, Education, and Welfare.

The New Frontier

John F. Kennedy continued and expanded the social programs started under Presidents Truman and Eisenhower. This included increases in social security benefits, minimum wage increases and extension to other people, and a housing bill. Other social legislation started by President Kennedy and passed the year following his assassination were the Equal Opportunity Act, the Tax Reform Act, and the Civil Rights Act.

The major premise upon which the "New Frontier" in economic growth was to take place was through a personal income tax cut that in turn would stimulate investment, consumption, and employment. Coming out of a period of the Eisenhower administration of a balanced budget, low inflation, and tolerable production increases and unemployment, this was considered a good approach to take, and one that worked well.

For the income tax cut to work effectively, both labor and management were supposed to maintain price and wage levels consistent with demonstrated increases in productivity improvements. However, U.S. Steel broke out of this pattern shortly after signing a noninflationary wage contract with the Steel Workers Union. U.S. Steel almost immediately increased the price of steel by $6 per ton and other major producers followed suit with similar price increases. The administrations reaction was immediate in that it threatened to transfer the purchase of all of its steel to only those producers who did not increase their prices. A few days later the major steel producers had rolled their prices back to their original level. This sent a message to big business that the administration was serious. As a result of these policies, price stability continued from 1961 through 1965 when the average consumer price index increase was close to 1 percent per year.

This was also the period of confrontation with the communists in Cuba to prevent them from placing missiles on Cuban soil within destructive range of much of the United States. It was also the period of extensive civil rights activity that the Kennedy administration was dedicated to solving and that resulted in the Civil Rights Act. It also was the beginning of the buildup of advisers and help to Vietnam, which was to break this country into opposing camps in following years and involve the United States in a frustrating war of containment that it did not win.

The Great Society

Lyndon B. Johnson took over as president upon the assassination of John F. Kennedy. He continued to support the social programs of his predecessor and was able to initiate a few more of his own. During the period 1964–1969 these included enactment or creation of such programs as support of medical aid for older Americans, improved housing, improved consumer information and product safety, the creation of an Office of Economic Opportunity to administer the war on poverty program, and the creation of a cabinet-level Department of Housing and Urban Development in 1965 and in 1966 a Department of Transportation.

The role of government continued to expand under the "Great Society." With increased government welfare programs and an expanding Vietnam conflict, the expenditures had increased to $200 billion in 1968 compared with $100 billion in 1960. The people seemed to be willing, and even eager, to let big government restrain big business and to take care of those who could not, and in some cases even would not, take care of themselves.

The Nixon-Ford Period

This period continued on with the passage of more socially oriented legislation such as the Agriculture and Consumer Protection Act, the Highway Safety Act, the Water Resources Development Act, the Safe Drinking Water Act, the Toxic Substance Control Act, and the Occupational Safety and Health Act (OSHA). A 1974 campaign law further legitimized business involvement in election by permitting the establishment by business of political action committees known as PACs. This permitted business legally to enter into collecting campaign contributions for candidates. All of this legislation led to more government control and what is claimed by many as improved social responsibility of business.

This period also continued and expanded the U.S. role in the Vietnam War and all of the problems associated with it. It also brought the downfall of President Nixon through the Watergate scandal, a combination of illegal, unethical, and immoral practices. Although most people appeared horrified with the Watergate illegal breaking and entering into unauthorized areas and the illegal, unethical, and immoral attempted cover up of the entire incident, it made very little impact on improving total moral and ethical conduct of people at large.

The Carter Years

President Carter and his administration continued to pass more socially oriented legislation such as the Railroad Revitalization and Regulatory Reform Act, Public Law 95–507, airline deregulation, and others. President Carter started a move to also cut down on the size of big government and try to streamline it. Other than to lay out some of the plans, not much progress was made along these lines.

Under President Carter the economy also worsened. Unemployment rates climbed all over the country and inflation continued to climb into the double digits. These conditions, in addition to his inability to obtain release of American citizens who were being held prisoners by the Iranians, led to his defeat and a landslide victory by President Reagan in 1980.

The Reagan Period

President Reagan and his administration came into power in 1981 after a landslide victory at the polls in 1980. His platform was a return to less big government, movement of many social programs back to the public sector with more involvement by the public sector, and improved economic conditions.

Shortly after he took office he was confronted with a strike by government workers involved in air traffic control. Since they would not settle their strike and refused to work, President Reagan replaced them. This set the stage not only in the government sector, but also in the private sector for unions to go on the defensive. With this new attitude of the government, high unemployment, high inflation, and increased foreign imports, the unions and labor in general gave back to management many of their early gains from years past.

With the Reagan policies in place, by early 1988 reduced inflation was still in the 4 percent area, employment was higher than ever before in the country, and unemployment was less than 6 percent of the labor force. Only once since 1974—in May 1979 when the rate was 5.6 percent—has the percentage of jobless Americans been lower.[4]

New federal legislation in the social arena fell off during this period, and deregulation and freedom from antitrust enforcement increased. More emphasis was placed on society controlling itself with the multitude of existing laws that were already in place. One major change that was made to help business and society help improve society in general was a change generated in the 1982 federal tax laws and retained in later tax revisions. This tax law change permitted a company to increase its contribution to social and philanthropic causes from 5 percent to 10 percent of taxable income. Even though this law has now been in place for several years, most companies still average in the 1 percent area. Only a few companies continue in the 5 percent club established under the old tax law, and most companies appear reluctant to even consider giving an amount up to 10 percent. This would amount to contributions of hundreds of millions of dollars from some of the larger companies.

The Reagan administration is also in favor of free trade and improved business efficiencies. The free trade attitude has caused some businesses to fail and others to change lines of business, improve efficiencies, or merge. It has kept inflation down, forced businesses to innovate and improve efficiencies, and forced a realignment in types of work available to employees. The basically hands-off attitude toward mergers and takeovers has resulted in considerable realignment of industry, increased foreign involvement and participation in U.S. business, and development of unique techniques to prevent takeovers and "greenmail."

The Reagan policies have also resulted in large federal budgets, high deficits, and a strongly negative balance of trade; although with improved American efficiencies and a reduction in the value of the dollar, the balance of trade is starting to turn around.

American Thinkers and Writers

This period was influenced by many thinkers and writers from many schools of management thought, which in turn have had considerable impact on social responsibility. The theories and concepts are so many and divergent one management writer has seen fit to call them the "management theory jungle."[5] The quantitative school places its emphasis on linear programming, calculus, statistics, and mathematical models for solutions to business problems; the systems school looks at the physical, biological, and managerial aspects and stresses the interrelatedness and interdependency of the parts to the whole; the human relations and behavioral movement emphasizes psychological aspects of motivation of people; and the contingency school (sometimes referred to as the situational approach) says use all tools available (know all of the theories) and pick the one or ones best suited for each situation. Major emphasis in this section will be placed on the human relations and behavioral school since this particular school of thought is the one most emphasized and taught in most universities in the country and its theories are predominant in the workplace.

The human relations and behavioral management movement began in the late 1920s and early 1930s with the Hawthorne studies and experiments conducted by Elton Mayo. Following these studies and publication of their results, the psychologists and sociologists began their move into the management and the business arena and tried to determine how it should and could best be operated for maximum happiness and output of employees and employers.

Abraham Maslow

The behavioral management concept was primarily triggered around 1943 by a psychologist, Abraham Maslow, who developed a hierarchy of needs model.[6] As shown in Figure 2, the needs range from psysiological as one of the first needs to be fulfilled on up the ladder to Maslow's peak of self-actualization. As originally proposed, each lower need had to be filled prior to stepping up to a higher need. Today, however, most behavioralists believe that the needs fulfillment can be going on in several steps at the same time. It should also be noted that the Maslow model can be considered as a selfish model in that the peak of his model ends with *self*-actualization, or "I have achieved my ultimate goal and peak"; "I am number one." The emphasis is on achieving one's own gratification and happiness, even at the expense of others. Almost every student who has taken a basic psychology course or a basic behavioral management course since World War II has been exposed to this model and theory. It is a model and theory that, if stopped at this point, promotes selfishness in the individual and leaves no one truly satisfied. As can be seen on the left hand scale of the figure, a person is only about 85 percent satisfied at most within himself or herself when the self-actualization state has been reached. James A. Kenny and his theory of "Beyond Self-actualization" continues on beyond that of Maslow.

James A. Kenny

Is there anything then beyond Maslow's self-actualization? Dr. James A. Kenny thinks that there is: "I see self-actualization as a step on the way to love and truism.... The self is never something that finally is.... The self can never be static. We are always developing, seeking, growing, reaching inward and outward."[7]

Dr. Kenny feels that self-actualization as a final goal would be a mistake that will shortchange the individual and those surrounding him or her. As shown in Figure 2 he feels that each person must go on to mutual actualization and finally to self-donation in order to reach 100 percent satisfaction. The step above self-actualization is mutual actualization. "Mutual actualization is the process whereby two individuals enrich each other and in so doing they grow both as individuals and as a couple...."[8] Dr. Kenny goes on to explain that mutual actualization is, however, still not the final goal; the final goal is self-donation. It is a stage where the self is learning to transcend itself. Some call it total love and some call it altruism.

Can anyone reach this final stage? Dr. Kenny feels that it can be reached. The Apostles of Jesus Christ certainly reached this stage. Dr. Kenny also mentions people such as Mahatma Gandhi, Tom Dooley, and Martin Luther King, Jr., as fitting into this category. The Good Samaritan discussed in Chapter

Figure 2
Hierarchy of Needs

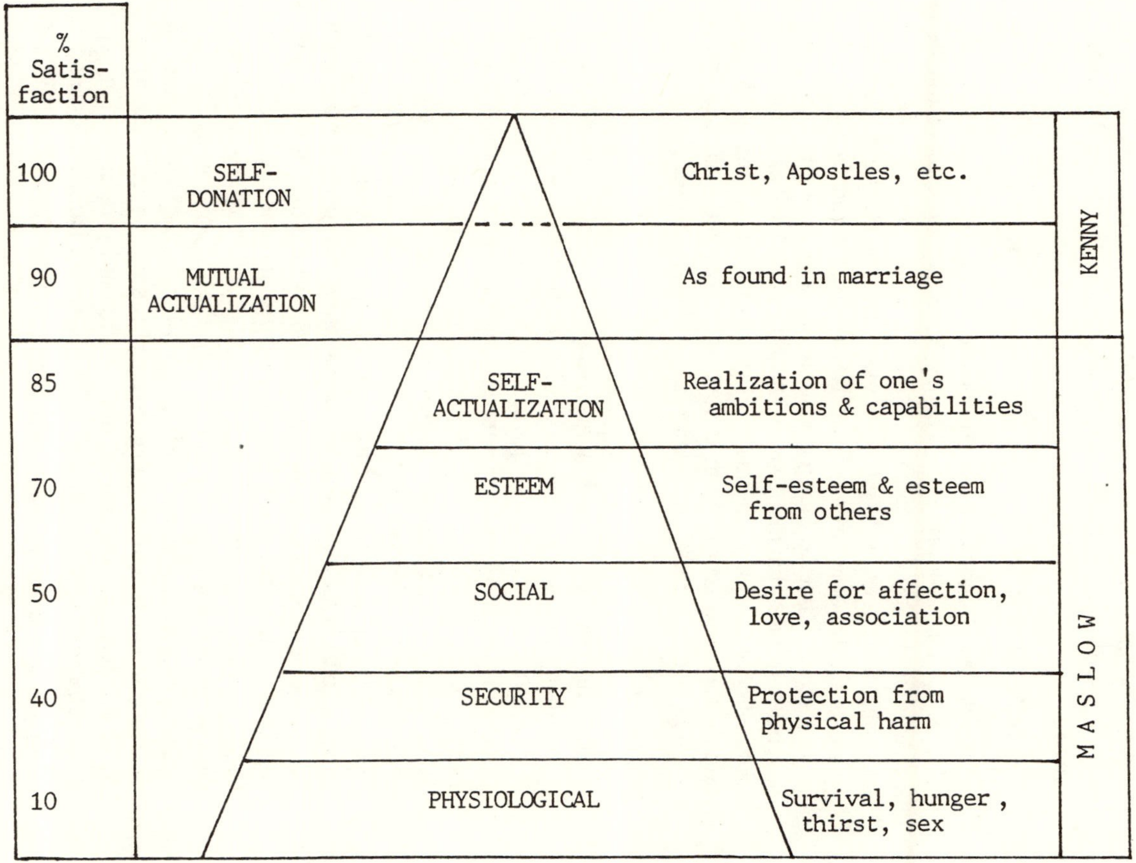

% Satis-faction			
100	SELF-DONATION		Christ, Apostles, etc.
90	MUTUAL ACTUALIZATION		As found in marriage
85		SELF-ACTUALIZATION	Realization of one's ambitions & capabilities
70		ESTEEM	Self-esteem & esteem from others
50		SOCIAL	Desire for affection, love, association
40		SECURITY	Protection from physical harm
10		PHYSIOLOGICAL	Survival, hunger, thirst, sex

KENNY

MASLOW

3, as well as those reaching the highest level of ethical and moral conduct listed in the early Jewish Talmud (also discussed in Chapter 3), would also reach this highest level of altruism. This certainly is a much superior level to reach for rather than stop at self-actualization.

Other popular motivational and behavioral theories have been developed by Douglas McGregor, Chris Argyris, Frederick Hertzberg, B. F. Skinner, and others.

Douglas McGregor

Douglas McGregor of the Sloan School of Management (MIT) developed "theory X" and "theory Y."[9] "Theory X" is at one end of the behavioral spectrum in that it states that man dislikes work and must be coerced, directed, and controlled in order to get work out of him; he can be made to contribute to the goals and objectives only by threatening the satisfaction of his psychological security needs. McGregor's "theory Y" sits at the other end of the spectrum. It states that man likes work and can and will exercise self-direction and self-control; the individual will participate in setting goals for himself and for the organization. In theory, most people and organizations fall some place in between these two extremes on the spectrum.

Chris Argyris

Chris Argyris was a psychologist from Yale who promoted the theory of "personality and the organization."[10] He felt that there was a conflict between the structure of the formal organization and the total personality. He stated that the organization was structured such that there was a task specialization, a chain of command, unity of direction, and a given span of control. On the other hand, he felt that the individual looks at life as a continuum from childhood to adulthood, which is defined as the total personality. It goes from passivity to activity, dependency to independency, behavioral inflexibility to behavioral flexibility, from a subordinate to a superordinate position, and from lack of awareness to full awareness and control of one's self. Argyris says that the formal organizational structure and the total personality are in conflict with one another. As a result of this conflict a person will develop one or several alternatives such as climbing the organizational ladder, quitting and seeking employment elsewhere, forming a group to gain remedial action or cause trouble, remain unhappy all of his life, or quit and form his own company. Without adequate understanding and proper working conditions there is bound to be continual conflict between labor and management.

Frederick Herzberg

Psychologist Frederick Herzberg developed, based on extensive testing and studies in all types of occupations and diverse cultures inside and outside the United States, what he called a "two-factor motivation–hygiene theory."[11] There are two groups of situations that influence the employee. He classified these as "maintenance or hygiene factors" and "satisfiers or motivational factors." The "maintenance or hygiene factors" are needed but do not lead to great motivation. They do lead to demotivation if they are not present. They include such items as interpersonal relations, supervision, company and policy administration, job security, working conditions, and salary. The "satisfiers or motivational factors," if present, lead to motivation but are not greatly dissatisfying if not present. They include such factors as the work itself, responsibility, advancement, growth, achievement, recognition, and status. Herzberg and his colleagues have been quite successful in applying this theory to actual industrial situations.

B. F. Skinner

The theories looked at so far have been primarily motivational theories. Behavioral theory, on the other hand, does not rely on any consent of motivation. Behavioral theory simply looks at behavior and its consequences. The behavioralists feel that it is the consequence of behavior, and not any supposed or imagined inner mental attitude or process, that shapes and determines any particular way of behaving. According to psychologist B. F. Skinner, the consequences of behavior determines behavior by a process known as "operant" or "instrumental conditioning."[12] He believes that a person's behavior can be every bit as controlled as a pigeon's (just that a person is a little more complex). This can be accomplished by positive reinforcement of good behavior or negative reinforcement of bad behavior.

Robert R. Blake and Jane S. Mouton

Although there are differences between the motivation theories and the behavioral theories, these differences may mean very little to managers in business because they tend to imply similar management practices. In fact, there are some theories that definitely use a combination of motivational and behavioral techniques. Three such theories are the Blake-Mouton managerial grid, management by objectives (MBO), and the world famous "carrot and stick" approach.

Beginning in the 1940s, studies conducted at Ohio State University and the University of Michigan looked into ways to produce the best management-worker relationship.[13] The feeling was that if a best style could be identified, it would be possible to train people to learn and adopt efficient and appropriate behaviors to improve leader-worker relationships. The studies first suggested that the subordinates of more people-oriented leaders made more productive leaders than those people working for more task-oriented leaders. Later results, however, showed that in actuality best leaders combined both people and task orientations into a more democratic and participative leadership style. Continued research has shown that for good leader-worker relationships the leader must be both people oriented (considerate in their relationships with other people) and task oriented (interested in getting the task accomplished).[14]

Perhaps one of the best known and the most popular models to evolve from this data is the Blake-Mouton two-dimensional managerial grid.[15] Using a vertical and horizontal axis, the crossover point of the two axes is given a value of zero. The horizontal or base axis is labeled "concern for production" (the task-oriented axis) and is measured off in equal spaces from zero (left) to nine (right); the vertical axis is labeled "concern for people" (the people-oriented axis) and is also measured off in equal spaces from zero (bottom) to nine (top). In both instances the nine level denotes the superior performance. The purpose of the grid is to train people and then measure their performance on the grid; a score of nine on each axis is the desired goal.

Peter Drucker and G. S. Odiorne

Another combined motivation and behavior process that has enjoyed relative popularity for several years is a concept known as management by objectives (MBO). Peter Drucker was one of the early proponents of this concept.[16] G. S. Odiorne has popularized it.[17] Basically it brings both management and worker together to discuss and jointly establish the goals and objectives and how they are to be measured. There are four to six major steps in the process, depending on which of many authors one might be following. In January 1979, Mark McConkie reviewed and compared 40 different articles and concepts of MBO and listed where they agreed and where they disagreed.[18] If four major steps are followed, the supervisor and worker will get together and (1) establish the goals and objectives in terms of specific measurable results; (2) develop action plans including costs, labor, and time to perform the tasks; (3) conduct periodic reviews and modify the plan as needed; and (4) evaluate and appraise the plan at the end of program or at the end of each year, whichever comes first.

MRS. PIC

Another combined motivational and behavioral concept is that which is called the plain old "carrot" (reward) and the "stick" (punishment) concept; for ease of remembering, it can be called the "MRS. PIC" theory. It helps establish the organizational process and behavior that is to be followed. First standards (S) by which one must work are established and a method of measuring (M) whether the standards are met must be developed and explained. Controls (C) must also be developed and in place to make certain that all standards, rules, regulations, policies, and procedures are met. Some forms of incentives (I) must be in place to induce the worker to want to meet the established standards. If the standards are met or exceeded, then the person is rewarded (R) and if the person does not meet the standards, then they are punished (P). This is a basic concept that has been around for many years and is practiced by many who have never been exposed to the more sophisticated theories previously examined.

Comments on American Writers and Thinkers

The better known and more popular theories discussed here are only a few of the multitude of theories that exist and have come into prominence since the 1930s; they are barely the tip of the iceberg. If this is the case then a valid set of questions that can be asked are: (1) Why has there been such a proliferation of theories since the 1930s? (2) Do these theories actually work? and (3) How, if at all, have these studies and theories helped make management and labor more socially aware and responsible?

The answer to the question on why there has been such a proliferation of studies and theories since the 1930s is threefold. First, the Western Electric Hawthorne studies showed that people were socially oriented human beings with brains who wanted to work for more satisfaction than just a weekly paycheck; therefore, ways must be found to satisfy this yearning. Second, there are many sincere people who are making sincere efforts to try and find techniques and concepts that will improve efficiency in the workplace while at the same time making the workplace and the participants therein happier and more satisfied. Third, and sad, is the requirement that exists in most universities that its professors must "publish or perish." This last requirement has resulted in the generation (if one examines the multitude of existing theories carefully) of numerous theories that are only slight variances of already existing theories or a repackaging of an older, antiquated theory. One case in point is the 40 or so articles referred to earlier on the subject of MBO.

On the question of whether these theories work and are effective in accomplishing their intended purpose, the answer is "yes" and "no" and "sometimes." Since many of these theories are in conflict with one another it is obvious that they can not all work under all conditions. On the other hand, a number of studies and theories are based on actual response of people under particular work conditions; if the theories are applied to similar groups of people under similar conditions they will normally produce the desired results—at least for a period of time. Since people and situations are in a constant state of flux and these studies and theories are based on conditions that exist at the time they are developed, the new theories and concepts tend to work for a period of time and then tend to lose their impact. It must be remembered that all of these theories involve a certain amount of psychology, which is far from being an exact science. Close examination of most of these theories will reveal that they contain an element of and even the potential for gross manipulation of the participants. If the proposed theories are to work at all they must be administered with great care, sincerity, and love and be devoid of any semblance of conditioning or manipulation. The moment a person feels that he or she is being conditioned or manipulated, the system will lose all of its force and effect. After following these theories and concepts and many others for over 40 years in industry, it appears that each major new theory is popular and widely accepted for a period of several years and then is replaced by the newest "improved" theory or set of theories. This constant change of theories and attitudes and feelings of people is why today there is so much confusion in industry on what is the best way to go. This is also why the "contingency theory" (use whatever theory or combination of theories that works best for the particular situation) is so popular today.

In response to the question of how, if at all, these theories have helped make management and labor more socially aware and responsible, the answer must be that it appears that progress has been made in this direction. A brief "broad brush" review of changes in the manufacturing processes and in employee benefits will show some of the progress that has been made along these lines. Prior to the 1930s and up through much of World War II, the production lines were set up on an assembly line basis where each person on the line did one frustrating and monotonous task day after day. This was referred to as "job simplification." The next move to help relieve some of this monotony and boredom was to move to "job enlargement"; this was still a horizontal assembly line process, but now a person performed as many as several operations on the line that were previously assigned to several people. Another similar system is "job rotation," where a person is periodically shifted from one job to another.

The next step taken for expanding employee responsibility was in the process of "job enrichment." This differed from "job enlargement" in that this new concept increased both the breadth and depth of the job. In addition to normal assembly line work it also involved some planning and evaluating duties that were formerly performed by supervision. It not only gave the employee horizontal assembly line responsibilities but also expanded them in the vertical direction to take over some previously supervisory duties. Cost, technological constraints, and union opposition may cause some problems in initiating "job enrichment" in some jobs.

Beyond "job enrichment" is what is referred to as "autonomous work groups." These are self-managed work teams responsible for the accomplishment of specifically defined performance requirements. They work as a group on an entire assembly project. It creates the atmosphere of a small workshop, which allows for decentralization and delegation. Volvo has used this concept to build its automobiles. The benefits reported from such a concept are (1) improved worker attitudes, (2) improved quality of output, (3) lower absenteeism and turnover, (4) ease of covering absent workers, and (5) reduced number of supervisory personnel. Some disadvantages of implementing this concept are (1) possible higher costs, (2) reduced production rates, (3) increased space requirements, and (4) the need for radically new plant designs.

One attempt to take advantage of the positive aspects found in "autonomous work groups" and minimize the negative aspects of the concept is the creation of "quality circles." A recent study concludes that "quality circles" have their distinct advantages, but they also have in their design certain inherent factors that often lead them to self-destruct.[19]

Other working concepts that attempt to accommodate the social desires of both the employee and the employer include "flexible working hours," where all people in the organization work a specific set of core hours but can normally adjust their starting and quitting times; "compressed work weeks" where employees may work four 10-hour days instead of five 8-hour days; "job sharing," where two or more people fill the same job but one may work mornings on Monday and Wednesday while the other person works in the afternoon or the other days of the week not worked by the other person; and "work at home" either by picking up work at a central location and doing it at home for redelivery back to the central location or the use of computer terminals in the home. All of these concepts give both the employee and the employer more flexibility and help meet the social needs of both parties.

In the area of social benefits to employees the list is almost without end. Some of these social benefits will be discussed in more detail in future chapters. It is sufficient here to say that they are plentiful and today in many companies are presented in a very palatable manner to the employees. Many companies present what they classify as the "market basket of social benefits." The employee may pick and choose, within limits, which social benefits he or she desires. For example, a person may choose dental care payments rather than child care coverage if they have no children.

It can therefore be said that although some of the proposed theories may be confusing or of limited value or use to the employer or employee, they have made both groups more aware of the desires and needs of one another and have promoted closer cooperation between the two groups in an attempt to arrive at equitable solutions.

THE ENTREPRENEURS AND BUILDERS

During this period, existing companies grew rapidly and new companies were started up all over the country. Route 128 outside of Boston is loaded with high technology companies, as is Silicon Valley in California. Companies grew, companies merged, and new companies were started.

Procter & Gamble began forward integration in the 1880s by building its own branch office network, while at the same time establishing an effective purchasing organization to ensure a steady flow of raw materials. After 1930 the company diversified into consumer products and captured a healthy share of the shampoo, detergent, diaper, toothpaste, deodorant, paper products, cake mixes, coffee, orange juice, and other markets. In more recent years it has gone into pharmaceuticals and is currently ranked as the largest over-the-counter (OTC) drug company.[20] The company sponsored the first radio soap opera ("The Puddle Family") and has spent as much as $500 million in a single year in mostly television advertising. P&G is only one of the many companies that have grown rapidly since the 1930s and after World War II. Some of the companies such as P&G, General Motors, General Electric, and Philip Morris have grown through both normal internal growth and through acquisitions. Minnesota Mining and Manufacturing has helped its growth by coming out with as many as 200 new products a year.[21] Other companies such as Texas Instruments, Wang Computer, IBM, Digital, Hewlett-Packard, and McDonald's have grown from small companies or nonexistent companies prior to 1930 into giants today. A recent book lists 365 companies whose stocks increased by a factor of 100 to 1 or better between 1931 to 1965 and the year 1971.[22] The book fits into this category such companies as Xerox, Avon Products, Polaroid, Georgia Pacific, Zenith Radio, Emerson Electric, Tampax, Magnavox, Minnesota Minning and Manufacturing, Black & Decker, Maytag, Gillette, and many smaller and less known companies. An initial investment of $10,000 in any of these companies would have been valued at $1 million or more in 1971.

New companies continue to proliferate each and every year. Tens of thousands of these new companies enter the business arena each year. Sadly, 65 percent of these new companies will not survive through five years of operation. This does not appear to deter the young new entrepreneur. Each one still has an opportunity to make it big.

This rapid expansion and growth of old line businesses, the explosive growth of numerous new companies, and the continued entry and exit of new entrepreneurs in the market place have helped the growth and improvement in social awareness and responsibility of both the government and the companies themselves. The government has generated many new socially oriented laws to protect workers and the environment from poor or negligent business practices. Business has also developed and implemented many new socially responsible features into their business operations as a result of greater social awareness and responsibility and as a protection against competitive pressures from other companies.

GROWTH OF LAWS AND COURT DECISIONS

Legislation has been passed in a number of areas requiring business and other organizations to meet with and fulfill certain social responsibilities. Included is legislation in the area of human resources, environmental protection, consumer protection, minority business, labor unions, exercise of religion, and many other areas. While cities, counties, and states have passed a number of laws in these areas, the major emphasis has come from the federal government. Compliance with these new rules and regulations has to a great extent been on a voluntary basis by business; where this has not occurred, administrative rulings and court tests are helping define the limits of compliance to the laws.

Although new legislation continues to be written and made into law, a large proportion of the new laws influencing social responsibility were passed in the decades of the 1960s and 1970s. To list and discuss all of these laws would require several books; therefore, they will be handled in two manners in this book. First, this section of this chapter will list significant pieces of key legislation in pertinent areas of social responsibility and give a brief description of the main impact of the legislation. Second, the remaining chapters in the book will discuss important aspects of certain pieces of legislation as it applies to the subject area under discussion.

Human Resources Legislation

Human resources legislation was passed by the federal government primarily to protect the worker from unfair and variable employment practices by business and various cities and states. Much of this legislation covers many of the areas where unions had been seeking protection for many years. Table 5 lists key legislation in this area along with the year of passage of the legislation and a brief description of what the legislation covers. A number of these laws and regulations have been amended, added to, or modified in some shape, manner, or form in later years. One example is Title VII, Civil Rights Act of 1964. In 1980 the Equal Employment Opportunity Commission (EEOC) in their role to monitor compliance with federal law, issued a variety of interpretive guidelines. In 1980, the EEOC published in the Federal Register guidelines directed toward sexual discrimination and harassment. This is listed as section 1604.11 of the guidelines.[23]

Environmental Protection Legislation

As businesses have grown and expanded throughout the country the amount of environmental pollution has increased in the areas of the atmosphere, water, noise, and chemicals. The key piece of legislation in environmental protection was the National Environmental Policy Act of 1969, which went into effect on January 1, 1970. It committed the government to preserving the country's ecology and established a White House Council on Environmental Quality that advises the president on environmental issues. Table 6 lists several pieces of key environmental legislation.

Consumer Protection Legislation

Consumer protection has always been a point of concern with the public. Some of the enacted laws protect both the consumer and business. According to Robert H. Harlat, during the last 30 years the focus of product liability law

Table 5
Major Federal Laws and Regulations Related to the Management of Human Resources

Year	Name	Purpose
1957	Civil Rights Act	Prevented interference with voting rights of others.
1963	Equal Pay Act	Prohibits pay differences based on sex for equal work.
1964 (amended 1974)	Civil Rights Act, Title VII	Prohibits discrimination based on race, color, religion, national origin, or sex.
1965	Executive Order 11246	Extends Civil Rights Act discrimination provisions to federal agencies, contractors and sub-contractors.
1965 (amended 1970)	Voting Rights Act	Requires protection to register voters in certain areas.
1967 (amended 1975)	Age Discrimination in Employment Act	Prohibits age discrimination against employees between forty and sixty-five years of age.
1970	Occupational Safety and Health Act (OSHA)	Requires employers to provide safe working conditions in the work place.
1972	Equal Employment Act	Provides equal employment rights in companies over 15 employees.
1973	Vocational Rehabilitation Act	Prohibits discrimination on the basis of physical or mental handicaps.
1974	Veterans Readjustment Act	Prohibits discrimination against disabled veterans and Viet Nam era veterans.
1974	Privacy Act	Gives employees the legal right to examine letters of reference concerning them.
1978	Pregnancy Discrimination Act, Title VII	Prohibits dismissal of women because of pregnancy alone and protects job security during maternity leave.
1978 (amended 1988)	Mandatory Retirement Act	Prohibits the forced retirement of most employees before the age of seventy.
1980	Sexual Harassment, Title VII	Prohibits sexual harassment of workers.
1988	Civil Rights Restoration Act of 1988	Clarifies and broadens scope of the 1964 Civil Rights Act.

Table 6
Laws Relating to Environmental Protection

Date	Name	Purpose
December 17, 1963	Clean Air Act	To improve, strengthen, and accelerate programs for the prevention and abatement of air pollution.
November 3, 1966	Clean Water Restoration Act of 1966	To provide technical and financial assistance in the development of waste treatment, water purification and water quality control programs.
January 1, 1970	National Environmental Policy Act of 1969	To establish a national policy on the environment and to establish a Council on Environmental Quality.
October 27, 1972	Noise Control Act of 1972	To control the emission of noise harmful to the human environment.
December 16, 1974	Safe Drinking Water Act	To assure that the public is provided with safe drinking water.
October 11, 1976	Toxic Substances Control Act	To regulate business and protect human health and the environment by requiring testing and necessary use restrictions on certain chemical substances.
October 21, 1976	Resource Conservation and Recovery Act	To provide technical and financial assistance to develop management plans and facilities for the recovery of energy and other resources from discarded materials and to regulate the management of hazardous waste.

has switched from emphasis on the conduct of the manufacturer and the marketer to the condition of the product. This has resulted in a variety of interpretations of the law in different states. He feels that this is confusing to both the consumer and the manufacturer and should be corrected. He recommends four standards that he feels if enacted by the federal government could establish uniform interpretation of the law in all states.[24] Table 7 lists some of the key consumer legislation passed in recent years.

Minority Business Legislation

For years, many companies have extended concerted efforts to hire members from minority groups as well as the handicapped. Much of the emphasis has been concentrated and aimed at hiring of the hard-core unemployed, such as black native American ghetto youths, and any other group that might have difficulties in obtaining jobs. In recent years increased emphasis has been placed on hiring the physically handicapped with the passage of the Vocational Rehabilitation Act of 1973. This act addresses discrimination against the handicapped people to anyone working on government contracts. A Department of Labor survey conducted several years after enactment of this law revealed that 91 percent of 300 companies surveyed were in violation of the act. Table 8 lists some of the more recent legislation affected minority business.

Labor Legislation

As will be discussed in much more detail in a separate section later in this chapter on unions, labor legislation and interpretations were made primarily by the judiciary in the period prior to the 1930s with increasing labor legislation occurring after the 1930s. Prior to 1930, big business held the upper hand over the unions; by the mid–1930s the power had swung over to the unions with the passage of the Norris-Laguardia Act of 1932 and the Wagner Act of 1935. The power swung back more to the center with the passage of the Taft-Hartley Act in 1947 and the Landrum-Griffin Act of 1959. With this legislation in place, many of the detailed areas of workers concern was taken care of by all of the various pieces of legislation already discussed in this section of the chapter. Table 9 outlines some of the more important labor legislation passed in recent years.

Government Deregulation

As shown in other sections of this chapter up to this point, the federal government appeared to be obsessed with the generation and implementation of new legislation in recent years. This new legislation has permeated almost every facet of how business and people must operate and behave.

Table 7
Federal Consumer Legislation

Date	Name	Purpose
1914	Federal Trade Commission Act	May attack unfair customer practices when there is a specific and substantial public interest involved in the presentation of a particular unethical practice in dealing with customers
1960	Fair Packaging and Labeling Act	Requires packages and labels to carry identity of article, manufacturer's name and location, quantity of contents in legible print
1966	National Traffic and Motor Safety Act	Requires auto manufacturers to notify buyers of defects discovered after delivery and to remedy these defects
1968	Consumer Credit Protection Act	Requires seller to disclose terms of sale and give facts of actual interest rate and other charges
1969	Child Protection and Toy Safety Act	Prohibits manufacture and distribution of toys and other children's articles sold in interstate trade that have electrical or other hazards
1969	Truth-in-Lending Act	Requires lenders to inform borrowers of all direct, indirect and true costs of credit. Both the amount of the finance charge and the annual percentage rate must be made clear
1970	Fair Credit Reporting Act	Requires consumer credit reporting agencies to adopt procedures for reporting personal information accurately and fairly
1972	Consumer Product Safety Act	Regulates product standards and creates a Consumer Safety Commission to maintain product safety standards and give more accurate facts about products on labels
1974	Privacy Act	Prohibits governments at all levels from requiring persons to give their Social Security numbers to receive a driver's license, vote or exercise other rights. Persons have a right to know what information is maintained by federal agencies about them. Sets up a commission to study problems of consumer privacy
1974	Real Estate Settlement Procedures Act	Requires lenders to disclose to home buyers all closing costs at least twelve days before closing the sale. Penalties for violations can run up to a year in prison and a $10,000 fine

Table 8
Recent Legislation Affecting Minority Business

Date	Name	Purpose
1969	Executive Order 11458	Established the Office of Minority Business Enterprises for mobilizing federal resources to aid minorities.
1971	Title 41 Federal Procurement Regulations	Required federal contracts exceeding $5,000 to contain clauses encouraging contractors to use minority businesses on a "best-effort" basis.
1971	Executive Order 11625	The Secretary of Commerce was given authority to: implement federal policy in support of minority business; provide technical and management assistance to disadvantaged business; and, coordinate federal activities to increase minority business activity.
1973	Vocational Rehabilitation Act	Addresses discrimination against handicapped on government contracts.
1977	Public Works Employment Act	Requires 10% of each federal construction grant be awarded to minority businesses.
1977	Public Law 95-89	Loan authorizations and surety bond guarantee authority improvements to minority businesses.
1977	Railroad Revitalization & Regulatory Reform Act	Recipients of financial grants and sub-contractors both must establish a goal of awarding 15% of all purchases to minority businesses.
1978	Public Law 95-507	Prospective bidders for federal contracts in excess of $500,000 ($1,000,000 for construction contracts) must submit before the contract award, a plan that includes percentage goals for utilization of minority businesses.

Table 9
Selected Labor Legislation

Date	Name	Purpose
1890	Sherman Anti-Trust Act	Declared certain types of business combinations and efforts to monopolize to be unlawful.
1914	Clayton Act	Supplemented Sherman Anti-Trust Act and dealt with many labor complaints.
1932	Norris-La Guardia Act	Protects unions from government and big business.
1935	Wagner Act	Encouraged Unionism.
1947	Taft-Hartley Act	Provided employees, employers and the public certain protections against union power.
1959	Landrum-Griffin Act	Extended the Taft-Hartley restrictions and also gave union members protection against their own unions.

This abundance of new laws and regulations, and the costs of enforcement of this legislation, has forced some people in government to take another look at it. As a result, significant steps have been taken (in the 1970s and 1980s) by the judiciary, the Congress, and the White House to deregulate certain sectors of the economy that had previously been heavily regulated by the federal government. Table 10 lists a number of important areas of deregulation that have taken place, including financial services, airlines and other forms of transportation, and the telecommunication industry.

This movement appears to have had important results, such as reducing prices, improving productivity and innovation, and awakening much of the business community to some of the virtues of more open competition. Although this deregulation has helped somewhat, the government is still deeply involved in business operations.

Exercise of Religion

As discussed throughout the book, this country was founded as a Christian nation and the "Christian work ethic" was what was behind the ethics, morals, and dedicated work habits of the majority of Americans. The earlier chapters also point out how the philosophers, economists, sociologists, psychologists, and even some businessmen have been slowly eroding these firmly founded beliefs and concepts and replacing the ethical-moral socially responsible Judeo-Christian background and work ethic with the "everything is relative," "if it feels good do it," and the "I am number one" philosophy of those who believe there is no black or white but that everything is gray. In recent years, this battle has entered into the court system and legislation system of this

Table 10
Major Steps Toward Deregulation

Date	Purpose
1968	The Supreme Court's Carterfone decision permits non-AT&T equipment to be connected to the AT&T system
1969	The FCC gives MCI the right to hook its long-distance network into local phone system
1970	The Federal Reserve Board frees interest rates on bank deposits over $100,000 with maturities of less than six months
1974	The Justice Department files antitrust suit against AT&T
1975	The SEC orders brokers to cease fixing commissions on stock sales
1977	Merrill Lynch offers the cash management account, competing more closely with commercial banks
1978	Congress deregulates the airlines
1979	The FCC allows AT&T to sell nonregulated services, such as data processing
1980	The Fed allows banks to pay interest on checking accounts
1980	Congress deregulates trucking and railroads
1981	Sears Roebuck becomes the first one-stop financial supermarket, offering insurance, banking, brokerage services
1982	Congress deregulates intercity bus services
1984	AT&T divests itself of its local phone companies

Source: "Deregulating America," *Business Week*, November 28, 1983, pp. 80–81.

country and has continued to erode the basic moral-ethical and religious foundations of the country, the educational system, and the workplace.

Surveys indicate that more people attend church today than ever before; however, when it comes to moral and ethical character, they tend to leave the 10 commandments inside the church building and the closed Bible. Many of them feel that minor lying, stealing (taking supplies home for their own use), and adultery do not apply to them. A recent survey conducted by *Forbes* magazine indicates that 40 percent of the general population attend church and 65 percent of the business leaders attend church.[25]

Most people, including some clergymen, are spending a major portion of their time dealing with and serving mammon rather than spiritual matters. Why then do business leaders spend some of their spare time on religious matters? Professor D. Quinn Mills, a Harvard business school professor, says: "Businessmen are comfortable with big institutions. I think that religious participation is part of their leadership role."[26]

Patrick O'Malley, chairman emeritus of Chicago's Canteen Corp., has a different explanation on the subject. He believes that maybe management realizes that they cannot do it all by themselves and are looking for some help and some faith.[27]

The survey also pointed out that some people believe that there is too little spiritual awareness in corporate America. W. A. Criswell, pastor at the First Baptist Church of Dallas, had this to say on the subject:

The actual horse truth is that we live in a secular society and the mind-set of our people is almost 100% materialistic. We judge things by material standards: prosperity, success. As I look at the commercial world, it seems to me that religion is far down the line in actual priority.[28]

J. Peter Grace seems to agree:

You call all these takeovers going on today "religious"? There is no thought given to people's security, their families, length of service, the loyalty they show. I think the whole business community today in the U.S. is more heartless and less caring than it was when I first went to work.[29]

The next area in question is that of new laws, and/or judicial interpretations of existing laws, pertaining to the exercise of religious practices. The First Amendment to the Constitution was originally a one-way street on religious matters. It simply states: "Congress shall make no law respecting an establishment of religion or prohibiting the free exercise thereof."

The First Amendment forbids the federal government from restricting religion in any manner; the establishment clause was only intended to stop the formation of a national church. The wall of separation between church and state did not come from the First Amendment, but from a private letter written by Thomas Jefferson in 1802 to the Danbury Baptist Church in Connecticut. (Jefferson by the way was not a member of the Constitutional convention.) In this letter he said there should be "a wall of separation between church and state." This is a key point in the argument. The First Amendment is a one-way street that restrains the federal government; Jefferson's letter opens up a two-way street. Over the years Jefferson's concept gradually gained preeminence, so that in practice the amendment became a two-way street. In recent years, the First Amendment has again been turned around until it is once more a one-way street but going in the opposite direction. The statement "separation of church and state" has come to be interpreted to mean what religion and, more specifically what the Christian church shall or shall not do; this is a turn around of 180 degrees from what the First Amendment says.

Backing up in time for a moment, perhaps one of the best evaluations of the part religion played in early America is written by a Frenchman, Alexis de Tocqueville, who visited the United States in 1831. He returned to Europe after two years in America and wrote his impressions of America in his book, *Democracy in America.*[30] Concerning religion in America de Tocqueville said: "On my arrival in the United States the religious aspect of the country was the first thing that struck my attention; and the longer I stayed there, the more I perceived the great political consequence resulting from this new state of things."[31]

De Tocqueville found that the school systems, especially those in New England, incorporated basic religious teachings right along with history and political science in order thoroughly to prepare the student for adult life. He wrote: "In New England every citizen receives the elementary notions of human knowledge; he is taught, moreover, the doctrines and the evidences of his religion, the history of his country, and the leading features of the Constitution."[32]

He continued on to emphasize that the clergy of that time believed implicitly that it was their duty to keep religious principles and moral and ethical values flowing out to the people throughout the country as one of the best ways to safeguard America's freedom and political security. "The Americans combine the notions of Christianity and of liberty so intimately in their minds that it is impossible to make them conceive the one without the other. . . . "[33]

In looking for what made America great, de Tocqueville turned to the church pulpits for his answer:

I sought for the greatness and genius of America . . . Not until I went to the churches of America and heard her pulpits aflame with righteousness did I understand the secret of her genius and power. America is great because she is good and if America ever ceases to be good, America will cease to be great.[34]

After the Civil War in 1868, the Fourteenth Amendment was passed. It required that all citizens within the state be treated on an equal basis.

Up until 1925, the Supreme Court continued to rule that the Fourteenth Amendment had not made the Bill of Rights apply to the states except where it was "implicit in the concept of ordered liberty." The First Amendment was still treated as a restriction on the power of Congress and not the states. Slowly, in a series of cases between 1925 and 1931 the Supreme Court made a number of judiciary decisions that began to claim the authority of the Bill of Rights to bind state governments rather than their own state constitutions.

In 1947 in *Everson* vs. *Board of Education*, the understanding of the First Amendment establishment clause was further changed. In the decision handed down, Hugo Black stated that the "establishment of religion" clause of the First Amendment meant at least: "Neither a state nor the Federal Government can set up a church. Neither can pass laws which aid one religion, aid all religions, or prefer one religion over another."[35]

The three words "aid all religions" added a new dimension to the First Amendment interpretation and was later used by the Supreme Court to attack the financial foundation of religious education in the United States and to remove all mention of God from the public schools.

In 1963 in the case of the *School District of Abington Township* vs. *Schempp* and *Murray* vs. *Curlett*, the Supreme Court ruled that it was unconstitutional for a state to have portions of the Bible recited in schools (despite excusing anyone who wished to be excused).[36] In an eight-to-one decision the Court called it an establishment of religion. Justice Potter Stewart, the lone dissenter on the Court, said that the ruling did not lead to a true neutrality with respect to religion but to the "establishment of a religion of secularism."[37] In a later case in 1980 (*Stone* vs. *Graham*) the Court upheld in a five-to-four decision that a Kentucky statute requiring the posting of the Ten Commandments in the classroom was unconstitutional.

It is fair to say that any reference in the public schools to the Ten Commandments, the principles of the Christian work ethic, or to any Bible scriptures, all of which served as the moral, ethical, work ethic, and social responsibility foundation in America in the past, is now completely null and void. Since the educational system is partially responsible for helping establish the ethical, moral, and social responsibility standards of the youth of America, it is not difficult to see why there are accelerating rates of crime of violence, narcotics addiction, hedonistic sexual aberrations, billion-dollar sales in pornography, high divorce rates, confused ethical and moral standards, and a deteriorating family life. Perhaps further examination of a de Tocqueville's final quote given earlier and the stirring words of Daniel Webster when he spoke to the New York Historical Society on February 22, 1852 should be reexamined:

Unborn ages and vision of glory crowd upon my soul, the realization of all which, however, is in the hands and good pleasure of Almighty God; but under his divine blessing, it will be dependent on the character and virtues of ourselves and of our posterity.... If we and they shall live always in the fear of God and shall respect his commandments...we may have the highest hopes of the future fortunes of our country.... It will have no decline and fall. It will go on prospering.... But if we and our posterity reject religious instruction and authority, violate the rules of eternal justice, trifle with the injunctions of morality, and recklessly destroy the political contribution which holds us together, no man can tell how sudden a catastrophe may overwhelm us, that shall bury all our glory in profound obscurity. Should that catastrophe happen, let it have no history! Let the horrible narrative never be written.

Table 11 shows some of the key judicial decisions that have been made in recent years. It should be noted that, similar to early labor union legal decisions, most of the religious legal decisions and interpretations are also made by the Court rather than through legislation passed by Congress. If the intent of the founding fathers (and the vast majority of American parents) is to be carried out and if these original ideals are to be restored and again

Table 11
Selected Decisions Affecting Religion

Date	Name	Purpose
1940	Cantwell vs. Connecticut	Free exercise clause extended to states
1943	West Virginia State Board of Education vs. Barnette	Compulsory Pledge of Allegiance voided
1947	Everson vs. Board of Education of Ewing Township	Establishment clause extended to states; government is prohibited from aiding all religion
1948	McCollum vs. Board of Education	Religious instruction may not be given on public school premises
1963	School District of Abington Township vs. Schempp	Bible selections, read in public schools are devotional exercises, and are therefore held unconstitutional
1972	Anderson vs. Laird	Compulsory chapel at military academies held unconstitutional
1980	Stone vs. Graham	State may not require display of the Ten Commandments in public schools
1987	Edwards vs. Agullard	State law requiring balanced treatment of creation science and evolution ruled unconstitutional

taught in the schools of America, it will probably not be done except through a constitutional amendment or new legislation.

Unions (1930–1988)

Although unions had made some progress, it was slow and difficult, being thwarted at almost every turn by business and rulings of the judiciary. The unions' first major positive step forward in this period occurred in 1932 under President Herbert Hoover with the passage of the Norris-LaGuardia Anti-Injunction Act. It was drafted to avoid the ambiguity of the Clayton Act and to curtail sharply the power of the federal courts to issue injunctions in labor dispute cases. It does not prohibit the issuance of injunctions by federal courts in labor dispute cases; however, it describes very carefully the circumstances under which a temporary restraining order or injunction might be issued. The law in no way eliminated labor-management conflict. Neither did it encourage unionism except to the extent that the new law did remove a substantial legal disadvantage previously encountered by the unions. Although now on the books, no significant court interpretation of the act was made until 1937 and afterward when even more powerful new laws had been enacted under a pro-labor administration.

By 1933 when Franklin D. Roosevelt took over as president, the stock market crash of 1929 had taken its toll in all areas of industry and farming, including a reduction of 25 percent in the work force. President Roosevelt and his group of economic advisers (his "brain trust") immediately went to work on his legislative programs. One of the major objectives of the trust was to help the working class by establishing a "greater social justice" for them. One of his first pieces of legislation was the National Industrial Recovery Act, enacted in 1933. This legislation was quite favorable to labor in that it suspended the antitrust laws to permit trade associations to draw up their own codes of conduct governing prices, hours, and output; the avowed purpose for this was to encourage production at "fair" rates of profit. Both labor and industry were encouraged to accept and endorse the NIRA. To encourage labor, a clause, section 7(a) of the Recovery Act, was included that provided employees the "right to organize and bargain collectively through representatives of their own choosing, free from employer interference, restraint or coercion." Employees that developed compatible codes of conduct were permitted to fly the "blue eagle" flag showing that they were in compliance with NIRA. Many manufacturers opposed the legislated right of labor to bargain collectively. After lengthy court battles, the legislation was declared unconstitutional in 1935 by a nine-to-zero vote of the Supreme Court. Labor had once again suffered a major setback in the courts.

Conflicting interpretations of section 7(a) of the Recovery Act necessitated the establishment of a board to hear and resolve conflicts. This was accomplished through the establishment of the National Labor Board (NLB) in August 1933. The NLB had three labor and three industry members, while Senator Robert Wagner of New York served as a public member and chairman of the group. Since the NLB had no enforcement powers and was riddled by internal differences and fighting, it was obvious that it would be short lived.

Anticipating the collapse of the NLB and the probable decision by the Supreme Court to declare section 7(a) of the Recovery Act unconstitutional, Senator Wagner had been working on a bill that would take care of the problems encountered with section 7(a) of the Recovery Act. Senator Wagner's bill was enacted into law in July 1935 and was called Wagner Act. Section 7 of the Act delegated and retained the lawful right for workers to join unions and bargain collectively. On the other hand, employers who had in the past enjoyed the right to oppose unionism in direct and explicit ways were now stripped of this right in section 8 of the act.

As might be expected, the constitutionality of this new pro-labor legislation was immediately labeled as unconstitutional by business and started winding its way through the court process up to the Supreme Court. In light of what the Supreme Court had been doing to new legislation, it appeared that the

Wagner Act might have a short life. Possibly because of the seriousness of the times, the fact that President Roosevelt won the 1936 presidential election by a landslide, and his threat to "pack the Supreme Court" in his favor by having all judges over 70 years of age removed and replaced on the bench by judges more attuned to what he envisioned as the social needs of the times, led the swing vote part of the Court to start siding with the policies of the second "New Deal" era. The Wagner Act was eventually found to be constitutional and was considered a very positive break for labor and the unions.

Another powerful policy declaration in the Wagner Act was constructed around the need to protect the flow of goods and services between states. The heavy emphasis on interstate commerce appeared to be in anticipation of the test of its constitutionality. This policy declaration had a profound effect on court decisions and eventually placed many things under the interstate commerce umbrella that had previously not been considered interstate commerce.

Union membership continued to grow rapidly during this period, now that labor had an administration that was sympathetic to it and labor was winning court battles for its causes. However, by 1945 union membership momentum had slowed down and membership had leveled off at close to 25 percent of the civilian work force where it plateaued until close to 1965; it has continued to slowly decline in the decade of the late 1970s and early 1980s.

By 1936 John S. Lewis could no longer stand the craft orientation attitude of the American Federation of Labor (AFL) and its reluctance to form industry-wide unions; in this year he broke with the AFL and formed the Congress of Industrial Organizations (CIO). The United Automobile Workers joined the CIO in 1936, quickly followed over the next few years by the steel workers and rubber workers. By 1939 most large businesses had recognized outside unions representing many of their workers.

With a few exceptions, during World War II there was a relative harmony between labor and management in their joint effort to produce all the goods and services needed to help win the war. Following the war, however, labor again started to flex its muscles and employers turned to the public with complaints about the now monopolistic powers of the unions and their negative effect on productivity. The pendulum had now swung too far in favor of labor and unions. This, plus the continued charges of communist infiltration into the unions, resulted in the passage of the Taft-Hartley Act in 1947. It was an attempt to bring into closer balance the power of both labor and management. It retained most of the union encouragement features of the Wagner Act, but superimposed upon them a number of union controls. Although initially vetoed by President Truman, the veto was quickly overridden in both houses and became the law of the land.

Probably the most controversial part of the Taft-Hartley Act was section 14(b) and state right-to-work laws. Under the Taft-Hartley Act, closed shops (a person must be a union member in good standing before being hired as an employee) were outlawed; however, union shops (all employees must belong to the union and newly hired employees must join the union within a certain number of days) and other forms of union security are permitted. Section 14(b) makes it possible for state governments to pass legislation that would prohibit union shops, maintenance of membership agreements, and other arrangements for compulsory union membership. Many state governorships and governments were made or toppled on this issue. In many of the northern strong union states, the right-to-work (a person did not have to join a union in order to keep his job) law did not pass. Many of the southern states, which were not strongly unionized, passed state right-to-work laws. As a result, with companies given relative freedom from unions and lower wage and tax rates, many companies moved to southern states.

By 1958 it was obvious that some changes had to be made in some of the provisions of the Taft-Hartley Act. This was brought about as a result of two major findings: (1) the impact upon public opinion of the McClellan committee on their exposure of corrupt practices in a number of local and national unions and (2) successive waves of price inflations, which were blamed on the excessive bargaining power of the unions. In 1959, the Landrum-Griffin Act was passed to help remedy these problems. The first six titles deal mainly with the regulation of unions and the rights of union members. The seventh includes amendments to the Taft-Hartley Act. Basically, the purpose of the act is to:

1. Safeguard the civil rights of union members (Title I)

2. Establish and define certain reporting and disclosure requirements of certain financial and administrative practices of unions, employers, and labor relations consultants (Title II)

3. Regulate the administration of trusteeships by labor unions (Title III)

4. Establish statutory regulations for the conduct of union elections (Title IV)

5. Provide safeguards for labor organizations in the areas of fiduciary responsibilities of union officers, bonding requirements, office holdings by communists and felons, and unlawful employer payments (Title V)

6. Empower the Secretary of Labor to investigate possible violations of the Act (Title VI)

7. Amend the Taft-Hartley Act (Title VII)

The four main pillars of national labor policy have now been examined. The Norris-LaGuardia Act sought to protect the union from the government and big business; the Wagner Act encouraged unionism; the Taft-Hartley Act provided employees, employers, and the public with certain protections against union power; and the Landrum-Griffin Act extended the Taft-Hartley restrictions and also gave union members protection against their own union.

Union membership today is slightly below 20 percent of the work force and projections call for a continued decrease. This decline in union membership in recent years can be attributed primarily to several causes, including changing times, changing characteristics of the work force, the changing legal environment, the unions themselves, and increased cooperation between labor and management.

Structural changes within the American economy itself have been significant since the end of World War II. Manufacturing, construction, and mining, the industries that have traditionally been unionized, have declined somewhat in importance in relationship to the emerging and rapidly growing areas of financial, service, and high technology industries. These newer areas of business have been more resistant to unionization.

The changing characteristics of the face of the labor force also has been a major contributor to the decline of unionization. Women and young workers, who are less apt to belong to unions, now make up a major part of the labor force. Also increasing in numbers in the labor force are more professional and white collar workers. By 1980, 40 million of the workers in the United States had completed four years of high school with almost an equal number having completed and graduated from college; these two groups represent almost 75 percent of the labor force. As each of these two groups has increased in the labor force, the proportion of the labor force belonging to unions has decreased.

The changing legal environment has also contributed to the reduction in unionization. Many of the things that the unions fought for in the past have been accomplished. In many instances, laws now exist and protect workers in areas where they were once unprotected (i.e., right-to-know laws, equal pay act, sexual harassment laws, and so on). As general legal protection for the employee has grown, the need to affiliate through unions has decreased.

Organized labor itself is also a strong contributor to declining union membership. Unions have been slow to react to the changing social and economic conditions and as a result many of their programs and goals fail to meet the needs of today's workers. Unions have also had problems discarding their somewhat negative image. The new union leaders are trying hard to change their image and update their causes and organizations.

Government deregulation and increased foreign competition during the 1980s have forced both labor and management to become more cooperative and work closer together to fight for a common cause against a common enemy—their business and their jobs against foreign encroachment. In many instances unions have made previously unheard of concessions and "give backs" to management in order for labor to keep jobs and to be competitive with both domestic and foreign companies. Joint labor-management committees and groups, under numerous names and titles, have been formed to work cooperatively to solve and resolve both technical problems and management-labor problems.

Union membership, although still in a declining trend, remains a powerful but weakening force in this country. If it becomes necessary, or to their advantage, they still have the power to shut down large companies and large segments of the economy if they so desire. Unions may be relatively docile at the moment; however, they cannot be ignored and are still a force to be reckoned with by management. This may not be as far off as some may think, or at least some hope. In four out of the last five years, union members have received smaller pay raises than nonunion members; and, in three out of the last four years, real wages of union members have fallen (wage raises have not kept up with inflation).[38] If past history is any example, management can expect union demands to start increasing in the very near future.

SUMMARY

This chapter covers the period from 1930 through the present. Major European and American influence of the period is discussed to show the impact of economists, philosophers, psychologists, business leaders, and presidential administrations on the growth and change in business moral-ethical thinking and conduct, and social responsibility. It is a period when American influence predominates, the country goes through a devastating depression and recovers, old and new business expand and prosper, unions come into their own, new social legislation is generated and passed at a rate and in a variety of areas never before seen in this country, and moral and ethical conduct continues to degenerate as all reference to the Bible and the Christian work ethic is removed from the school system and replaced by what Supreme Court Justice Potter Stewart called a "religion of secularism."

NOTES

1. John Maynard Keynes, *The General Theory of Employment, Interest, and Money* (hereafter referred to as *Theory*) (New York: Harcourt Brace, 1936.)

2. Thomas C. Cochran, *American Business in the Twentieth Century* (Cambridge, Mass.: Harvard University Press, 1972), p. 176.

3. Quoted in Louis W. Koenig, ed. *The Truman Administration: Its Principles and Practices* (New York: New York University Press, 1956), p. 93.

4. "Jobless Rate Hits Lowest Since 1980," *Cincinnati Enquirer*, March 5, 1988, p. A–1.

5. Harold Koontz, "The Management Theory Jungle," *Academy of Management Journal* 11, no. 9 (1968): 174–188.

6. Abraham Maslow, "A Theory of Human Motivation," *Psychological Review* 50, no. 4 (1943): 370–396.

7. James A. Kenny, "Beyond Self-Actualization—What?" *The Catholic Telegraph Register*, special supplement (May 1978): 26.

8. Ibid.

9. Douglas McGregor, *The Human Side of Enterprise* (New York: McGraw-Hill, 1960).

10. Chris Argyris, *Integrating the Individual and the Organization* (New York: John Wiley & Sons, 1964).

11. F. Herzberg, B. Mausner, and B. Synderman, *The Motivation to Work*, 2d ed. (New York: John Wiley and Sons, 1967; Frederick Herzberg, "One More Time: How Do You Motivate Employees," *Harvard Business Review* 47 (January–February 1968): 53–62.

12. B. F. Skinner, *Walden Two* (New York: Macmillan, 1948); *Science and Human Behavior* (New York: Macmillan, 1953); *Contingencies of Reinforcement* (New York: Appleton-Century-Crofts, 1969); *About Behavior* (New York: Vintage, 1976).

13. Rensis Likert, *New Patterns of Management* (New York: McGraw-Hill, 1961); Bernard M. Bass, *Stogdill's Handbook of Leadership* (New York: Free Press, 1981).

14. Robert H. House and M. L. Baetz, "Leadership: Some Generalizations and New Research Directions," in Barry M. Staw, ed., *Research in Organizational Behavior* (Greenwich, Conn.: JAI Press, 1979).

15. Robert R. Blake and Jane S. Mouton, "The Developing Revolution in Management Practices," *Journal of the American Society of Training Directors* 10, no. 7 (1962): 29–52.

16. P. S. Drucker, *The Practice of Management* (New York: Harper and Row, 1954); "What Results Should You Expect? A User's Guide to MBO," *Public Administration Review* 36, no. 1 (1976):12–19.

17. G. S. Odiorne, *Management by Objectives: A System of Managerial Leadership* (New York: Pitman Publishing, 1965); "Management by Objectives and the Phenomenon of Goals Displacement," *Human Resources Management* 13, no. 1 (1974): 2–7.

18. Mark L. McConkie, "A Clarification of the Goal Setting and Appraisal Process in MBO," *The Academy of Management Review* 4, no. 1 (1979): 29–40.

19. E. E. Lawler III and Susan A. Mohrman, "Quality Circles after the Fad," *Harvard Business Review* 63, no. 1 (1985): 64–71.

20. Patricia Gallagher, "P&G Widens Pharmaceutical Sector," *Cincinnati Enquirer*, March 9, 1988, p. D–4.

21. Christopher Knowlton, "What America Makes Best," *Fortune* 117, no. 7 (1988): 45.

22. Thomas W. Phelps, *100 to 1 in the Stock Market* (New York, McGraw-Hill, 1972).

23. *Federal Register*, 45, no. 72 (1980): 25024.

24. Robert H. Malott, "Let's Restore Balance to Product Liability Law," *Harvard Business Review* 61, no. 3 (1983): 66–74.

25. Barbara Kallen, "Praying for Guidance," *Forbes* 19, no. 4 (1986): 220.

26. Ibid., p. 221.

27. Ibid.

28. Ibid.

29. Ibid.

30. Alexis de Tocqueville, *Democracy in America*, 12th ed., 2 vols. (New York: Vintage Books, 1945).

31. Ibid., vol. 1, p. 319.

32. Ibid., vol. 1, p. 327.

33. Ibid., vol. 1, p. 317.

34. Quoted in Ezra Taft Benson, *God, Family, Country: Our Three Great Loyalties* (Salt Lake City: Desert Book Company, 1975), p. 360.

35. *Everson* vs. *Board of Education*, 330 U.S. 1, at 15–16, quoted by Robert L. Cord, *Separation of Church and State* (New York: Lambeth Press, 1982), p. 109.

36. *School District of Abington Township* vs. *Schempp*, 374 U.S. 223.

37. Alfred H. Kelly and Winfred A. Harrison, *The American Constitution: Its Origin and Development* (New York: W. W. Norton, 1976), p. 976.

38. Vivian Brownstein, "Here Comes the Pay Packet Price Push," *Fortune* 117, no. 6 (1988): 73–76.

PART III

Legal, Ethical-Moral, and Philanthropic Business, Government, and Public Internal and External Interaction and Issues

7

Legal Aspects of Social Responsibility: Business and the Government

At no time in the history of this country have local, state, national, and international governments played as extensive a role in the regulation, control, and operation of what takes place in the business and public sectors of the economy. This movement proceeded fairly slowly during the early days of the country's growth but started to gather speed and strength in the 1930s after the Depression and exploded in a multitude of new legislation at all levels of government during the late 1950s, 1960s, and 1970s, after which it again slowed down somewhat. This heavy load of new legislation induced some in government to take a route of deregulation in various areas of industry to help offset some of the multitude of new laws and regulations; most of this deregulation activity has taken place during the 1970s and 1980s but still leaves the government with an abundance of new legislation.

This new government legislation leaves practically no corner of society untouched. It has had a strong impact on the interaction and the issues that involve the government, business, and the public. The government has imposed laws, regulations, and other forms of persuasion on both business and the public. In turn, business has used lobbying and its own form of persuasion on the government for favorable treatment, while the public in general has used the political process, voting, and pressure and interest groups to make their voice heard by the government. Business has relied heavily on advertising, education, and public relations to influence the public, while the public has relied on tactics such as public interest groups, influencing various levels of government for more legislation, not purchasing selected products, and protest groups of various kinds in order to direct business to comply with their wishes. This interaction process is not static but is one that is ever changing with time. Part II has outlined and discussed some of the history that led up to the interaction process now in place. Part III will in turn examine the interaction process in more detail.

BUSINESS AND THE GOVERNMENT

Today, business cannot operate without contact and interaction with the government and its myriad of rules and regulations. This chapter will discuss in some detail the legal external aspects of social responsibility of business and its relationship and interaction with the government, the environment, the consumer and the community.

Government Role and Influence on Business and Society

The role of government in business and social actions today is broad in scope. It extends all the way from local community laws and regulations to international laws and regulations. Multinational companies are involved with laws and regulations at all levels of government from local laws to international laws, while domestic companies are influenced and controlled primarily by local, state, and national laws.

The National Government

During the early days of its existence the federal government took a "leave business alone" or "laissez-faire" attitude toward its development and operation. The government went even further than this through support and encouragement of business with enactment of tariffs on foreign goods and support of some businesses, such as the growth and expansion of the railroads in the 1800s, through special government grants. By the time the late 1800s had arrived the tone of the federal government was starting to change. Due to numerous abuses by big business and the "robber barons," the federal government started passing legislation to control some of these abuses. It passed the Interstate Commerce Act in 1887 followed by the Sherman Antitrust Law of 1890 and the Clayton Act in 1914. Following the Depression and the election of President Franklin D. Roosevelt, new legislation and judiciary decisions started to flow from the federal government in increasing abundance; most of these new decisions and laws were restrictive of business. With the people now turning to the federal government for help, the federal government took advantage of this opportunity to pass innumerable new laws during the period of the 1950s, 1960s, and 1970s, with some abatement during the 1980s and some increased deregulation of various businesses during the 1970s and 1980s.

The federal government bases its authority to pass these laws and regulations on the Constitution of the United States and its interpretation thereof. Although it relies on the entire Constitution to pass and enforce these laws, great emphasis is based on two major clauses. The first is what is referred to as the "general welfare clause," which states in part: "Congress shall have the power to lay and collect taxes, duties, imports, and excise, to pay the debts and to provide for the common defense and general welfare of the United States." The second clause is referred to as the "necessary and proper" clause, which reads in part: "to make all laws which shall be necessary and proper for carrying into execution the foregoing powers, and all other powers vested by this Constitution in the government of the United States, or in any department or office thereof."

A fairly recent example that takes both of these clauses into consideration is the passage of the Fair Packaging and Labeling Act of 1966. This act assures the customer that the company will accurately label the quality and quantity of a package. It is "necessary and proper" to do so in addition to being in the best interest and general welfare of the consumer. Unfortunately, this law became necessary in order to force some in the business community to meet their obligations to the public.

Government has seen its role as the helper, promoter, and protector of the general health and welfare of the nation, business, the community, and the consumer. With this view of its role, along with the interpretation placed by President Franklin D. Roosevelt and his administration on the Constitution (anything not strictly forbidden by the Constitution falls under the jurisdiction and control of the federal government), the period of government legislation, control, and even infringement took hold with increasing rapidity after the mid–1930s.

Not only does the government enforce its will upon business, public affairs, and social responsibility through legislation but also through persuasion or "arm twisting." Prime examples of arm twisting are: (1) when President Truman had the Army operate the railroad trains during a crucial time period when the railway employees went out on strike, (2) when President Kennedy threatened to purchase steel products only from small steel companies who did not raise their prices at a time when the larger companies had raised their prices, and (3) several administrations that have threatened to release scarce materials from government stockpiles onto the commercial market when private enterprise has either indicated it would or actually did raise the price of the materials to their customers.

With this complexity of new laws and regulations the federal government has become all powerful in its role with business and the public. Almost every move or decision made by either business or the public today is affected by one or more of these rules and regulations. George Steiner has compiled a list of varied roles the federal government plays in its relationship with business and the public. An examination of this list is worthwhile since it shows, or at least implies, the power and influence, the interrelationships, and the complexities induced by the federal government as it exerts its influence over the government-business-public domain. Government:

1. Prescribes the rules of the game for business

2. Is a major purchaser of business' products and services

3. Uses its contracting power to get business to do things it wants

4. Is a major promoter and subsidizer of business

5. Is the owner of vast quantities of productive equipment and wealth

6. Is the architect of economic growth

7. Is a financer of business

8. Is the protector of various interests in society against business exploitation

9. Directly manages large areas of private business

10. Is the repository of the social conscience and redistributes resources to meet social objectives.[1]

Upon examining this list and the smattering of legislature discussed in Chapter 6, it is no wonder that one becomes confused as to what are the critical relationships and interconnections between the government, business, and the public. One thing is certain, however, and that is the federal government is certainly the power broker and the navigator of the course that this country is presently following; business behavior and social responsibility are being dictated to a major extent by the government. The question that everyone that reads this book must then answer is what should the respective roles of business, government, and the public be in today's society? This question is certainly easier to ask than to answer and will probably produce as many different answers as people asked. In attempting to answer the question several areas should be explored and examined.

Of all the tasks that must be considered and handled by society today, which ones can best be handled by, or should be handled by, the government, the private business sector, or the public? In attempting to answer this question one must look at all areas of production, distribution, marketing, engineering, work environment, product safety, advertising, equal employment opportunities and practices, fair pay, a clean environment, and hundreds of other areas. Prior to the late 1800s, the decision leaned very heavily in the direction of business and private citizens taking the leading role in running the economy and setting the social responsibility standards of the community and the nation. From the late 1800s to the mid–1930s, the government began to slowly get more involved in running the entire country and setting social responsibility standards. It was, however, still only a "drop in the bucket" compared with what was to follow. From the mid 1930s through the 1960s and into the 1970s, new legislation and the establishment of new social responsibilities came off of the government presses with rapid fire succession. Only in the 1980s, under the Reagan administration, have some of the big government's role been reversed slightly. Even though business and the public has had more freedom in many areas under the Reagan administration, big government still has the prime power to control business and society.

Much of this battle that goes on between government, business, and society is a result of the conflict that exists between these three areas and their different views on economic and social responsibility goals. Opinions differ between the goals and objectives of government, business, and society and how best to achieve these goals and objectives. The bottom line is that someone has to pay for any changes or dislocations that result from new laws and legislation; it does not come free—even though some people seem to think that it does.

Local and State Governments

The federal government has held no privileged position in generating new laws and legislation in recent times. Even though the local and state governments lost much of their "state's rights" control over their own territories to the federal government with the passage of new federal legislation, the local governments and state governments have generated a proliferation of new rules, laws, and regulations of their own.

With the growth and expansion of towns and cities the local and state legislatures felt compelled to write new legislation which would "protect the social welfare" of the increased and higher density population. New zoning laws were passed on lot sizes, fence heights and locations, sidewalk requirements, and on every imaginable subject one might think of. Many of the laws were initially passed in the 1950s and 1960s by state and local communities with little concern for federal legislation and prime concern for their own problems. As the new federal legislation was implemented and started to be enforced throughout the country, local and state laws were modified so as to not be in conflict with the higher level laws. In many instances, however, local and state laws are more restrictive than federal laws and, in some cases, local or state laws exist in areas where federal laws either do not exist or are relatively broad by comparison. In all cases, the local business must still comply with these additional laws and regulations at a cost to someone. Lower taxes, an abundant and/or low cost labor supply, convenience to raw materials and/or markets, or other desirable factors may offset the other more restrictive laws and regulations of a particular location. All of this must be taken into consideration when choosing a plant or business location.

International Government

The United States is diverse in nature with its complexities and differences between local, state, and national laws. Educational systems and requirements vary between school systems; tax laws and other business requirements differ from state to state and locality to locality; and attitudes, climate, resources, transportation, and history vary all over the United States.

When a business moves across international boundaries, the cultural, educational, economic, political, legal, ethical and moral, and social differences are compounded manyfold. The chance for mistakes or misunderstanding are multiplied many times. What might be considered a commission in one locale could very well end up being considered a bribe somewhere else; what might be considered by the business as being helpful to the host government might be considered by the host government as being hostile and an attempt to take advantage of and dominate the local or national economy. The role that women, the number of U.S. workers used versus number of local workers used, pay levels, work schedules, and type of business permitted can vary from place to place and country to country. It is not an easy task to pick where and when, if at all, a business will attempt to journey into the international arena. It can serve as a place of great conflict and controversy.

Perhaps one of the first multinational moves was made by the German chemical producer, Bayer, when it purchased an interest in an aniline plant in Albany, New York, in 1865.[2] On the other hand, it might be more correct to assign the title of true multinational to Singer. From its sewing machine plant, which it built in Glasgow, Scotland, in 1867, it manufactured, shipped, and mass marketed an almost identical product throughout the world.[3] As it grew, it developed manufacturing and marketing capabilities in each of the areas where it sold sewing machines.

In spite of the problems and difficulties discussed earlier, multinational companies have spread and grown rapidly since the time of the initial plunge into this area by Bayer and Singer. England held the title of being the leading nation in direct foreign investment in other countries in the early twentieth century. These investments were primarily in the area of development of mineral and other resources and the investment and development of processing, packaging, and distribution of goods in a host country for export back to England. Direct foreign investment in other countries by America started to exceed those of England in the early 1900s. It first started in Mexico in 1919, followed by Canada in 1922, and Latin America in 1929.[4] This multinational expansion from the U.S. grew rapidly. In 1914 only 19 major companies were identified as falling into this category; whereas by 1929 the list boasted of 50 such companies.[5] Prior to the 1920s, mining was the major area of U.S. foreign investment.[6] By 1929, manufacturing had surpassed mining as the leading sector of direct U.S. foreign investment; with the emergence of oil companies, petroleum became the second major area of direct foreign investment by U.S. companies.

Direct investment by the United States in foreign lands has continued to grow through the years, with little apparent concern for foreign direct investments in the United States. As late as 1980 the investments and holdings held by U.S. companies in foreign lands exceeded by $100 billion the value of foreign owned assets in the United States.[7] Today, however, the positions are reversed.

Foreign-owned companies are shaking the foundation of the U.S. construction industry, chipping away at domestic semiconductor manufacturers, and colliding with U.S. car producers. U.S. children are riding to school in buses operated by a Canadian company. American firemen depend on hydrants made by an Arab company in Illinois. Foreigners have bought land in practically every state, a piece of virtually every industry, and one-seventh of the federal debt.[8]

In total, foreigners took over 260 American corporations in 1986 with total asset value held by foreigners by the end of 1986 in the $1.3 billion range; this is up from $2.6 million at the end of 1976 and $1.0 billion in 1985.[9] In dollar amounts in 1985, England led the list of direct investors in the United States, followed by Netherlands, Japan, Canada, West Germany, Switzerland, Netherlands Antilles, France, Sweden, and Belgium.[10]

The United States has not only been welcoming foreign investment but actively courts it. City mayors and state governors are colliding with one another as they tour the European and Asiatic continents in attempting to induce foreign governments, usually through tax incentives or free land, to invest in their city or state. Nestle recently purchased Carnation for $3.0 billion; Celanese was purchased by a West German company, as was Doubleday and Company and RCA Records; Japanese landlords now own and operate the Maui Marriott in Hawaii, the Exxon Building in Rockefeller Center, and the Tiffany Building on Fifth Avenue; American Express sold a part interest in its Shearson Lehman Brothers subsidiary to Nippon Life Insurance Company, Japan's largest insurance company; Campeau of Canada bought out Allied Stores for $3.2 million in 1986 and paid over $6.5 billion in 1988 for Federated Department stores, the fifth largest retailer in the United States; "golden parachute" clauses for top Federated executives, legal and investment banking fees, a deferred compensation program, and other assorted costs will bring the total estimated cost to $8.8 billion. Land purchases also have been extensive in some states. In Connecticut and Rhode Island foreigners own less than 0.1 percent of the farmland; in Maine, New Hampshire, Vermont, Florida, Arizona, Washington, Oregon, and Hawaii they own 2 to 10 percent of the farmland; while in all of the remaining states they own between 0.1 to 1.9 percent of the farmland.[11] A section of the new trade bill now under consideration by Congress calls for the registration of all foreign property ownership in the United States.

This foreign investment and ownership of businesses and farmland in the United States is applauded by some as wonderful, while others take a dim view of it. Those in favor of it argue that it enriches the U.S. economy by bringing in new industries, increases employment, and increases local and national purchasing power, as well as bolstering the GNP and balance of payments.

Jobs and increased purchasing power are the two strongest reasons for support of the foreign investments. In 1985, foreign companies directly employed about 3 percent of the American work force with some nonunionized states such as Georgia claiming 900 foreign companies and Houston alone claiming 600 foreign companies.[12] Local merchants also like the foreign investments because of the increased money and the indirect increase in employment by them to sell merchandise to the foreign employed workers; this spinoff of indirect increased employment extends on to the goods supplier and manufacturer and all associated middlemen.

Those who object to foreign ownership of American assets pose interesting arguments and questions about the "selling off of America." Some people are upset with this general influx of foreign multinationals, primarily on the basis that they do not want foreigners taking over the country's banks, businesses, and farmland, or as it has been stated by some, "what the foreigners could not do through war they are now doing through economics." Others question whether the United States is giving up its technology edge and relying too much on foreign technology; how it influences U.S. competitiveness in world markets; and most importantly, whether it jeopardizes national security.[13] This last concern was brought into the limelight when Commerce Secretary Malcolm Baldridge and Defense Department officials opposed the $200 million bid by Fujitsu Ltd. of Japan to buy 80 percent of the Fairchild Semiconductor Corporation, one of United States' major producers of computer chips in California's Silicon Valley.

The expansion of multinational corporations into foreign countries is not always an easy one. To a great extent they are at the mercy of the political actions of the host country. If the host country attitude is or becomes hostile, such as was the case in Lebanon and Iran and some Central American countries, the corporation can lose part or all of its investments in that country. South Africa has produced a host of other problems with its apartheid policy. In this case a number of outside multinational companies have tried, with little success, to reshape the political policies of South Africa. If this could not be done, then the approach of many was that if American companies were going to do business in South Africa, they at least should not be an extension of South Africa's apartheid policy. In 1977, to assist in this philosophy, Reverend Leon Sullivan (the first black to occupy a seat on the board of General Motors) argued for a policy that has come to be known as the Sullivan principles, of which there are six:

1. Integration of all company facilities

2. Establishment of equal and fair employment practices

3. Equal pay for employees performing equal or comparable work for the same period of time

4. Development of training programs for nonwhites

5. An increase in the number of black people in managerial positions

6. Improvement in housing, transportation, education, and health facilities for employees[14]

In 1977, twelve major U.S. corporations adopted the Sullivan principles. This number grew to a total of 145 companies but by 1983 had decreased by 29 companies.[15] Companies have not only continued to drop out of practicing the principles because of the difficulties in some cases of actually practicing and enforcing them, but also because many companies have pulled out of South Africa altogether. In many cases, the companies and South African officials felt that some of these principles, as well as other imposed sanctions on South Africa, hurt the South African blacks much more than it hurt the South African government.

When sanctions did not work and the Sullivan principles did not produce the desired results, many companies slowly pulled out of South Africa, some of them at great loss to the company and riches to some South Africans:

Sanctions have made them [South Africans] rich. This has happened because foreign corporations couldn't simply pick up their factories and go home, as advocates of divestment seemed to think they would. They have had to sell them, frequently to the incumbent managers in the form of leveraged buyouts, often for a fraction of market value, because everyone knew they were desperate.[16]

Some multinational companies that have recently pulled out of South Africa include Coca-Cola, IBM, Procter & Gamble, Pepsi-Cola, Kentucky Fried Chicken, Exxon, Barclays of Britain, Eastman Kodak, Revlon, and Honeywell. Numerous companies still remain in South Africa with many considering a possible pull out. In early June of 1987, Rev. Sullivan abandoned his 10-year effort to end apartheid in South Africa through the principles that bear his name. He also urged companies to pull out of South Africa as the only solution at this time.[17] Two major California state pension funds have also tried to help get companies to leave South Africa by no longer purchasing the stocks of more than 200 of the nations largest companies.[18] Several colleges have also tried to force U.S. companies out of South Africa by using similar techniques. Companies, however, are starting to fight back by hitting the schools where it hurts the most—in their bank accounts. Some corporations under fire, where colleges either have sold off or have threatened to sell off stocks of companies that do business with South Africa, are putting counterpressure on the colleges by refusing to contribute grants, scholarships, and faculty bonuses to the schools.[19]

This brief discussion of a few of the complex issues involved in the operation of multinational companies suggests some of the possible difficulties involved in managing these enterprises and corporate social performance.

Businesses' Role and Influence on the Government

The previous section has shown some of the tremendous influence that all levels of the government has over business. Business, on the other hand, has much less power to influence the government. Its main power to influence the government is primarily through lobbying groups, political action committees, political power, and public relations.

Lobbying Groups

Lobbying groups for almost every cause imaginable exist in the nation's capital. Companies can either support existing groups or hire, form, and support their own people to form a lobbying group for a specific cause. It is then the responsibility of these lobbying groups to contact all involved lawmakers and their staff members who draft the legislation to make certain that they are fully aware of businesses' view on the subject. They also appear before regulatory agencies that are involved in drafting legislation.

Letter writing to legislators is also an important aspect of lobbying. Federal agencies quite often ask for comment letters on proposed rules and regulations; it helps them decide how to set policy. The procedure calls for a request for comments to be posted in the *Federal Register*, along with a summary of the rule in question. An estimated 4 to 5 percent of the letters received come directly from the group affected. Most of the letters received come from trade associations, individual firms, and large corporations.[20]

Opposing lobbying groups also exist in abundance and since the 1960s have been quite successful in getting their views before the regulatory agencies and congressional staff members who were drafting legislation. As a result, business and trade associations became more sophisticated and active in presenting their ideas and views at the federal, state, and local levels of government.[21]

Political Action Committees

In 1974, an amendment to the Federal Election Campaign Act made it legal, for the first time, for companies to set up political action committees. These committees are permitted to solicit funds from employees and stockholders and make contributions to political candidates. The number of PACs active in congressional election campaigns grew from 971 in 1977 to 2,729 in 1985–1986, with total PAC contributions to congressional candidates growing from $11 million to $71 million over the same period.[22]

One might ask where all this money comes from and to whom does it go? In 1986, the top PAC donors to the congressional candidates included the National Association of Realtors ($1.4 million), National Education Association ($1.0 million), National Association of Home Builders ($950,000), and the National Association of Letter Carriers ($840,000).[23] It appears that the bulk (over $52 million) of the money is aimed at the incumbents in positions of power. In 1986, the top amounts of money went to: Chairman Bob Packwood (R-Oregon) of the Senate Finance Committee ($992,000); Steve Symms (R-Idaho), who is a member of the Senate Finance Committee ($871,000); Sam Gibbons (D-Florida), who is a member of the House Ways and Means Committee ($483,000); and House Budget Chairman William Gray (D-Pennsylvania) ($368,000).[24]

While some congressional and senatorial incumbents receive as much as 35 to 45 percent of their campaign cash from PACs, there are still a number of members of both Houses who will not accept contributions from this source. Some senators, without success so far, have attempted to eliminate or to at least reduce from $5,000 to $3,000 the maximum amount that the groups are permitted to contribute to the candidates. Those who oppose PACs feel that they place public office on the auction block and permit those who are inclined to do so to buy political influence. One example used to support this point is the 286-to-133 House of Representatives vote that killed a Federal Trade Commission rule that would have required used-car dealers to inform prospective purchasers of a used car of any known defect that existed in the car at the time of purchase. A study conducted by Ralph Nader's Congress Watch pointed out that a total of $742,371 was contributed by the car dealers' PAC to the 286 members of Congress who voted to kill the rule.[25]

Those who support and defend PACs deny any hint of influence peddling through them. They feel that they help expand participation in elections by encouraging and enabling the average American taxpayer the opportunity to pool his or her money with other people in like positions in order to compete with the wealthier interests for the attention of the same lawmakers.

Business is heavily involved in both the electoral and governmental process. When business and trade association PACs combine and coordinate their activities with the powerful Business Roundtable and other lobbyists sympathetic to their cause, they represent a powerful and influential voice to be heard. This trend is continuing to increase but some feel that it is not as powerful, influential, or representative of all the people as it could and should be. The corporation per se does not directly influence political affairs because it is governed by a written charter authorized by a state and in many cases is not permitted by law to contribute money to political leaders. Ira G. Conn, Jr., feels that it is therefore the managers of the corporation who must take the responsibility, as individuals, to fulfill their duties to their stockholders and to the public at large by extending themselves further by making more personal contact among employees, business management, the academic community, and political groups. If sincerely and properly done, an effective communication, interaction, and ongoing relationship can be developed. This in turn will permit corporate leaders to become influential in political affairs to an extent never before realized.[26]

Negotiations and Court Actions

Two other mechanisms available to business in its attempt to obtain more favorable conditions for its problems or cause is through negotiations or court action. When new legislation is to be considered, regardless of the government level at which it occurs, business has the right to express its view on the impending legislation. In many instances, changes or modifications can and will be made in the legislation to accommodate some form of business or other hardship. Waivers or release from certain sections of laws, rules, and ordinances can sometimes be negotiated and obtained through a formal appeal to the responsible government agency.

Sometimes a new law is passed and all negotiating attempts and political action have failed to result in any relief to the business. The business then has the option to move to another location or country (depending on whether a local, state, federal, or another country's law is the offending trouble maker) or go to court and sue for a change of the law, a new interpretation of the law, relief from the law or troublesome parts of it, or invalidation of the law. Court dockets are full at all levels of government of all types of cases generated by business. They range from simple clarification of certain laws or portions of laws to cases where the company does not agree with the law or cannot effectively operate under it with the present conditions or requirements.

SCENARIO

The remaining chapters will contain several short scenarios at the chapter end. Each scenario is a mini-case or situation problem. No answer will be given to the scenarios; however, there is sufficient information in each chapter preceeding the scenario to help evaluate the situation. The prime purpose of the scenarios is to initiate discussion and thought and, hopefully, some solutions to real world problems facing everyone today. Most of the scenarios are based on true situations.

You live in a quiet, pleasant, suburban residential area where most houses are placed on approximately one-half acre lots. On cool clear evenings and nights you prefer fresh air to air-conditioning, so you have had the habit of opening your windows to let the cool, fresh air circulate through the house. However, over the past year or so every time you do this the house becomes filled with the stench of burning garbage shortly after midnight. You have toured the neighborhood but have not been able to locate anyone burning trash. There is a local ordinance prohibiting all outside burning, but nothing covering what can or cannot be burned in the fireplace. You are certain that someone is burning trash in their fireplace late at night, but are not certain what to do about it. You feel that your rights to breathe fresh air and obtain a peaceful nights' sleep are being infringed upon. If you were in this situation, what would you do?

NOTES

1. George A. Steiner, "Societal Change and Business—Government Relationships," *MSU Business Topics* 23 (Autumn 1975): 5–6.

2. Christopher Tugendhat, *The Multinationals* (New York: Random House, 1972), p. 12.

3. Ibid., p. 13.

4. Mira Wilkins, *The Emergence of Multinational Enterprise: American Business Abroad from the Colonial Era to 1914* (Cambridge, Mass: Harvard University Press, 1970), p. 155.

5. Mira Wilkins, *The Maturing of Multinational Enterprise, American Business Abroad, 1914–1970* (Cambridge, Mass.: Harvard University Press, 1974), p. 142.

6. Neil A. Jacoby, "The Multinational Corporation," *Center Magazine*, no. 3 (1970): 39.

7. Jaclyn Fierman, "The Selling Off of America," *Fortune* 114, no. 14 (1986): 44–45.

8. Ibid., p. 45.

9. "American on the Auction Block," *U.S. News & World Report* 102, no. 12 (1987): 56–57; Fierman, "The Selling Off of America," p. 45.

10. "America on the Auction Block," p. 57.

11. Fierman, "The Selling Off of America," p. 45.

12. Ibid.

13. "America on the Auction Block," p. 56.

14. John Omicinski, "Influential Pastor Urges S. African Pullout," *Cincinnati Enquirer*, June 4, 1987, p. A–4.

15. Tamar Lewin, "Rev. Sullivan Steps Up His Anti-Apartheid Fight," *New York Times*, November 6, 1983, p. F–12.

16. Peter Brimelow, "Why South Africa Shrugs at Sanctions," *Forbes* 139, no. 5 (1987): 101.

17. Omicinski, "Influential Pastor," p. A–4.

18. John R. Emshwiller, "South Africa Ban in California Places 200 Big U.S. Firms Off Limits to Funds," *Wall Street Journal*, January 1, 1987, p. 17.

19. Dennis Knele, "Firms Tied to South Africa Strike at Colleges That Sell Their Stock," *Wall Street Journal*, December 10, 1986, p. 33.

20. R. M. Lakin, "Administrative Law . . . Decision Making . . . and Second Opinions," *Bottomline* 1, no. 8 (1984): 33–36, 48.

21. George Schwartz, "Lobbying Effectively for Business Interests," *Business Horizons* 24, no. 5 (1981): 41–46.

22. "Greening of the Candidates: When the PACs Turn on the Money Spigot," *U.S. News & World Report*, 101, no. 14, 1986, p. 22.

23. Ibid.

24. Ibid., p. 23.

25. Norman C. Miller, "The Pernicious Influence of PACs on Congress," *Wall Street Journal*, February 17, 1983, p. 36.

26. Ira B. Corn, Jr., "The Changing Role of Corporations in Political Affairs—Corporate Free Speech," *Vital Speeches* 47, no. 15 (1981): 463–468.

8

Legal Aspects of Social Responsibility: Business, Government, and the Environment

BUSINESS, GOVERNMENT, AND THE ENVIRONMENT

The earth is warming up, ice caps are melting, the tillable top soil layer of the earth is getting thinner, drinking water is in short supply and contaminated, surface and underground water supplies and tables are shrinking in size and becoming contaminated, forests are being stunted and shrinking in size, the ozone layer is thinning, buildings and ancient art objects are rapidly deteriorating and eroding away, fish and wildlife are dying, all types of waste material are accumulating, the population is ever increasing, and easily available energy sources are rapidly being depleted. This sounds almost like a horror motion picture where sooner or later some type of monster is going to "grab you" and "do you in "; however, the above scenario is a true-life drama now taking place on good old planet Earth. Without proper care, one or a combination of these conditions could deal the planet a death blow (at least as far as people living on the Earth are concerned) and the true monster would be none other than the selfish inhabitants of the Earth itself. All of the above items either generate pollution or are the result of pollution. Not all of this deterioration from pollution is caused by business alone but by a combination of business, government, and the general public; however, business practices are by far the main contributor to these problems.

Business Responsibility for the Environment

The answers and solutions to the problem are not simple ones but ones that will take much continuous work and care. Business and everyone else must be diligent and aware of what causes certain conditions and what can be done to hold them within tolerable limits. An example to amplify this last point might be the company executives who listened to the local area citizen representatives complain about the company polluting a local lake by dumping its waste chemicals into the lake. The executive indignantly responded that it was not his waste chemicals being dumped into the lake that was causing all the pollution but those smelly dead fish floating in the water. The business executive went on to say that all the citizens had to do was to clean up the smelly dead fish and the local pollution problem would be solved. This may solve the smelly fish part of the pollution but does not solve the root cause of the problem.

Before examining some specific areas of pollution and what can be and is being done about them, it will be worthwhile to look at what the total debate is about. Pollution is, unfortunately in most cases, a by-product of everyday living. The operation of a "free market" system may fail to serve the best interests of society because of the inability of the market to adjust itself independently and adequately to certain kinds of side effects such as pollution. Also, the buyers and sellers in the marketplace often lack the quantity and quality of information necessary to undertake effectively and efficiently the proper transactions to optimize the side effects for the best interests of both parties involved.

Under a free market economy, private industry, local governments, and county, state, and federal governments (hereafter referred to as "emitters") can, and do, sometimes relieve themselves of certain costs associated with disposal of waste materials by using the atmosphere, oceans, lakes, rivers, and landfills, as free waste receptacles. If it is to the economic advantage of the particular emitter to do so, it will normally take advantage of this free resource. The cost problem is, however, passed onto another party (hereafter referred to as the receptor) and the ultimate costs for the entire pollution region may not be reduced; in fact, if the costs to the receptors are in excess of the costs to the emitters to reduce their discharge or disposal of pollutants, the ultimate costs to society as a whole may be increased. This is basically a variation of the same problem presented and discussed by Pigou many years ago in part 2 of his "The Economics of Welfare" when he discussed the problem of "uncompensated damage done to surrounding woods by sparks from railway engines.[1]

Pollution arises when waste materials (pollutants) are dumped into or onto the earth's surface or into the atmosphere by emitters. Following Pigou's lead, this discharge of pollutants by the emitters places on the receptors costs that are not adequately charged to the emitters by the free market; this in turn, results in more pollution being expelled by the emitters to settle on the receptors than is desirable from the point of view of society as a whole. The pollutants whose costs are not adequately imputed to the emitters results in what is today commonly referred to as "technological externalities." These technological externalities can, and in many instances do, keep the free market mechanism from operating in such a manner as to bring the economic system into a state of Pareto optimality.

For many unthinking people, the solution to the problem is as simple as prohibiting the externalities; that is, that since the emitters are inflicting harm upon the receptors, then the emitters should be prohibited from doing so. This is, of course, not the solution since the problem being dealt with is reciprocal in nature. If all harm were to be removed from the receptors, then great harm would be inflicted upon the emitters; on the other hand, to place no restraints whatsoever on the emitters inflicts great harm on the receptors. Either one of these approaches is in conflict with the concept of Pareto optimality. Optimality does not require that all externalities be eliminated. Rather, optimality requires that externalities exist in the "correct" amount. Diagrammatically the correct amount of pollution can be depicted in a simplified manner by referring to Figure 3. Costs and gains are measured in dollars on the Y axis and the level of pollution control is measured on the X axis. The rising incremental cost of control line (IC) represents at each potential level of control what the last small increment of control costs. The falling incremental reduction in damage cost line, or incremental benefit to the receptor line (IB), portrays at each potential level of control how much the last increment of control benefits the receptors by reducing damage. By using incremental lines the areas under them represent the total value of what they show an increment. For example, if incremental costs and benefits are examined at point X_1, there would be an incentive for society to increase controls because additional benefits from further controls exceed the additional costs at this point. If controls are extended to point X_2 the area ACX_2 under the IC line shows the total cost to the emitters for that level of control; similarly, the area X_2CD under the IB line shows the total residual damage that is left to the receptors after control level X_2 has been achieved. At position CX_2 incremental costs and incremental benefits are equal and the correct amount of pollution (externality) now exists. The reciprocal interplay of too much damage to the receptors or too much damage to the emitters has been optimized.

The primary problem and task then is to determine the optimality point through the development of two types of functional relations. One of these functions must establish the emitters' costs of pollution abatement at each level of pollution reduction. The second function must relate the benefits (or cost savings) received by the receptors at each level of pollution reduction. This is no easy task to accomplish if one examines the early literature of the 1960s and 1970s when the government was trying to establish the proper and safe level of pollution. There was much conflicting evidence between the "experts" in the area of pollution.

It was not sufficient to sit and complain that the available data were inadequate to reach a Pareto optimum position at that time. A start had to be

Figure 3
Incremental (Marginal) Cost and Incremental Benefit of Pollution Abatement

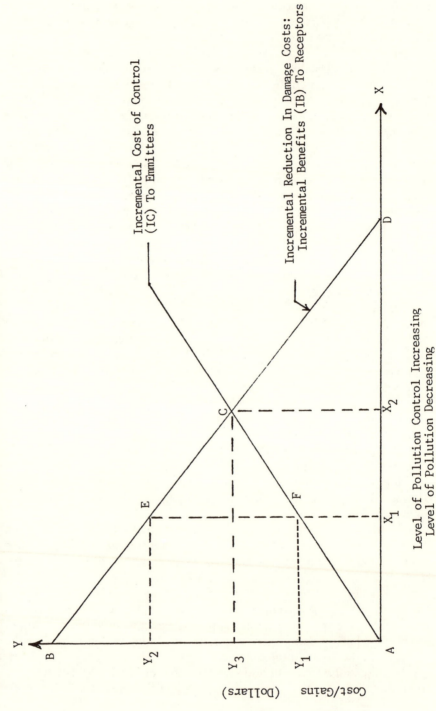

made somewhere with the information that was available. The solution at that time was that the government took the best information available and established what it felt were achievable and realistic levels of pollution; it then forced the emitters to meet these standards, by legal action if necessary. Right, wrong, or otherwise, it is the responsibility of business to meet the established levels of pollution unless and until it can prove other levels of pollution will be more beneficial to society as a whole.

Even though pollution levels have been established for most types of pollution, there is much concern and interest in encouraging business to reduce the levels below those now established. In certain instances the government gives incentives for accomplishing such feats.

Examination of the pollution literature is full of data that show where and how, especially when taken in the aggregate, both emitter and receptor can save money by reducing pollution levels. For example, more efficient energy production will help reduce pollution and conserve natural resources. The United States does quite poorly in energy production efficiency when compared with other countries. When energy efficiency is measured in energy use per dollar of GNP the United States rates as the most inefficient energy user of all the market-oriented countries of the world (France, Sweden, Japan, Spain, West Germany, Italy and Britain); in fact, France, Sweden, and Japan are twice as efficient as the United States in this area.[2]

Regardless of whether a political or economic approach is taken to reduce environmental pollution, a major share of this reduction must be borne by the business concern. Table 6 lists a number of pollution laws now existing that must be addressed by business.

Another dislocation area associated with pollution abatement is the question of who should pay for this reduction in pollution? It is obvious that in the long run the customer pays for the improved environment in which he lives, so perhaps the question should really be rephrased to ask how the customer should pay for it and which customers should pay for it? If the government subsidizes pollution abatement in any manner, then the entire population will pay for the reduced pollution level through increased taxes. If the business pays the cost of the pollution abatement the customers (through higher product costs), the stockholders (through possible reduced dividends) and possibly even the employees (through possible reduced wages or smaller wage increases) will pay for the pollution level reduction. Should all three of these groups suffer money losses or should all cost increases be passed on to the customer? If all costs are passed on to the customer will it hurt business sales through increased prices? Is it fair to distant customers who must pay for the pollution reduction through increased goods costs but may not reap any of the benefits of the pollution reduction because they are in a different unaffected locale? Business has been handling these problems in various ways and should continue to do so. They should, however, periodically reevaluate their system for doing this to see that it fairly respects all involved people.

Causes of Environmental Deterioration

It is often difficult to find any one cause on which to blame the tremendous increase in pollution. It is quite often a combination of factors. To list all the factors that contribute to this problem would be an endless task; however, they can probably be lumped under three major social forces and discussed in a general manner. These three social forces are intertwined and may be categorized as population growth and relocation, technology growth, and affluence.

Population Growth and Relocation

The population increase and the movement of people from the countryside to more central locations has intensified the environmental problems. The sheer number of people brought about by the postwar baby boom and continued legal and illegal immigration, along with movement of these people into concentrated city areas, have put a strain on the physical environment. This strain has come from such things as overcrowding, increased waste material and its disposal, traffic congestion, transportation overloading, increased energy usage with its undesirable by-products, increased use of artificial pesticides, increased water consumption, and congested living conditions.

Waste material and pollution has always existed, but at one time there were plenty of places to dispose of it. Waste material becomes a serious pollution problem when there is a shortage of places to dispose of it. At one time small quantities of waste were dumped into streams and lakes with a minimum of detrimental impact, but as quantities of waste material increased, streams, lakes, landfills, and other previous waste depositories could no longer be used without seriously harming all living creatures.[3] Only by practicing restraint, consideration of others, and improved technology can excessive pollution be held in check.

Technological Growth

Technological growth is a multiple-edged sword. First, it has made people more fully aware of detrimental pollutants that at one time received only minimal concern; in this category can be found lead in paint and gasoline, asbestos in many buildings, and numerous chemicals. Second, it is a direct and indirect creator of pollution; through its expanded manufacturing facilities and increased energy consumption it directly creates air, water, chemical, and noise pollution; through the increased manufacture of throw-away products, consumer chemical products, and artificial fertilizers it creates secondary increased pollution sources when these products fall into careless hands or are not properly used. Third, it can contribute greatly to the solution of many pollution problems; in many cases waste materials are being turned into saleable by-products that were once thrown away, and garbage and trash is being efficiently turned into heat and electricity.[4] The United States still has a much longer way to go to be truly efficient in this area.

If this world is to continue to support life on its surface, some part of technology must continually be directed toward improvement of the environment. A *Business Week* article expressed this feeling by saying: "Properly directed by business and government, it (technology) can undo much of the environmental damage it once wrought."[5] Not only must technology continue to undo much of the damage it has created, but it must also find ways to keep from creating new and worse environmental problems.

Affluence

The rapid and continuously growing standard of living is another prime cause of the increased pollution. Real personal income has continued to grow almost uninterrupted since the mid 1940s. The people of the United States have as a result purchased more goods and services, traveled more miles, and generated more waste than in any other comparable period in history. With ever rising single and double incomes in families the people have become less concerned with long-term durable goods and have opted for the convenient throw-away goods. Business has been happy to oblige with these new disposable items because it means more repeat sales. Unfortunately for the environment, it means that it must also have a large appetite to accommodate all of the increased waste, a total of 1,547 pounds per person per year in the United States.[6] The country is rapidly running out of space to take care of all of this new waste material. In the United States, 86 percent of the household and commercial waste ends up in landfills; in land-poor Japan, 50 percent of the household and commercial waste is recycled, 34 percent is incinerated, and only 16 percent of it goes to landfills.[7] How bad does waste have to get in the United States before more constructive and innovative approaches are taken for its disposal?

Types of Environmental Pollution

Pollution is a serious problem not only in the United States but throughout the world.

With no place to hide, boys in Cubatao, Brazil, cover their faces as they try to avoid breathing a cloud of lung searing fumes from a fertilizer plant. Called the "valley of death" by residents, Cubatao may be the most polluted community on earth. Scores of plants including a petrochemical complex pump at least 75 pollutants into its frequently stagnant air, raising contamination levels in parts of town to twice those considered safe for humans. "Some days it is so bad you can't breathe," says one resident. "If you go outside, you will vomit."[8]

This one quote alone shows how serious a problem only one category of pollution (air pollution) is when in this one location alone it has 75 different pollutants carried through the air and is bad enough to make people so sick that they vomit.

Types and forms of pollution abound throughout the world and in the United States and cause all types of problems. Neither the space nor the time permit an examination of all the pollutants to which one might be exposed; however, a realistic overview of the pollution problem, what must be done about it, and where possible, what is being done about it, can be briefly examined if pollution is broken down into fairly standard major categories. Any list on major categories of pollution would contain at least: (1) air pollution, (2) water pollution, (3) chemical pollution, (4) solid waste pollution, (5) noise pollution, (6) visual pollution, and (7) odor pollution. Each of these main categories of pollution then has many subcategories under it. In order to be better aware of some of the social problems pollution creates and industry's social responsibility for helping solve some of these problems, each major category and some of the subcategories or types of pollution will be briefly reviewed in the next few pages. It should be noted that even though the various forms of pollution are placed primarily in one category it does not mean that it has no impact on another category. Certainly, solid waste pollution has an impact on water pollution if the solid waste is dumped into the water; likewise, chemical pollution also may be a part of air pollution, water pollution, solid waste pollution, or odor pollution or fall into all categories at the same time. Very simply, pollution is a complex problem that requires integrated supervision and control.

Air Pollution

Air pollution exists everywhere and is one of the most visible forms of pollution. Rarely does a locality suffer from only one form of air pollution; almost every major city or metropolitan area is plagued by complex mixture of pollutants.

The original theory of setting air pollution levels was that there was a "threshold" level that had to be reached before the pollutant adversely affected health. With this concept in mind the Environmental Protection Agency had to determine fairly quickly what these levels were. The main problem with this line of thinking was that no one truly knew what these levels were— and we still are not certain what the actual threshold for health damage from the most common air pollutants are. Since each person reacts differently to different conditions, they may never know for certain what this level is; for some people it will be relatively high and for others it may be close to zero. In spite of these problems, levels of pollution were established on the best information available and enforced for each pollutant and each community. This has not, however, necessarily reduced the total pollution level throughout the United States or the world:

For example, the concentration of sulfur dioxide in the atmosphere of cities is about 20% lower than it was a decade ago. But to achieve this reduction in ground-level pollution outside the plant gate, many companies have built new plants in the countryside or have erected tall smokestacks to disperse the pollutants.[9]

What this accomplishes is to spread the sulfur dioxide, at lower concentrated levels, over a wider range of the countryside.

While traveling across the countryside, both sulfur dioxide and nitrogen dioxide react with the moisture in the atmosphere to form minute particles of sulfate or nitrate and eventually reach the earth either in that form or as sulfuric and nitric acid when mixed with rain. These and other combinations of airborne pollutants have been credited with worldwide problems of stunting and destroying forests, fish, and wildlife; eroding and disfiguring historic buildings and art objects; contamination of water supplies; temperature increase of the world; and depletion of the earth's protective ozone layer and an animal and human health problem.

Acid rain presents a great problem and dilemma for all of society. In Europe, forest trees are being stressed and killed.[10] Canada is claiming that acid rain from the United States is hurting its forest industry and contaminating its lakes and streams and has requested the United States to take corrective action.[11] President Reagan agreed to consider an acid rain pact with Canada[12] and then almost immediately delayed action on it.[13] At the same time, a study conducted by a group of scientists for the EPA on the detrimental affects of pollution on lakes and streams in the Northeast came to the conclusion that, " . . . the agency's data suggest little or no lake acidification is occurring in the Northeast from acid rain, EPA officials said."[14] This supplied ammunition to the coal and electric utility industries who claimed that there was no proof that lakes and streams would suffer from sulfur dioxide emissions from coal-fired plants if they continue fuel usage at current levels. The toughening of air pollution standards for utilities could result in increased costs to the utilities and to the public, as well as make nuclear power plants more attractive and more popular, according to the utilities.[15] Is this true or a scare tactic on the part of utilities to use low-priced, high-sulfur coal and get back on schedule with nuclear power? A relatively new electronic method that controls particulate air pollution at reduced pollution levels and that considerably reduces control costs has been installed and tested at a trash burning incinerator at Langley Air Force Base, a coal-burning power plant in Saskatchewan, Canada, a cement plant in Michigan, and a steel mill in Kentucky.[16]

Possibly the two most dramatic air pollution incidents to occur were the Three Mile Island, Pennsylvania, nuclear power plant breakdown on March 28, 1979, and the destruction of the Chernobyl nuclear power plant in April 1986. In the accident at Three Mile Island, three backup water pumps were turned off in violation of the Nuclear Regulatory Commission's rules. Then an important valve became stuck in the incorrect position, and a false signal on a water level gauge caused the operators to temporarily turn off the emergency cooling system. This caused the water level to drop two feet below the top of the core and some of the exposed fuel rods to overheat and burst, permitting extensive amounts of radioactive material to fill the containment building.[17] Fortunately, the radioactivity released to the surrounding areas remained below the safety limits established by the government.

The aftermath of the breakdown of the Chernobyl plant was extremely destructive in comparison with the Three Mile Island incident. When it exploded, it spewed radioactive cesium–137, iodine–131, strontium, and other poisonous substances into the atmosphere to be carried around the world by winds. The radiation from the complete destruction of the Chernobyl plant was carried by the wind in heavy dosages for over a thousand miles and at higher levels completely around the world. The explosion killed more than 20 people and created over 100,000 refugees from the Ukraine countryside close to the site; contaminated food and drinking water for hundreds of miles away (drinking water from the Dnepr River, Kiev's main source of drinking water, was declared unfit for drinking until December 1,1986—over seven months after the explosion); contaminated food supplies in northern Norway, Sweden, and Finland, over 1,300 miles away; and will eventually cause up to 1,000 people in Western Europe and over 150,000 worldwide to die of cancer over the next 50 years.[18]

These two incidents, plus increasing costs to build, operate, and eventually retire the facilities, along with documented operational carelessness, has caused many to turn against the use of nuclear power as a viable power source. Any malfunction of a facility, which can take place quickly, can put thousands of lives at risk. The Nuclear Regulatory Commission has tried to avert such a catastrophe from happening because of careless operators who, after years of drudgery watching banks of gauges, were nodding off to sleep at the switches at Philadelphia Electric's Peach Power reactors in Delta, Pennsylvania. The Commission initiated a punitive shutdown of the nuclear plant where they had recorded at least five incidents of sleeping on duty since 1981.[19] Other plants had previously been fined in amounts from $50,000 to $635,000 for people sleeping on the job (usually on the 11:00 P.M. to 7:00 A.M. shift) and for other acts of carelessness.[20]

It is not uncommon for the nuclear power industry to spend up to $250,000 in preparing key operators and paying them $30,000 or more per year for diligently and accurately performing their tasks. If operators and business do not decrease carelessness in plant operations, the nuclear industry may deservedly go out of business. They are not only risking their own lives but possibly millions of others. Nuclear plants can be safe if constructed properly and operated carefully and conscientiously. If workers and employers are not willing to work within these rules, then they should not be in the nuclear power business.

Air pollution not only causes acid rain and nuclear radiation fallout and its side effects, but also other troublesome problems, such as overheating of the earth and ozone layer depletion. Carbon dioxide is the prime culprit that is helping heat up the earth's atmosphere. The levels of carbon dioxide have been increasing since before the time of the industrial revolution. Basically, the carbon dioxide layer acts in a similar manner to that of a window of a greenhouse. The sun's short-wave radiation penetrates this increasingly denser carbon dioxide window with relative ease; however, when the sun's rays hit the earth's surface, the reflected rays have been transformed into long-wave radiation and have greater difficulty in penetrating the carbon dioxide shield in order to escape back into the outer atmosphere. The net result is a gradual warming of the earth's atmosphere. The National Aeronautics and Space Administration's Goddard Space Flight Center in Greenbelt, Maryland, said that this buildup of carbon dioxide in the atmosphere is a fact and "Atmospheric buildup of chemical compounds from human activity will change the earth's climate more over the next 50 years than it has since agriculture began."[21]

Estimates are that the northern hemisphere will warm up by one to two degrees Fahrenheit by the year 2,000 and by three to six degrees by 2020. This increase in temperature will continue to melt the ice caps, which will in turn raise the level of the water in the oceans. Sea levels have risen by as much as one foot over the past 100 years and according to EPA projections is expected to rise an additional three feet by the year 2030.[22] If this happens, cities and river outlets along the Gulf Coast and Atlantic Coast could have water encroach another 100 feet further inland. Cities such as Boston, New York, Baltimore, Washington, D.C., Norfolk, Charleston, Miami, St. Petersburg, and New Orleans, as well as the Florida Keys, could be in serious trouble. The additional warming also influences food-growth patterns; with excessive heat food supplies will diminish.

The depletion of the natural protective ozone shield in the earth's upper atmosphere is also another serious problem. The ozone layer is supposed to screen out the type of ultraviolet light that causes skin cancer. Over the last 17 years, levels of ozone have dropped an average of 2 to 3 percent in Canada to 1.7 percent in the southern states; estimates indicate that there are roughly 500,000 new cases of skin cancer per year for each 1 percent decrease in the ozone layer.

The ozone debate began in 1974 when two University of California chemists argued that chlorofluorocarbons (CFCs) do not decompose in the lower atmosphere as do most other compounds but instead slowly drift into the upper atmosphere where they break down and start a complex chemical action that destroys ozone. In 1978, the EPA banned the use of CFCs in aerosol products. Chemical companies let out a howl of protest and mounted a powerful lobby to conduct further study on the controversial, yet unproven theory. Federal regulators backed off of the ban and complied with industry's request. The study is now over and the evidence that CFCs do harm the environment has become more compelling.[23] In the face of mounting pressure from world governments from outright bans to the establishment of "reasonable" limits of CFCs, industry is changing its tune.

In an attempt to resolve the worldwide problem, 45 nations, including the United States and Canada, met in Geneva, Switzerland, in an attempt to hammer out global limits on ozone-destroying chemicals.[24] They hope that these decisions might set the pattern for solving and resolving other worldwide industrial pollution problems.

DuPont, one of several major producers of CFCs, has undertaken moves to curb them.[25] This is a good beginning but others have to follow if a dent is to be made in the ozone problem. Even if all other manufacturers of CFCs did as DuPont is doing, it would not immediately solve the problem. They have an extremely long atmospheric life span; it may take years for the chemicals to reach the ozone layer (an average of 7 to 11 miles above the earth). "The springtime ozone hole over Antarctica will last 100 years even if the world cuts emissions of ozone-destroying chemicals by 90% immediately, the Environmental Protection Agency was told...."[26]

Where the governments have not moved fast enough to solve pollution problems or adequately enforce regulations, private citizens have stepped into the breach. Citizens' lawsuits are proliferating all over the country. These suits began in the 1970s as a result of federal legislation. Nearly all U.S. environmental laws empower the private citizen to sue companies that release pollutants, whatever the type, and collect for both damages and legal fees if successful in the suit. Initially, the suits were aimed at the state and federal governments, but in the early 1980s the emphasis shifted toward the pollutors themselves. Many lawyers consider these cases against companies as "no-risk lawsuits" and as easy as "shooting fish in a barrel."[27] Even though a number of the settlements have been substantial (some over $1.5 million), nearly all of the suits are quickly settled. The companies can pay settlement awards to the state or federal government but in most instances prefer to give the money to an environmental group or specific project as a donation; this is because contributions are usually tax deductible.[28]

Attempts are being made to decrease the levels of air pollution through several techniques, including such items as improved equipments for removing pollution from the air prior to its release from smokestacks; use of low sulfur coal and oil; use of new techniques (or reversion to old techniques) of energy generation such as the sun, wind, ocean, and waterways; and the use of cogeneration techniques where energy generated as a by-product or in excess of need by a private individual or by a business is channeled into the power company's distribution system. All of these sources can, and in most instances do, produce energy in a cleaner manner; they are also, in most instances, more costly at this time.

U.S. energy demands are expected to grow 1 percent per year up through the year 2000 except in the Northeast where they are scheduled to grow at a 2 to 3 percent rate into the 1990s, with demand outpacing supply.[29] It is projected that much of the increased U.S. demand will be supplied from conventional oil, coal, nuclear, and hydroelectric power, with decreasing contributions from natural gas. In New England, the proponents of cogeneration are hoping for increased usage of new power sources, especially if the Seabrook nuclear plant opening is blocked. The data from the Three Mile Island nuclear spill in Pennsylvania and the Chernobyl nuclear power plant disaster in Russia might make it a little more difficult to bring more nuclear power plants on line. Regardless of the direction taken in New England to meet the above energy needs, as well as the national energy demand, new methods of power generation are needed in this country if it is not to become heavily dependent on foreign sources, such as Canadian power in New England and OPEC oil imports for the entire country; U.S. oil import dependence is expected to rise from slightly less than 30 percent in 1985 to between 50 and 75 percent by the year 2000.[30]

Water Pollution

Deterioration of water quality is not a new problem. It has existed ever since mankind began; however, it was fairly well localized and limited until the advent of the Industrial Revolution. With the coming of the Industrial Revolution, first in Europe and then in the United States, the growing concentration of both people and factories added new complex dimensions to the problem. In the past several decades, with the increasingly rapid growth in both the population and the economy, it is now regarded as a serious problem that calls for new approaches and solutions.

Other than for air, water is perhaps our most precious resource. On the average, a person uses 87 gallons of water per day but only 2 gallons per day of this total usage is for the purpose of cooking and drinking; the remaining 85 gallons is used for flushing, bathing, laundering, dishwashing, and filling swimming pools.[31] This, however, is only the direct personal use of water. To this must be added the water used, for example, to irrigate land for growing food and natural fibers for clothing and the water that keeps industry operating. All told it is estimated that the American way of life requires 2,000 gallons of water every day for each person.[32]

This precious water supply is polluted from many sources, such as acid rain, leakage from landfills and strip mining processes, and pollutants either leaked or dumped directly into rivers, streams, and lakes. Easy detection of those who continue to dump pollutants illegally into the rivers and lakes can be accomplished through the use of infrared equipment.[33] By now, about 90 percent of industries and 37 percent of municipalities are in compliance; however, the nation is far from its goal of water aesthetics and fishing and swimming goals for all lakes and rivers.[34]

The Clean Water Act actually created almost as many problems as it solved. When industry was forced to withhold pollutants from rivers, they often buried them in pits all around the countryside. These pollutants have, in many cases, percolated down through the earth and contaminated the underground water supply. Even in cases where the pits have been outfitted with liners, the plastic or rubber liners have torn. At the U.S. Department of Energy's Fernald uranium refinery plant, 20 miles northwest of downtown Cincinnati, Ohio, a one-sixteenth inch rubber plastic liner in a thirty-foot deep pit was supposed to prevent approximately 194 million pounds of radioactive chemicals from leaking into and contaminating the groundwater in the Great Miami Aquifer, a vast underground sand and gravel deposit saturated with water. About one million people in the southwest Ohio region receive their drinking water from this source. The rubber liner has been torn at least twice. For 20 years, plant managers have issued reports every three or four months describing contamination of the plant's wells—and the aquifer—from its six waste pits.[35] It is estimated that about one-half of America's drinking water comes from these underground water supplies and not enough is being done to protect them.[36] In fact, almost all of rural America is still dependent on underground water supplies. Unlike most surface water, which is treated before it is consumed, most underground water receives no treatment before consumption on the assumption that it is pure. In rural areas it is estimated that it can cost up to $2,000 per household for a complete analysis of the water; treatment of the water, if contaminated, can cost even more.[37] It appears that it would be much cheaper to prevent it in the first place and certainly much safer. In order to try and help this problem, Senators Daniel Moynihan, George Mitchell, Max Baucus, Frank Lautenberg, and Quinten Burdick introduced S. 20, the Groundwater Protection Act of 1987, into the first session of the One Hundredth Congress.

River pollution is another serious area of water pollution. In Europe rivers run from country to country and one country's pollution adversely effects the next downstream country. In the United States, rivers run from state to state with the same results. One of the worst waterway spills occurred in Pittsburgh, Pennsylvania, on January 2, 1988. A 40-year-old Ashland Oil Company diesel fuel storage tank ruptured and dumped 3.8 million gallons of its contents. A dike prevented 2.5 million gallons from leaving the area and crews of workmen, operating in subzero temperatures, recovered another 400,000 gallons. This left about 900,000 gallons of diesel fuel oil to start its way slowly down the Monongahela River into the Ohio River and eventually into the Mississippi River. As temperatures remained below freezing in much of the Midwest, faucets went dry in thousands of homes along the Monongahela and Ohio Rivers in the Pittsburgh area as the oil spill started its journey down the Ohio River. Up to as many as 100,000 people in the Pittsburgh area were affected by either loss of water or low water pressure. As the oil slick moved down stream it was stalled in the Steubenville, Ohio, area by ice jams. Tugboats tried to break up the ice jams as schools and businesses closed in an attempt to conserve water supplies. Wheeling, West Virginia, closed its water intake on January 9 and relied on 9 million gallons of stored water to get them through the crisis. By the time the oil slick reached Cincinnati, Ohio, over three weeks later, after a 470 mile downriver trek, it was 60 to 80 miles long and still emitting a slight odor. As in other cities along the river, all water intakes in the Cincinnati area were turned off during the oil slick passage, which by then was considerably diluted since its departure from Pittsburgh.

The ruptured storage tank was over 40 years old and had been disassembled from another sight and moved to Pittsburgh and reassembled. After assembly, it was tested with only five feet of water in the tank, rather than being completely filled. Whether Ashland had received an official building permit for the tank's construction is unclear. The tank ruptured while it was being filled. John Hall, chairman and chief executive officer of Ashland Oil Co., apologized for the oil spill and said Ashland would pay for the cleanup.[38] In the meantime, Ashland is preparing for a wave of lawsuits.[39] Ashland is not the only company in lawsuit trouble for contaminating water. The Kentucky Division of Water has cited the Filon-Silmar plastics plant for dumping sludge used in its manufacturing plants into Banklick Creek near its plant.[40] Amco Corporation was ordered to pay $85.2 million to France and other plaintiffs for damage suffered when one of Amco's supertankers ran aground off the Brittany coast a decade ago and spilled 68 million gallons of oil.[41]

Water cleanup is far from complete and many dangers exist still. For example, there are over 100,000 such storage tanks along rivers similar to the tank that ruptured in Pittsburgh. They contain everything from fuel oil to deadly chemicals. Some plants still dump waste into the rivers and lakes either intentionally or through carelessness. The cost of cleanup is not getting any cheaper and federal money for assistance is shrinking. It went from a low of $0.8 billion in 1974 to $4.3 billion in 1980 and retreated to $2.8 billion in 1987; the latest money, totaling $20 billion, allocated by Washington for clean water is scheduled to be gone by 1994.[42] Unless Congress enacts new legislation, when this money is gone, cities and states will be pretty much left on their own to clean up the remainder of U.S. water supplies.

With all of the problems associated with obtaining clean water, the two gallons per day used for cooking and drinking is the area of greatest concern. Lead is one of the detrimental contaminants most readily found in today's drinking water. It is also found in air, soil, on banisters, walls, window sills, furniture, most toys, and many other items painted before the mid–1970s, and even under new coats of paint. It comes from lead solder used to join copper pipe, from leaking gasoline tanks, and natural lead in the ground in some areas. Ingested lead, whether from water, paint, gasoline fumes, or any other source is a serious health hazard. It can stunt growth, cause mental retardation, and even kill people if consumed at excessive levels or over a prolonged period of time. The human body can only eliminate a certain amount of lead each day, so if the body takes in more than it eliminates it slowly builds up in the body in an additive process. The EPA estimates that every year lead poisoning slightly lowers intelligence up to five IQ points in 143,500 children; and lead increases the risk for 622,000 pregnant women of bearing a child with clubfoot, or with neurological, mental, or physical abnormalities. Lead may also cause hypertension, stroke, and heart attack in middle-aged men.[43] Nearly one in five Americans, according to the EPA, drinks tap water containing excess levels of the highly toxic lead.

With bans on lead in paint, and leaded gasoline being phased out, lead from these sources should be slowly eliminated and the major source of lead in drinking water will then come from leaded solder used in copper joints in home water pipes. This lead can be eliminated or dissipated through the use of filters at the tap or by letting the tap water run three or four minutes prior to drinking it.

Even if the lead problem in drinking water is solved, there still remain other contaminants. In June 1986, Congress approved amendments to the Safe Drinking Water Act that gave the EPA three years to set limits for 64 other contaminants out of over 200 that have been found in groundwater. Groundwater is a natural solvent and readily dissolves and absorbs heavy metals such as lead and cadmium as well as gases (such as radon) and industrial chemicals. Up to one-fourth of the houses in the United States use water that contains radon; most of these homes are found in the New England area. Radon, which is found in much of North American rock, is a radioactive gas emitted when uranium decays. If water that has picked up and absorbed radon is heated, up to 80 percent of the gas is released; this then makes the water a little safer to drink. If, however, the emitted gas is inhaled, just as if the basic radon gas is inhaled, it can produce lung cancer.

The third largest area of drinking water contaminants comes from synthetic organic compounds such as pesticides and solvents; these include benzene, chloroform, and ethylene dibromide and comprise the largest class of water contaminants released by industry. Just as lead solder is a problem area in copper plumbing, the special adhesives used to connect polyvinyl chloride (PVC) pipes can also be a household problem.

Although the above discussion on water pollution barely scratches the surface, it does suffice to awaken everyone to the fact that this is a serious social responsibility area in which much more work must be done. It also shows that some of the cures that have been recommended and implemented have resulted in "cures" that are as bad as or worse than the original problem. It appears that it is time for someone, or some agency, to sit down and examine the entire problem, accurately define the problem areas, and develop proper legislation to handle the entire problem, rather than using "Band-Aid" remedies that sometimes create new problems. Band-Aids will never stop a person from bleeding to death when a tourniquet is needed to stop the blood flow; neither will "patchwork" or legislation solve the water pollution problem when a uniform integrated piece of legislation is needed.

Chemical Pollution

Much in the area of chemical pollution has already been touched on in the discussion of air and water pollution, since that is the way chemical pollution is usually transported to the human body for ingestion. Much of the chemical pollution process is also a concern in the solid waste area. There are some areas of this category, however, that should be and will be expanded upon.

"At an abandoned dump near Swartz Creek, Michigan, a technician scoops up an oily sludge containing PCBs, toxic organic chemicals. Thousands of such sites clogged with deadly waste present the nation with a monumental cleanup task."[44] For four weeks during the summer of 1984, 50 trucks a day rumbled down the street carrying contaminated soil from Swartz Creek to a landfill in Ohio. In 1972, Charles Berlin and a partner had opened a hazardous waste incinerator in Swartz Creek. Quite often it was overloaded and the countryside was covered with dark and dense acrid smoke so corrosive that it drastically reduced housing values, deteriorated convertible car tops into literal ragtops, reddened children's faces with rashes and swelled their eyes shut, and presented an overall area health hazard. It took four years for infuriated area residents to get state officials to permanently close the dump. To purge the dump of toxic metals, used motor oil, drug and dye products, and industrial waste, bulldozers and backhoes removed 120,000 tons of earth as a first cut at cleaning up the dump.[45]

There are hundreds of waste dumps around the country. By October 1984 the EPA had designated or proposed a total of 786 waste sites for its national priorities list. It estimates that the list will eventually grow to 2,500 sites. Of the 264 million metric tons of waste material regulated in 1981, 71 percent come from the chemical and petroleum industry, 22 percent from the metal-related industry, and the remaining 7 percent from other sources. About two-thirds of the total amount was treated by various methods to reduce its volume and toxcity; the remainder was stored or disposed of.[46]

One of the most publicized chemical spills was the one that occurred in Bhopal (in central India) during the night of December 2/3, 1984; toxic methyl isocyanate gas escaped from a Union Carbide Corp. subsidiary plant and by government estimates quickly killed 1,600 people, with an additional 700 dying later of aftereffects. This death figure is expected to increase since many still living Bhopal residents continue to suffer from shortness of breath, eye irritation, and depression months after the accident. The government of India is paying $115 to victims. Unfortunately, many of the victims of the disaster die before they receive their $115.[47]

With the Bhopal accident still fresh in its mind, Congress passed the Superfund Amendment and Reauthorization Act (SARA) in 1986. It is the responsibility of the EPA to implement the new law that is gradually being phased in. By 1989, companies nationwide will be required to report on over

60,000 chemicals; they will have to report on where they are kept, why they are dangerous, how they leak into the environment, and what to do if they spill. It is estimated by the EPA that over the next decade this will generate about 13 million hours of paperwork, which in turn will cost U.S. businesses over $4 billion.[48]

Because of its magnitude and severity, the Bhopal situation received world-wide attention; however, much smaller spills and leaks take place constantly. Three years after a major radiation accident in Cuidad Juarez, Mexico, 80 of its residents are suffering from infertility, headaches, tiredness, wine-colored spots on their skin, and odd fluctuations in the number of white cells in their blood; this all came about after a cobalt 60 accident that subjected these people to widespread radiation exposure at limits as great as five times higher than the yearly limit permitted for U.S. radiation workers.[49] Nuclear contamination has been discovered in six spots by the General Accounting Office; groundwater contamination and contaminated soil was found at the six sites and in four of the locations the contamination had migrated off site.[50] Congress is looking for an explanation to why the Energy Department is making plutonium for bombs in aging problem-laden plants. Cracks appeared in a reactor producing plutonium at the Savannah River, South Carolina, plant because engineers had miscalculated the ability of emergency reactors on the site to prevent a meltdown in the event of an accident; power was cut back by 20 percent and eventually to half power on the recommendations of an independent panel at the National Academy of Sciences.[51] The Hanford, Washington, reactor was shut down for six months to correct safety problems; decades of radioactive waste has accumulated at Hanford and Savannah River and pose another serious problem.[52] The target date for selecting a permanent nuclear waste repository in the eastern part of the country has been tentatively put off until the year 2007.[53]

Two other important chemicals that are much in the news and need some comment on are dioxin and asbestos. Small doses of dioxin cause miscarriages, birth defects, liver damage, or death in laboratory animals; to laboratory animals it is as much as 200 times as lethal as strychnine. Humans that have been exposed to dioxin seem not to suffer such severe results. It is not known, however, about long-term affects of dioxin on people. To point out the difficulty of showing and proving "cause and effect" in the case of dioxin a trial went on for hundreds of days in Belleville, Illinois, in the case of *Kenner* vs. *Monsanto*. The trial is trying to determine whether 65 residents of Sturgeon, Missouri, were harmed when 22,000 gallons of wood-preserving chemicals spilled from a railcar in the center of town in January 1979; the chemicals contained minute traces of dioxin. As the case dragged on, Monsanto was accused of using delaying tactics, which they denied, to make the case so costly that no one would want to attempt suing Monsanto again. Illinois Supreme Court Chief Justice William G. Clark was reported to have said "I find this whole situation disturbing. It may come to pass in this case that justice delayed is justice denied."[54]

Asbestos causes a nonmalignant scarring of the lungs that has been blamed for the deaths of 7 to 10 percent of asbestos workers surveyed in epidemiological studies.[55] The EPA estimates that 733,000 or 20 percent of the nation's public and commercial buildings contain asbestos, and that in two-thirds of the buildings the asbestos has been damaged, making release of dangerous fibers more likely.[56] Some banks, fearful of lawsuits, refuse refinancing an asbestos-laden building unless the owner first agrees to remove all of the asbestos. In other cases, it is believed that in some nonthreatening cases it is better off leaving it alone since some experts feel that the danger to those removing the asbestos is greater than to just leaving it there.

The Asbestos Hazard Emergency Response Act and its implementation requires all schools to have an asbestos assessment completed by October 12, 1988. This means that asbestos must be tracked down in approximately 107,000 schools in the country with a penalty of $5,000 to $25,000 for each day the law is not carried out.[57] Where will all the inspectors come from to do all this inspecting? Anyone can become certified under the Asbestos Emergency Response Act by taking a five-day training course; some long-established asbestos firms feel that it can be dangerous to have an inspector with only five days' training certify or not certify a building.[58] In the meantime, lawyers are out offering free X-rays as they look for new groups of asbestos victims to represent.[59]

Pesticides, plastics, and a list of many other chemicals could be listed as areas of pollution concern and discussed in some detail. It is not the purpose of this book, however, to do that but rather to show the social responsibility that business, the government, and society have in this area. After over two years of deliberation with industry, environmentalists, and enforcement officials, the EPA announced a new revised national policy on PCB cleanup that is less stringent then some of the agency's past settlements.[60] This and other directives from the EPA to clean up contaminated sites and reduce pollution has been a boon to many small businesses. In many instances, these small companies are especially suited to the industry because they are able to supply the specialization that it requires. Previously the EPA contracted with a single company to do emergency cleanups in each of the EPA's four administrative areas. Now, competition from small business specialists should result in better, more efficient, and less costly cleanup.[61]

Solid Waste Pollution

The present day throw-away lifestyle carries a hidden price tag and that is simply that the United States, especially city areas, are running out of room to dispose of their trash. These disposable items extend over the range from used cardboard milk containers to the rockets used to power space vehicles;

they include such items as razors, ballpoint pens, napkins, food containers, diapers, wrist watches, cameras, and you name it. Opposition to plastic packaging and other nonbiodegradable items is intensifying as they pile up along roadsides and waste disposal dumps.[62]

Convenience packaging moves much of the garbage from the household back to the dump, quite often into areas where the crops are grown. Most of the solid waste from households, stores, and offices is a volume problem. Other than for small quantities of pesticides, paints, and illegally dumped motor oil there is no special hazard from this material. It is a matter of space (don't dump it in my back yard) and economics (the cost of the landfill sight and the cost of getting the trash to the sight). This situation, however, does not hold for those that dump toxic waste such as PCBs, chemicals, and other illegal items into purely trash dumps. PCBs seem to be one of the major items illegally placed in trash dumps and landfills.[63]

What is the solution to this problem and what is being done about it? One solution, or possibly it should be called a combination of solutions, is to recycle tin and aluminum cans, prime paper, cardboard, glass, newspapers, oil and scrap metal and then either incinerate or compost the remainder of the solid waste or use a combination of both methods. This combination accomplishes several things: it extends the life of the waste dump sight; it recycles scarce materials; it can make compost available to local residents; if the city is large enough it permits generation of heat and electric power for use by the city or excess electricity can be funneled into the local utility system as part of the cogeneration process; and, if done properly, it should pay for itself or even make a profit.

There are advantages to recycling as part of the process rather than just incinerating the trash. To incinerate the entire trash load does not reduce the trash volume as much as some proponents say; there are ashes from the burned debris, but more importantly the tin, aluminum, glass and some other products do not burn and still must be disposed of in a landfill. Although mass burning is quite popular in Europe, the technology is not directly transferable to the United States. One of the main reasons is that U.S. trash burns differently from European trash because the U.S. trash contains more plastics and toxic material. Additionally, the U.S. employees who run the incinerators have had less training and experience than their European counterparts. Composting, which allows debris to return to its natural state, also requires recycling as part of its process. Although quite effective, it is not used too much in this country. Germany is slowly turning away from incineration and going to the composting and recycling process.

As available land space for dumping shrinks, more communities will have to consider the recycling-incineration-composting process. In 1969 there were 644 landfills in Ohio; this number has now shrunk to 198, and 25 percent of those that are still open are limited to industrial users. Similarly, Hamilton County, Ohio, had 22 landfills in 1969 and today has only 2 that are active. This reduction in available landfills is happening all around the country.[64]

Several states and communities are taking action to use the incineration process, either separately or in conjunction with the recycling and compost process. The Marion County, Oregon, incinerator (outside of Salem, Oregon) is a state-of-the-art plant where both recycling and incineration are used. A state law passed in Oregon in 1969 requires that tin and aluminum cans, prime paper, cardboard, glass, newspaper, oil, and scrap metal all be recycled. With this law in effect residents of the community were required to separate their trash into two containers for trash pickup; one container was to be filled with material that could be recycled while the other container was to be loaded with burnable material. The plant cost $47 million to build and can handle 550 tons of trash per day. In Camden County, New Jersey, most of the almost one-half million people have been separating their garbage into recyclable and burnable cans since 1985. By the end of 1986 22 percent of the residential waste was recycled.

Although more communities are going either to mass burn incinerator systems or to combined incinerator-recycling processes, there are still those who look at them from the negative side. They cite the initial cost of building the units, the cost of operation, and potential air and water pollution problems as well as the increased noise from trucks hauling trash. Several communities have reported problems. In Rutland, Vermont, the incinerator cost considerably more to build than expected; in Tuscaloosa, Alabama, they lost an average of $20,000 a month during their first 34 months of operation. Since the utility companies must by federal law purchase all cogenerated power from these sources (which is usually more costly than the price at which the utilities themselves can generate the power), the cost of electricity for all users will increase. Opponents of mass incineration also point out that unless the fire is kept above a certain temperature, items such as solvents and plastics can produce highly toxic chemicals called dioxins, which will be carried up through the smokestacks and spewed over the countryside.

In spite of the problems associated with the discussed processes it appears that unless people dramatically change their habits—which is not too likely— in the short run, garbage is going to increase and will have to be disposed of by some means. It appears that with landfills becoming scarcer that some form of incineration, recycling, and composting is a realistic and workable alternative. Instead of worrying that it will not work or it is too costly, business and government should be working on more efficient and effective ways to undertake these operations. Space to bury all the garbage is quickly running out.

Noise Pollution

Noise has always existed in the workplace, in congested cities, and around airports. New York City dwellers made it a major social issue in the 1960s when a three-year-long subway construction project, affecting several thousand residents, disrupted the home environment.[65] There has been much debate over the establishment of acceptable standard levels. There are several problems that arise when trying to establish sound levels that might be detrimental to hearing and health:

1. Loudness does not hold precisely for tones of different frequencies and intensities.

2. Loudness also varies widely according to the pitch of the sound and the individual.

3. Loudness does not increase directly in proportion to the power delivered to the ear but varies roughly as the logarithm of the power.

4. Absorption levels of nearby materials and reverberation times affect the persistance of the sound.

5. The total time duration of the sound influences the impact of the noise upon the body.

Almost everyone will agree that persistant noise is more aggravating than short-term noise. Sound persistency is caused by echoes repeated in rapid succession; that is called reverberation. When a source is set into vibration it produces sound (or noise) waves that travel to the wall and other surfaces and bounces back and forth from one surface to another. If none of the sound energy were absorbed, then in theory the resulting sound intensity would continue to increase indefinitely. Fortunately, however, absorption does take place and the sound is dissipated and eventually reaches zero again. Absorption coefficients (ability to absorb sound) have been measured for many materials and are expressed as fractions (or percentages) of the absorption that would occur if all the sound was directed out an open window. For example, felt is a good sound absorber because it contains many tiny channels in which the air vibrations are damped out and their energy is dissipated as heat. On the other hand, glass and metals are bad absorbers. The higher the value of the absorption coefficient the more quickly the sound level is reduced.

Also tied in with the reflection of the sound waves off of the walls and ceilings is the fact that they tend to reinforce one another or cancel one another out depending on the shape and size of the room and repetition of the sound. It is possible to get no sound at one point in a room and extremely loud sound in another area of a room. Therefore, equipment location is important.

In areas of high noise levels steps should be taken to control the noise, dampen the noise, or have the people wear protective ear muffs. It is always preferable to locate people and noisy equipment away from one another whenever possible.

Visual Pollution

Visual pollution is another area that presents problems. Certainly if the light level is too low people cannot see to do their work; on the other hand, if the light level is too bright or intense or a person is in an area where the light is highly reflected this can quickly tire the eyes and reduce employee effectiveness and efficiency and possibly eventually cause a person to go blind. People who use high-powered microscopes to do work on miniature components must periodically rest their eyes or suffer severe headaches. There is much controversy over the color, intensity, and contrast needed on computer screens so that people using them do not end up with eye fatigue, headaches, and blindness. This is all a form of visual pollution. The other form of visual pollution that arises is when the air becomes so polluted that it is difficult to see through it, and under even worse conditions when it gets so bad that the eyes water or actually swell closed from the contaminants being transported by the air.

Any and all of these forms of visual pollution require constant vigilance and corrective measures to keep them within tolerable levels, which vary from individual to individual, from location to location, from day to day.

Odor Pollution

Odor pollution is an area that by itself does not get too much attention in the press; this is because it is quite often associated with air and water pollution. Anyone that lives near a trash dump, an incinerator, a chemical factory, or numerous odor-generating sources will not hesitate to advise you, however, about how obnoxious it is. Regardless of what little concern others may have for the odor, all odors cannot be totally eliminated. Foul odors have as negative an effect on property value as does the damage from air pollution fallout. In fact, it is not uncommon for both to go hand in hand.

Quite often odor pollution is a telltale symptom of more serious pollution problems such as chemical spills, malfunctioning pollution equipment, illegal burning of certain types of trash, or landfill leaks. If it occurs, it should be tracked down to find its cause so it can be determined whether it is a symptom of some serious problem that needs to be taken care of.

The Role of the Environmental Protection Agency

There are two agencies that are involved in setting standards in the just discussed pollution areas. Where it involves the environment, the primary responsibility falls on the shoulders of the Environmental Protection Agency; where the health, safety, and welfare of the worker is involved then the government looks to standards authorized by the Occupational Safety and Health Act. In overlapping areas, it is not uncommon for the two agencies to disagree on what levels are safe.

The Clean Air Act was passed in December 1963 and the Clean Water Restoration Act was passed in November 1966. Although these laws were on the books, they were of limited effectiveness. This situation changed dramatically, however, in the late 1960s with the active ecology movement and the creation of the Council on Environmental Quality (CEQ) and the EPA with the passage of the National Environmental Policy Act of 1969, which became effective in January 1970. The purpose of the CEQ was to consider policy on new environmental legislation and programs. The EPA was given the responsibility for administering and enforcing a wide range of environmental protection programs; these programs included air pollution control, water pollution control, solid waste management, and the control of noise, pesticides, and radiation.[66]

The EPA activities focus on its power and ability to establish and enforce standards in all the above areas. With its regulatory authority over these forms of pollution, the agency has available several avenues of enforcement when it observes a violation of the established standards, including seeking voluntary compliance, court action, fines, and even prison sentences.

The power of the EPA to enforce standards, and their pressure on business to abide by the standards, has resulted in much controversy between the EPA, business, and the environmentalists. Business says the EPA is moving too fast; environmentalists say that the EPA is not tough enough and is moving too slowly; the EPA tells business that compliance is essential with its standards and it tells the environmentalists changes cannot be made overnight. Each group has valid arguments to support its position; a quick examination of some of the problems, challenges, and complexities encountered by each of these groups will help you understand why solutions are not simple or "cut and dried" situations.

Business, Government, and Environmentalists Working Together

Every person is concerned and interested in having a clean environment; that is, they are interested up to a certain limit that they can afford. This then very simply gets into a cost versus benefit analysis of the situation. This is what the discussion surrounding Figure 3 was all about. Someone must pay for a clean environment and in the end analysis it is the average everyday citizen who ends up getting hit with this cost increase through higher prices paid for merchandise. The citizen may pay for the pollution control in other ways also. For example, too little air pollution control may devalue nearby private homes because of dirty paint, dying or stunted shrubbery, foul odors, and so on; on the other hand, too stringent controls on the plants may cause some of them to close because it is too costly for the company to remain open. When a plant closes, and many have because of pollution control requirements, there are many people in the area thrown out of a job.[67]

Involvement of U.S. corporations in pollution control carries with it a requirement and demand for a measurement and reporting system to account for corporate environmental performance. Reporting systems to date are primarily voluntary, mostly because no standard system has been adopted. As a result the voluntary disclosures have been incomplete and inadequate.[68]

In addition to no standards having been adopted for disclosure, there may be other reasons for only a brief disclosure and that is the way that stockholders view company participation in pollution control. Pollution control expenditures do not necessarily lead to lower profitability or seriously affect cash position; however, some investors view pollution control expenditures as a drain on resources that could have been invested profitably elsewhere and do not reward the companies for their socially responsible behavior.[69] In another recent study, however, the conclusion was that there is evidence to substantiate the existence of a moderate to strong relationship between the investment value of a company's common stock and its social performance record.[70] To help in this area, large corporations have significantly increased their voluntary disclosure of socially oriented information in annual reports.[71] In spite of this improvement in reporting, industry is still seen as doing only the minimum required by law, and a negative perception of industry has been fostered by its failure to communicate its efforts (investment of over $100 billion for pollution control equipment and operating costs from 1973 to 1980) in the areas of maintaining and improving environmental quality in air, water, and land.[72]

To overcome some of these problems that exist between the three groups, an attempt has been made to understand the makeup of the three conflicting groups. The profiles of the EPA and business have been fairly well established for quite some time; however, only recently has a profile of the ecologically and socially minded been studied. This study shows that the profile of a typical ecologically and socially concerned consumer includes some of the following traits: (1) young male or female of the high strata in respect to income, education, and general socioeconomic standing; (2) persons tending to be open minded, liberal, and secure; and (3) persons who are rational and conservative in respect to their consuming behaviors.[73] These people in the past have joined together as citizens groups or have joined existing environmental groups or founded new groups and have presented their case to both the government and business for stricter environmental control. In recent years improved cooperation between the government, business, and environmentalists have reduced some of the friction between the groups. In 1976 when Jerry D. Geist took over as president of Public Service Company of New Mexico (PNM) he decided cooperating with environmental groups was easier than fighting with them; PNM spends heavily on pollution control equipment and even allows the Sierra Club to review specifications and technical data for pollution control equipment. This has gained PNM the respect of the environmental leaders and has made it much easier for the utility to obtain money for new construction projects.[74] In another case of cooperation, The National Wildlife Federation met with major U.S. corporations in an attempt to hammer out strategies to blend the goals of economic growth and environmental protection. Conservation groups are stressing that corporate contributions can be mutually profitable as well as environmentally sound. There are tax benefits, as well as image enhancement, to donating large tracts of land to private conservation groups or state governments.[75]

Pollution abatement is still not perfect and needs much improvement. Business and other groups could improve their image considerably by co-operating more with one another and making the public more aware of what accomplishments they have truly produced. Industry is going to have to help police itself by identifying flagrant violators of environmental standards. A few violators, for whatever reason, hurt the image of all.

SCENARIO

You are the president of a utility that owns and operates a nuclear power plant. You have spent $250,000 training an operator and now pay him $35,000 a year to watch all the crucial gauges to make certain that all of the needles stay in the green. An NCR inspector reports seeing the operator with his eyes closed and his head tilted back as if asleep while attending the crucial controls at the 1,000-megawatt nuclear plant. The operator said he was just joking and not really asleep. What would you do?

NOTES

1. A. C. Pigou, *The Economics of Welfare*, 4th ed. (London: Macmillan, 1932), p. 134.

2. William U. Chandler, "Efficiency in Energy Use—Free Market vs. Centrally Planned Economics," *Strategic Planning and Energy Management* 6, no. 3 (1986/1987): 28.

3. Faye Rice, "Where Will We Put All That Garbage," *Fortune* 117, no. 8 (1988): 96–100.

4. Ibid., p. 100.

5. "Technology Isn't the Villain—After All," *Business Week*, February 3, 1973, 38.

6. Rice, "Where Will We Put All That Garbage," p. 98.

7. Ibid., p. 100.

8. Noel Grave, "Air: An Atmosphere of Uncertainty," *National Geographic* 171, no. 4 (1987): 505.

9. Tom Alexander, "A Simpler Path to a Cleaner Environment," *Fortune* (1987): 235.

10. Grave, "Air," p. 305.

11. John Urquhart, "Canada Asks U.S. to Boost Spending to Curb Acid Rain," *Wall Street Journal*, January 1, 1987, p. 3.

12. Ellen Hume, "Reagan Agrees to Consider Acid-Rain Pact," *Wall Street Journal*, April 7, 1987, p. 10.

13. *New York Times*, "Reagan Stalls on Acid Rain, Critics say," *Cincinnati Enquirer*, April 8, 1987, p. A–12.

14. Robert E. Taylor, "Acid Rain Damage to Lakes Minimal, EPA Advisors Say," *Wall Street Journal*, March 26, 1987, p. 62.

15. Mark Braykovich, "Acid Rain Law Could Be Costly," *Cincinnati Enquirer*, November 11, 1986, p. D–1; Myron Magnet, "How Acid Rain Might Dampen Utilities," *Fortune* 108, no. 3 (1983): 58–64.

16. "Electronic Method to Control Particulate Air Pollution Finds Much Success," *Research & Development* 29, no. 1 (1987): 55.

17. Edmund Faltermayer, "Nuclear Power after Three Mile Island," *Fortune* 99, no. 9 (1979): 115.

18. Tom Shanker, "Chernobyl's Fate: Soviets Try to Squash Fear, Concern," *Cincinnati Enquirer*, December 21, 1986, pp. F–1, F–6; "The Legacy of Chernobyl: Disaster for the Lapps," *U.S. News & World Report*, March 23, 1987, 34–35; "Chernobyl Will Kill 1,000 in Europe," *Cincinnati Enquirer*, March 26, 1987, p. A–13.

19. "Nuclear-Power Industry Geta a Wake-up Call," *U.S. News & World Report*, April 13, 1987, 14.

20. Ibid.

21. "Facing Life in a Greenhouse," *U.S. News & World Report*, September 29, 1986: 74.

22. Ibid., p. 75.

23. "Ozone: Industry Is Getting Its Head Out of the Clouds," *Business Week*, October 12, 1986, 110.

24. Barry Meir, "Hard Choices Await Industry as Ozone-Layer Fears Rise," *Wall Street Journal*, December 2, 1986, p. 4.

25. "Ozone: DuPont Moves to Curb CFCs but Many Others Need to Follow," *Cincinnati Enquirer*, April 4, 1988, p. A–8.

26. "Scientist: Ozone Hole Will Stay for 100 Years," *Cincinnati Enquirer*, January 8, 1988, p. B–9.

27. Barry Meier, " 'Citizens Suits' Become a Popular Weapon in the Fight against Industrial Polluters," *Wall Street Journal*, April 17, 1987, p. 11.

28. Ibid.

29. Conoco, Inc., "U.S. Energy Outlook Through 2000," *Strategic Planning and Energy Management* 6, no. 3 (1986/87): 4; Julia Lichblau, "Northeast Electricity Picture May Spur Development," *Energy User News Magazine*, March 1987, 26.

30. Conoco, Inc., "U.S. Energy Outlook," p. 15.

31. Thomas Y. Canby and Ted Spiegel, "Our Most Precious Resource: Water," *National Geographic*, August 1980, 144.

32. Ibid., p. 143.

33. Jerry W. Anderson, Jr., "Infrared: What Is It, How It Works, and How and Where It Can Be Used in Energy Evaluation and Analysis," *Energy Engineering* 81, no. 6 (1984): 29–33.

34. Alexander, "A Simpler Path to a Cleaner Environment," p. 239.

35. Anne Brataas, "Pit Liner Failed Twice: Tears Let Waste into Underground Water," *Cincinnati Enquirer*, October 19, 1986, p. A–1.

36. Sen. Quentin Burdick, "Saving America's Ground Water," *American Legion Magazine* 124, no. 1 (1987): 16.

37. Ibid.

38. "Permits in Question for Collapsed Tank," *Cincinnati Enquirer*, January 7, 1988, p. A–6.

39. "The Oil Spill That Snaked Through Mid-America," *U.S. News & World Report* 104, no. 2 (1988): 12.

40. Jim Calhoun, "Kentucky Pollution Officials Cite Filon-Silmar Plant," *Cincinnati Enquirer*, March 18, 1987, p. G–2.

41. James Litke, "Amco Must Pay $85 Million for Decade Old Spill Damages," *Cincinnati Enquirer*, January 12, 1988, p. C–6.

42. "Clean Water: Adding up the Balance Sheet," *U.S. News & World Report* 102, no. 6 (1987): 23.

43. "Pouring Lead from the Tap," *U.S. News & World Report* 101, no. 21 (1986): 70.

44. Allen A. Boraiko and Fred Ward, "Storing Up Trouble...Hazardous Waste," *National Geographic* (1985): 319.

45. Ibid., pp. 320–321.

46. Ibid., p. 322.

47. Matt Miller, "Two Years after Bhopal's Gas Disaster, Lingering Effects Still Plague Its People," *Wall Street Journal*, December 5, 1986, p. 26.

48. Scott Burgins, "Braced for SARA: From Paint Stores to Chemical Plants, Firms Will Tell You What's a Hazard,"*Cincinnati Enquirer*, April 24, 1988, pp. A–1, A–12.

49. David Hancock, "Mexicans Suffer from Radiation," *Cincinnati Enquirer*, December 21, 1986, p. F–6.

50. "Nuclear Contamination Discovered in Six Spots," *The Cincinnati Enquirer*, April 24, 1987, p. A–3.

51. "Uncle Sam's Risky Bomb Plants," *U.S. News & World Report* 102, no. 20 (1987): 75.

52. Ibid.

53. "Nuke Waste Site Ruling Postponed Until 2007," *The Cincinnati Enquirer*, April 24, 1987, p. A–3.

54. Patricia Bellew Gray, "Endless Trail: Dioxin Damage Suit Ties Up Courthouse and Angers Judiciary," *Wall Street Journal*, January 13, 1987, p. 1.

55. Stephen Solomon, "The Asbestos Fallout at Johns Manville," *Fortune* 99, no. 9 (1979): 196–206.

56. Jeffery L. Sheler, "Asbestos Cleanup Gets Tougher," *U.S. News & World Report* 104, no. 10 (1988): 25.

57. Lynda Houston, "Asbestos Law Burden to Schools," *Cincinnati Enquirer*, March 29, 1988, p. A–9.

58. Lynda Houston, "Asbestos Law Proves Boon for Inspectors," *Cincinnati Enquirer*, March 30, 1988, p. B–2.

59. Bill Richards and Barry Meier, "Lawyers Lead Hunt for New Groups of Asbestos Victims," *Wall Street Journal*, February 8, 1987, p. 1.

60. "EPA Announces National Policy on PCB Cleanups," *Wall Street Journal*, March 24, 1987, p. 6.

61. Steven P. Galante, "Toxic Waste Cleanup Provides Fertile Ground for New Firms," *Wall Street Journal*, March 9, 1987, p. 19.

62. Steve Bernfield, "Throwaway Products May Throw Environment Out of Balance," *Cincinnati Enquirer*, March 30, 1988, p. E–7; Elliot D. Lee, "Opposition to Plastic Packaging Is Intensifying as the Nation's Solid Waste Problem Grows Acute," *Wall Street Journal*, November 25, 1987, p. 36.

63. Robert E. Taylor, "Four More Pipeline Concerns Disposed of PCBs in Earthen Pits, EPA Aids Say," *Wall Street Journal*, February 26, 1987, p. 4; "Legislator Says Company with Four Indiana Sites Burned PCBs Recently," *Cincinnati Enquirer,* February 28, 1987, p. D–3.

64. John Eckberg and Anne Fitzhenry, "Trash: Running Out of Room," *Cincinnati Enquirer*, January 10, 1988, p. A–1.

65. Robert Alex Baron, *The Tyranny of Noise* (New York: St. Martin's Press, 1970), p. 12.

66. Murray L. Wiedenbaum, *Business, Government, and the Public* (Englewood Cliffs, N.J.: Prentice-Hall, 1977), pp. 74–75.

67. Robert E. Curran, *The Foundry Industry* (Washington, D.C.: U.S. Department of Commerce, Bureau of Domestic Affairs, March 24, 1975); "Steel: Clean Up or Close Up," *Business Week*, April 6, 1974, 72–73.

68. Joanne Wiseman, "An Evaluation of Environmental Disclosures Made in Corporate Annual Reports," *Accounting, Organizations & Society (UK)* 7, no. 1 (1982): 53–63.

69. Sitikantha Mahapatra, "Investor Reaction to a Corporate Social Accounting," *Journal of Business Finance & Accounting (UK)* 11, no. 1 (1984): 29–40.

70. Leo A. Smith and James L. Smith, "The Relationship Between Pollution Control Records and Financial Indicators Revisited and Further Comment," *Industrial Engineering* 14, no. 2 (1982): 38–43.

71. Philip B. Shane and Barry Spicer, "Market Response to Environmental Information Produced Outside the Firm,"*Accounting Review* 58, no. 3 (1983): 521–538.

72. Gerald R. Prout, "Industry and the Environment: A Communication Gap," *Public Relations Review* 9, no. 4 (1983): 41–52.

73. "Ecological and Socially Concerned Consumer Profiled," *Marketing News* 13, no. 16 (1980): 8.

74. William H. Miller, "New Mexico's Environmental Peacemaker," *Industry Week* 213, no. 5 (1982): 49–50, 53.

75. "Offering Business a Peace Pipe: Conservationists Are Taking a More Conciliatory Stance in Settling Disputes," *Business Week*, February 21, 1983, 98H.

9

Legal Aspects of Social Responsibility: Business, Government, and the Consumer

BUSINESS, GOVERNMENT, AND THE CONSUMER

One in every five purchases of products and services by the consumer results in dissatisfaction with something other than price and roughly one in every three complaints is not satisfactorily resolved, according to a survey conducted a few years ago.[1] No wonder the issue of consumer complaints against business is in the headlines so much today.

The Consumer Movement

As far back as people can remember there have been outcries about how the consumer has been improperly taken into consideration and has been mistreated. In 1914 the Federal Trade Commission Act was passed to protect consumers when a specific and substantial public interest was involved in an unethical practice. This did not, however, solve many of the problems that bothered people. As a result, their voices became louder and more clearly heard in the 1950s, 1960s, and 1970s and continue on into today. It was not until the 1960s and 1970s, however, that much new legislation was passed to protect the consumer. This entire movement, labeled by many as consumerism, has been simply defined by Kotler: "Consumerism is a social movement seeking to augment the rights and powers of buyers in relation to sellers."[2]

There are a number of factors that have contributed to this rise in consumerism, including increasing income and education, product technological complexity, size of businesses, inflation, pollution, shoddy and dishonest products, consumer interest groups, consumer awareness, mass media exposure, and political considerations. This entire area is one in which legal and ethical considerations overlap and where in some instances legal action and legislation have followed questionable ethical practices to make what once was considered an unethical or questionable ethical practice an illegal practice. The Pinto case, which will be discussed in detail in the chapter on ethics and morals, is a case in point.

The Federal Trade Commission (FTC)

The Federal Trade Commission has broad and sweeping powers and is the federal government's law enforcement arm in handling product information in advertising, packaging, and labeling, deceptive practices, consumer credit, warranties, and other related areas. The FTC was established under the Federal Trade Commission Act (1914) and now has the responsibility of policing and enforcing all aspects of the consumer-oriented legislation listed in Table 7 (See Chapter 6), as well as ones not listed.

The FTC was not too active from 1941 to 1969, a period referred to by Thomas Krattenmaker as "decades of neglect."[3] Under Miles Kirkpatrick, a Nixon appointee, the agency became active and aggressive to the point that business has in some instances referred to it as being overzealous. For example, at one time, in the area of advertising, the FTC only took issue with the most outlandish cases of advertising deception. In most recent years the FTC has taken issue with advertising where deception was not nearly as clear. One example in this category was in the case of Firestone implying that their tires were safe under any conditions.[4]

The FTC is also responsible for seeing that the customer obtains the proper information in order to make a safe and wise choice. It is assumed that a customer knows what he wants (not always the case) and can get all the information that he needs (again, not always true) to obtain his greatest needs satisfaction. When either or both of these situations are not fulfilled the FTC and many consumers feel that the FTC must step in and rectify the situation. In many instances it does just this and either by persuasion, court action, or through newly recommended legislation is able to force the businessman into doing what is desired by the consumer or required by law. As consumers have become more sophisticated, and products more complex, the concept of "what is good information" has changed. It is also not clear to most people what the term *full disclosure* truly means. It is apparent, then, that there is much dialogue needed between business, government, and the consumer in order to determine fair and appropriate actions to be taken. A brief examination of some of the major issues involved in advertising, packaging and labeling, deceptive practices, product liability, and consumer credit will help determine how best to handle responsibility for product liability and information.

Advertising

Advertising serves three basic purposes. First, it makes the consumer aware of products; second, it informs the consumer of the characteristics of the product in a manner that will make the consumer purchase the item; and third, it is hoped by the seller that the advertising and the quality of the product itself will make the customer insist on demanding that particular product by name. Some items that have achieved this success level are Kleenex, Coke, Bayer aspirin, Kodak film, and Clorox. Some people criticize that the massive advertising often required to achieve customer product awareness and acceptance produces unnecessarily high prices; others claim that in the long run it reduces prices through competition, advertising costs per item because of increased volume, and cost of production per item because of economics of scale.

Advertising has an impact on three major areas: the economic area, the social area, and the information area. The economic area of advertising gets involved in the costs versus benefits and improved well-being of society as a result of advertising. The social issued involves the influence of advertising on persuading people to buy things they do not need or really want, insulting their intelligence, and its adverse influence on changing longstanding social customs; on this issue, David Potter argued that:

...advertising now compares with such longstanding institutions as the school and the church in the magnitude of its social influence. It dominates the media, it has vast power in the shaping of popular standards and it is really one of the very limited groups of institutions which exercises social control.[5]

The third area involves the truth and the information disclosure aspects of advertising as well as the content, taste, and aesthetics involved. This is the main area of concern of the FTC and most people.

Advertising expenditures in all media were $2 billion in 1940.[6] They were, by estimate, at $43 billion in 1978. This advertising helps sell over $1 billion worth of analgesic drugs to the public each year as well as billions of dollars worth of toys and other children's products. Over $1 billion a year is spent on advertising of alcoholic beverages that encourages increased consumption by current drinkers and new drinking for those who yet do not drink.[7] It is, therefore, not unreasonable to make advertisers who make objective claims of product capability and/or superiority supply evidence to justify their claims. What about the aspirin makers who run heart attack prevention ads that claim taking aspirin every day will help prevent heart attacks? There is apparently medical evidence showing both good and bad effects in this area, depending on the health and condition of the individual involved; this latter part of the story is quite often played down or hardly mentioned in the ads. The FDA is now investigating these ads and their claims.[8]

Parents, private groups, the Federal Trade Commission, and researchers at universities are concerned with both children's advertising, teenage advertising, and even adult advertising. In the children's area, they are concerned especially with Saturday morning shows and claim that young children are unable to distinguish between the television program content and the commercial where they are deluged with commercials by cereal, "junk food," and toy manufacturers. In recent years a new concern has been expressed by various groups and organizations; this area of concern is where the cartoon show is based on existing toys and games. Shows that fall into this category are "The Smurfs," "G.I. Joe," "Pac Man," and many others. These people express concern that TV programs and commercials are gradually being blended together to manipulate children through blurring the distinction between entertainment and advertising.[9]

Ads for teenagers also solicit outcrys of horror and rage. For example, according to the *Wall Street Journal*, a new teenage magazine for 14- to 19-year-old girls, called *Sassy* plans to include material in their magazine that competitors call offensive and exploitive. One of the headlines in the magazine reads, "Losing Your Virginity–Read This Before You Decide." While the final decision is left to the reader, the article discusses such things as pregnancy, AIDS, venereal disease, and such questions as "How long will it take?" "Should I talk during sex?" and "Will it hurt?"[10] A full-page ad for condoms in the magazine reads in part, "They're easy to buy—you'll find them in any drugstore, usually on a display rack."[11] Liquor and tobacco advertising is strictly prohibited, yet articles that many feel condone and even encourage promiscuity amongst teenagers are permitted. No wonder so many people are upset about such advertising. Some people are even questioning some of the new adult ads and whether they insult the intelligence of the potential purchaser. A recent Lever Brothers ad for Sunlight detergent showed, in animated cartoon format, Bud storming out of the house because his wife Sally had unsightly spotted drinking glasses. Sally, in the meantine, sought comfort from her friend Marge, who naturally recommended Sunlight detergent. Sally, of course, uses Sunlight and it gets rid of the spots and also solves her problem with Bud. Bud returns home, complimenting her on how beautiful her glasses are, and telling her that he will never stray again.[12].

Ads that are not illegal but foster unsafe practices are some of the types that the National Advertising Review Board (NARB) review and try to get modified or eliminated. The NARB is an organization established for self-regulation in the advertising industry. Such ads included commercials showing children grilling hot dogs in a microwave oven without adult supervision or parents placing insect spray on the edge of tables where children can get hold of them; these are not considered safe consumer practices by the Board.

Packaging and Labeling

The package and label of a product serves a threefold purpose. First, the package serves as a container to hold and preserve safely the contents; second, the package itself can serve as a form of advertising; and third, the label presents an opportunity for the manufacturer to communicate the contents and merits of the package contents. The package and label must also meet the legal requirements imposed upon the piece of merchandise. Consumers want the label to tell them clearly and quickly about the product so that they can arrive at a decision on which, if any, product they wish to purchase. Most labels, as a minimum, carry the name; net weight or volume; price per unit of weight or volume; producer; distributor, if different from producer; the contents and its makeup and nutritional value (if a food product); last date of purchase or use; and applicable standards; warrantied life; cost of operation; list of major components that are guaranteed and for how long; and, in the case of automobiles, the sticker price.

Information on packages cost money; that is, obtaining some of the information that goes on package labels costs money. The Fair Packaging and Labeling Act, passed in 1968, imposes certain minimum information to be on every package. Later legislation strengthened the act. For example, required on food packaging is food grading, disclosure of all ingredients, nutritional value, identification of the manufacturer, packer, and distributor, and expiration date. Other information desired by some people will increase the cost of the item; this additional desired labeling information includes ingredient content, percentage of ingredients, fat and oil content, and which ingredients are natural and which are artificial. These may actually be easier to bet on labels than standardized package size.

When the final version of the Fair Packaging and Labeling Act was passed, the standardized package size requirement was eliminated from the act. The major reason given was that it was not necessary and manufacturers believed it would be costly and quite undesirable. They want to use what they call "packaging to price." If manufacturing costs increase, then the package size and contents can be reduced and the price remains the same. Candy manufacturers have used this concept for years as the price of ingredients, such as chocolate, increased or decreased; it is not uncommon for the candy bar to remain at a fixed price while the actual size increases or decreases in response to ingredient price.

All in all, packaging and labeling have improved considerably over the past couple of decades. It can still stand improvement in some areas, but whether it is of sufficient importance to people to pay the extra money is still a question.

Deceptive Practices

In 1938, the passage of the Wheeler-Lea Amendment to the Federal Trade Commission Act gave the FTC jurisdiction over unfair acts and practices for consumer protection to the same extent that the original FTC Act gave jurisdiction over unfair methods of competition for the protection of competitors. The amendment declared certain advertisements of foods, drugs, medical devices, and cosmetics to be unfair or deceptive acts or practices in commerce.

There are a number of well-known sales practices that have come under federal control and action in recent years. These include such practices as bait-and-switch (advertising a low-priced model and then talking the customer into purchasing a higher priced model after he has been enticed into the store), lowballing (advertising prices lower than that actually charged for the product), fear selling, pyramid selling, and free gifts. Many of these practices and other deceptive selling practices are also controlled by state and local laws.

Some of the medical and health food claims for products that are now on the market range from the relatively harmless to the life threatening. In October 1986, General Nutrition, Inc., a health food chain, pleaded guilty in federal court to promoting primrose oil as a cure for high blood pressure. General Nutrition promoted the primrose oil solely as a dietary supplement, but the Federal Drug Administration found that the company was distributing it to the stores with literature that claimed it could cure arthritis, hypertension, and multiple sclerosis; the salespeople then repeated these claims.[13] In the case of aging creams, the FDA told 22 cosmetic companies on April 4, 1988, that they had 30 days to stop claiming their over-the-counter creams can reverse or retard aging of skin.[14] In a recent letter to Rep. Claude Pepper (D-Fla.), the FDA reported that in 1985 it has seized 10 products; this was 14 less than the year before. They filed criminal charges in only one case.[15]

One step beyond but still a part of deceptive practices is outright fraud in selling. Much of this is done by manufacturing and selling counterfeit or bogus products as name-brand products; in recent years counterfeit items have been sold under the name of "Gucci," "Cartier," and "Levis." Another area where this is not uncommon is when one goes to purchase antiques; it is not uncommon for some unreputable dealer to claim a reproduction item is the original item, either through ignorance or through intent.

Product Liability

Another area with which the government, business and consumers are concerned is unsafe or impure products. Again, this is an area that moved into the forefront in the 1970s with the founding of the Consumer Product Safety Commission (CPSC); the Commission was authorized by the Consumer Protection Safety Act of 1972. A government study group, the National Commission on Product Safety, had investigated injuries in the area of hazardous household products and determined that 20 million American were injured around the home each year in incidents involving household products; of this number, 110,000 were permanently disabled and 30,000 were killed (not counting automobile accidents).[16] This information, along with pressure and lobbying by consumers, resulted in the Consumer Protection Safety Act.

Since its inception, the CPSC has enforced product safety rules in numerous areas such as bottles for medication, refrigerator door latches, and slat spacing in baby cribs. As a result of this enforcement by the CPSC, business has also become more aware and responsible for its actions; however, there are still many problem areas to be overcome.

Johnson & Johnson immediately removed Tylenol from the market when it was thought that there might be a product safety problem. Procter & Gamble quickly removed Rely tampons from the market when it was found that they could cause toxic shock syndrome. Johnson & Johnson is recalling three crib toys that the CPSC has found unsafe.[17] *Fortune* magazine recently listed 100 U.S. products that were the world's best with respect to product quality.[18] Many businesses are trying to build safe, quality products and if they run into a problem they tend to be cooperative and remove them from the market.

There are cases where business has not been quite as quick to remove or fix unsafe products on the market and in some cases has even resisted any such moves. Examples of this are the Ford Pinto case, where Ford resisted for several years the change of the gas tank. According to one observer, Ford successfully lobbied against Federal Motor Vehicle Safety Standard 301, which would have made them redesign the Pinto's fire-prone gas tank, even in the face of conservative estimates that the Pinto has been responsible for between 500 and 900 burn deaths to people who would not normally have been seriously injured by the accident impact.[19] Firestone repeatedly tried to block the investigation of its Firestone 500 series of steel-belted radial tires and publicly questioned the motives of the investigators; according to federal authorities the tires were prone to blowouts, tread deformation, and other dangerous deformities.[20] Stopping the sale of all-terrain vehicles (ATVs) was resisted by manufacturers even though more than 900 people, many of them children, were killed over a 5-year period riding the ATVs; there were nearly 7,000 injuries. The manufacturers agreed to stop making the vehicles but no effort or requirement was made to recall the approximately 2.3 million ATVs now in use.[21] Audi automobiles had problems with sudden acceleration, which the National Highway Traffic Safety Administration said had prompted reports of 513 accidents, 271 injuries, and 5 deaths. For nearly a year Audi insisted that drivers were to blame for any acceleration problems, but finally agreed to recall all 1978 through 1986 Audi 5000 series cars.[22] Audi's "blame the customer" approach backfired on them. Car prices dropped as much as $500 to $600 a month and new car sales dropped dramatically. People expected a better response and attitude out of the manufacturer of a $20,000 car.[23] Those manufacturers who do not take responsibility for their products' problems will either face legal action or, as in the case of Audi, boycott or other action from the consumer.

According to Nancy Steorts there are 10 regulatory trends that will affect the future product safety regulatory environment:

1. Increased concern by company executives for product safety
2. Increasing cooperation between business, regulators, and consumers on reaching product safety goals

3. Increasing compliance by business in meeting safety regulations in order to reduce the involvement of lawyers and expenses from litigation
4. More sharing of product hazard information between business and regulators
5. Continued improvement in product safety from food and drug manufacturers
6. Increased customer education by business and regulators
7. Increased emphasis on product safety attributes through marketing endeavors
8. Increased participation by retailers in product safety
9. Greater international cooperation in the promotion of product safety
10. Greater involvement of both business and the consumer in establishing safety priorities and regulations.[24]

Consumer Credit

Consumer credit issues can be divided into two major categories: those that primarily concern the poverty level consumer and those that concern the "middle class" consumer.

Low income people are quite often taken advantage of. They are often exposed to "enticement, the bait of easy terms, fraudulent practices, shoddy merchandise, unreliable dealers, garnishment, and oppressive collection methods."[25] On the other hand, the credit issues facing the middle class American are often more subtle in nature. For example, there are several valid ways to compute service charges and all of them will show the same yearly percentage rate, but the total cost to the consumer will differ under the different methods of computation. Some of the key variable ingredients that go into the computation are the date from which the interest is computed, whether there is also a fixed service charge added on up front, and whether the final payment is deducted before the calculation is made.

In the case of the low income person, the techniques used are quite often illegal or borderline legal tactics where the person is afraid to, unable to, or not knowledgeable enough to take remedial action. In the case of the middle income person, the techniques used are more likely to be legal but of a nature where it is difficult to determine precisely what is going on without considerable effort on the part of the consumer, and where the business is more knowledgeable about the subject under discussion than is the customer. It is primarily an information gap where the odds are stacked in favor of business.

SCENARIO

You have just completed washing and drying your 14-year-old daughter's clothes and are putting them in her dresser drawer in her bedroom when you notice a magazine sticking out from under some of her clothes. Innocently and curiously wondering why the magazine would be tucked away in your daughter's drawer under her clothes, you move the clothing over to see what it might be. To your surprise, a teenage magazine is folded open and you see an ad for condoms and how and where to get them staring you in the face. What would you do?

NOTES

1. Alan R. Andersen and Arthur Best, "Consumers Complain—Does Business Respond?"*Harvard Business Review* 55, no. 4 (1977): 93.

2. Philip Kotler, "What Consumerism Means for Marketers," *Harvard Business Review* 50, no. 3 (1972): 48–57.

3. Thomas G. Krattenmaker, "The Federal Trade Commission and Consumer Protection," *California Management Review* 18, no. 4 (1976): 94–95.

4. "FTC Rules Firestone Ads Deceptive," *Advertising Age* 42, no. 43 (1972): 1, 77.

5. David M. Potter, *People of Plenty* (Chicago: University of Chicago Press, 1954), p. 167.

6. Helmut Becker, "Advertising Image and Impact," *Journal of Contemporary Business* 7, no. 4 (1979): 77–78.

7. Michael Jacobson, George Hacker, and Robert Atkins, *The Booze Merchants* (Washington, D.C.: Center for Science in Public Interest, 1983), p. 16.

8. Ronald Alsop, "Aspirin Makers Face FDA Scrutiny for Heart-Attack Prevention Ads," *Wall Street Journal,* February 1, 1988, p. 28.

9. Kathleen Selvaggio, "Putting a Label on Fun," *Multinational Monitor,* December 1983, p. 17.

10. Cynthia Crossen, "Sexual Candor Marks Magazine for Teen Girls," *Wall Street Journal,* February 17, 1988, p. 25; Gail Baruck, "Magazine Gives Teens Facts of Life," *Cincinnati Enquirer,* April 14, 1988, p. B–16.

11. Crossen, "Sexual Candor," p. 25.

12. Ronald Alsop, "Ads that Make Fun of Ads Are In, As Firms Face a More Jaded Buyer," *Wall Street Journal,* February 22, 1988, p. 21.

13. "New Snake Oil, Old Pitch: For Every Malady, a Cure—But Some of Them Are Downright Dangerous," *U.S. News & World Report*, December 3, 1988, 68.

14. "Time Runs Out on Aging Creams: FDA Gives Companies 30 Days to Change Product Labels," *Cincinnati Enquirer,* April 5, 1988, p. B–9.

15. "New Snake Oil, Old Pitch," p. 68.

16. R. David Pittle, "The Consumer Product Safety Commission," *California Management Review* 18, no. 4 (1976): 105–109.

17. "Johnson & Johnson to Recall Three Crib Toys," *Cincinnati Enquirer,* October 27, 1986, p. D–8.

18. Christopher Knowlton, "What America Makes Best," *Fortune* 117, no. 7 (1988): 40–54.

19. Elizabeth Gatewood and Archie B. Carroll, "The Anatomy of Corporate Social Response: The Rely, Firestone 500 and Pinto Cases," *Business Horizons* 24, no. 5 (1981): 9–16.

20. Ibid., p. 13.

21. Lee Byrd, "Sales of Off-road Vehicles Curbed," *Cincinnati Enquirer,* December 31, 1987, p. A–11.

22. Douglas R. Sease, "Audi Problems with Sudden Acceleration May Not Be Over, Despite Recent Recall," *Wall Street Journal,* January 20, 1987, p. 31.

23. Ibid.

24. Nancy Harvey Steorts, "New Direction in Product Safety Regulation," *Directors & Boards* 8, no. 4. (1984) 28–32.

25. Homer Kripke, "Gesture and Reality in Consumer Credit Reform," *New York University Law Review* 44, no. 2 (1969): 1.

10

Legal Aspects of Social Responsibility: Business, Government, and the Community

BUSINESS, GOVERNMENT, AND THE COMMUNITY

The relationship of business with the community has had a long and changing role and involves many areas. It starts out by creating and supplying an employment base within the community where the business resides; from this point it expands into involvement in the areas of education, the arts, environment, urban development, job training, volunteerism, minority enterprises, summer jobs for youth, health, housing, alcohol and drug abuse, nutrition, philanthropy, prison rehabilitation, and many other areas.

Community Involvement

It is almost impossible for any business not to become involved in some kind of community affairs. Some of this involvement is primarily charitable, while other community affairs with which business becomes involved pays a direct return to the company. It is difficult to separate one from the other because in most instances both community and business reap positive rewards from any business participation in community affairs. The general theory behind much of it is that by business participating in community affairs it makes the community a better place in which to live. By making the community a better place to live, it helps improve the community for all those who live there and as an inducement for hiring new employees from distant communities—possibly needed experts from other cities. By being able to bring in needed key people from other localities, the business will be able to remain competitive, increase sales and profits, and make more money for the stockholders and the IRS. The result is that everyone is happy and better off because of community involvement by business—the community, the business and its employees, the stockholders, and the local, state, and federal government.

What, Where, Why, When and How Deeply?

Whenever the subject of community involvement is discussed it immediately brings to mind such questions as *what* is it; *where* is it practiced; *why* get involved in it; and if the business does want to get involved in it, *when* and *how* should it get involved? The question pertaining to what is community involvement, or of what does it consist, has been briefly answered in the opening paragraph. It encompasses all areas of involvement between the community and business and sometimes the government.

In the not too distant past, when one spoke of community involvement, it usually meant the immediate or close vicinity (town, city, county, or state) of where the business was located. In today's modern world of high-speed travel and communication and many multiple business locations, it has in many instances expanded so that today it can encompass total regions, nations, or even the entire world. National and multinational businesses thus have a large complex of communities with which to concern themselves. When this situation arises, all communities where the businesses reside do not necessarily fare equally. In 1972, when the Xerox Corporation started its Social Service Leave Program, it only covered employees in the United States.[1] In the case of the Dayton Hudson Corporation, in the early and mid–1970s a major portion of their income came from outside of Minnesota while the majority of community funds were spent within the state of Minnesota—the share of contribution dollars going back to the operating companies was not proportional to the individual operating companies earning results (in the mid–1970s attempts were being made by some members of the company to correct this inequity).[2]

With respect to why business should get involved in community affairs, this can be simply and quickly expressed with the use of a quote from Robert Cushman, president of the Norton Company in Worcester, Massachusetts. He states: "Business does not operate in a vacuum, but as a social institution interacting with other social institutions. What business does affects its community; in turn, the people's good will and trust are essential for business to fulfill its primary role, which is to provide goods and services...."[3]

When and how deeply should a business involve itself in community affairs, other than supplying basic jobs to the people of the community, presents a set of questions that each business will have to evaluate on an individual basis. Certainly economics enter into the picture. If a business is new and just starting up it can be expected to participate only minimally; if it is long established, stable, and profitable then it will be expected to get more deeply involved. The how deeply part of the question involves other economic and political considerations. The owners and employees deserve decent incomes and working conditions; the stockholders deserve a reasonable return on their investments; the business must stay competitive; and the community expects some form of support from the business. This is a balancing act that each business must evaluate for itself as a part of its total social responsibility commitment.

Some large companies are very sincere and quite adept at handling corporate urban development and other social responsibility problems. For example, IBM UK Ltd., a company on the leading edge of corporate social responsibility, applies its resources of cash management expertise and technology to three major areas of social responsibility, including work creation, educational programs, and community welfare. Each of these areas has an issue manager who is responsible for research, preparation, and implementation of an action plan; specific criteria are then applied to determine project selection.[4] This may take more time and resources than some smaller businesses can afford; however, the concept used by IBM UK can be used by both small and large businesses.

Urban Development

The Ralston Purina Co., a $5 billion agribusiness giant, transformed the area surrounding its headquarters in St. Louis, Missouri, from a general slum area into a "delight to behold" community, with new homes, apartments for the elderly, low-income housing, rehabilitated 100-year-old town houses, churches, and commercial and light industrial facilities. A total of $4.5 million was spent on the project, with $1.1 million given by Ralston and matching funds from the federal government. To keep speculators out of the region, Ralston required purchasers to begin work within 30 days, with the work to be completed within 18 months. The company real estate in the area increased in value and the company received public relation accolades for its efforts.[5] Detroit Renaissance is a commercial venture by 51 Detroit firms that shows what local authorities and private business can accomplish in restoring depressed inner cities. Detroit Renaissance was started by Henry Ford II, who persuaded 50 companies to join together with him in a task to create a $350 million renaissance center, to be composed of a complex of offices, shops, and hotel accommodations. General Motors also has been active in rehabilitating decayed neighborhoods in the Detroit area as has Honeywell and Continental Bank in Chicago.[6] In Baltimore, Maryland, the Greater Baltimore Committee, which included heads of some of the largest firms in the area, developed a plan for clearing 22 acres of land and constructing self-financing public and private buildings and other facilities.[7]

Sometimes where there is cooperation between the city government and the private sector things can be accomplished rapidly. The Greater Indianapolis Progress Committee (Gipsy), made up of 300 business leaders, attorneys, and elected officials working with the mayor and other city officials, is pushing revitalization plans for the downtown Indianapolis area with amazing speed.[8]

These are but a few examples of many to show how business and communities are working together throughout the country to make it a better place in which to live. With federal government cutbacks in funds, and tight state and local government funds, improvements can come only through private business participation.

Volunteerism

Another way that business can help communities and local, state, and federal governments is to let some of its employees volunteer for community service. This volunteer contribution of time and experience includes such things as discounts on service, free professional services, volunteer sabbaticals, volunteer projects, and civic volunteerism.

In 1972, Xerox Corporation started a social service leave program that provided the opportunity for approximately 20 U.S. Xerox employees to take up to one-year leave of absence with full pay and benefits and devote their time to working with a social service of their choice. They were also guaranteed the same or equivalent job when they returned. To be eligible, they had to have been with the company for three years and the social agency had to sign a paper saying that their services were needed and required. Some problems have been encountered on a smooth reentry into the work force, but on the whole the program has been quite successful, with returning employees, after a short period of time, being better employees after their return.[9]

Baltimore would have had to pay an additional 12.1 million, which it did not have, for work done in the 1981 fiscal year if it had not been for volunteer corporations. Cleveland, Ohio, has used the help of 89 business people to help with projects, studies, and services the city could not afford. The J. C. Penney Co. publicizes the need for volunteers and fits the volunteers to the jobs, with awards going to the top volunteers.[10] Levi Strauss volunteers both manpower and monetary assistance to smaller businesses as a public relations gesture.[11] Many companies also volunteer people to help out in community fund drives for the arts and charitable organizations.

Volunteer programs are necessary for the survival and rejuvenation of many cities and communities. Melanie Lawrence feels that business support of community activities improves workers' attitudes, because it recognizes workers' personal values and encourages them to act upon them.[12]

Job Training

Job training to keep unemployment rates down is of vital concern to both business and the community. Both have been sympathetic to this area and have employed and trained people whenever practical. Today, most programs are operated by individual firms. It is imperative, however, if these people are not to end up in the unemployment lines of the future that the training be in meaningful work areas and not just "handout" jobs where the person is paid something like summer work but actually gains very little useful work experience.

Companies such as General Electric Co. have set up retraining programs in areas where they have had to close down plants. They retrain the laid-off employees in new skills so that they have a better chance of being employed by other businesses in the area or elsewhere, or even starting up their own business.[13] More companies each year are letting released professional people return to the office for three to six months and use an office, a secretary, a telephone, and a copy machine to make resumes and try to locate a new position.

In 1983, the federal government passed the Federal Job Training Partnership Act (JTPA). This act replaces the inefficient Comprehensive Education and Training Act which lasted from 1973 to 1982. JTPA concentrates on training rather than other social goals. Under JTPA, employers and local governments negotiate the type of training that will be offered by the employers, based on their perception of the local job vacancies and requirements.

These are only a few of the different job training programs that are available to the employer and employee. As long as the job and the training is useful and productive to both the employer and employee, the community should benefit from it.

Managing Community Involvement

Any time that a business becomes involved in community affairs it must be concerned with at least four major areas: knowledge of the company's resources, knowledge of the community, which projects to select, and monitoring and feedback of the projects.

In order to know what the business can do for the community, it must first thoroughly know and understand its own resource capability in the areas of money, manpower, equipment, space, and managerial and technical expertise. Once this is known, then it can be correlated with the various community needs to determine how helpful, if at all, the company can be to the community. It may be as simple as supplying a few employees for local volunteer work to assisting the community in an in-depth study program or building program in a particular area.

It is just as important to know the community and its needs as it is to know the company's capabilities. Someone within the company must work with the community to become familiar with the community needs, or the company must establish some type of internal committee or board to study community problems. The committee or board should be composed of people from the company and various representatives of community organizations.

Once both company capabilities and community needs are established, then some form of selection process must be established for determining which project or projects will be undertaken by the company. The Dayton Hudson Company uses a system of six criteria, which it rates on a one (highest) to five (lowest) scale, in order to determine which projects and charitable grants it will support. The six criteria used are: (1) quality of leadership, (2) quality of management, (3) financial strength and stability of the institution, (4) potential favorable impact of grant in relation to size of grant, (5) degree of risk involved in awarding the grant, and (6) overall rating, based on comparison with other grants previously awarded, immediate needs of the grantee, and merits of supporting a particular project.[14] In making these selections and decisions they must be made with the same care and involvement as that devoted to other parts of the business.

Finally, once a program selection has been made it must be carefully monitored; this must involve both review and control. Proper monitoring will enhance the image of the company and improve the chance of program success. Project feedback and follow-up will ensure that the project is being executed within time and funds limitations.

If these four major concerns are soundly evaluated and followed, then a realistic and workable community involvement program can be undertaken by almost any business.

SCENARIO

As the owner and president of a medium-sized company you have been actively recruiting professional people all year long. You have made job offers to seven new May graduates; five of them accepted the offer and came to work for your company. In September of that same year you find that your business has not grown as you had anticipated and you must release at least five professional people. Would you release the new employees who have not yet had time to contribute much to the company or would you release some of the older, long-time employees with higher salaries or would your release a combination of the two groups? How would you release them? What might be the repercussions under each situation?

NOTES

1. C. Roland Christensen, Kenneth R. Andrews, Joseph L. Bowers, et al., *Business Policy: Text and Cases* 5th ed. (Homewood, Ill.: Richard D. Irwin, 1982), pp. 458–484.

2. Christensen et al., "Dayton Hudson Corporation," pp. 510–532.

3. "Community Action Manual" (Worcester, Mass.: Norton Company, April 1978).

4. Len Peach, "Managing Corporate Citizenship," *Personnel Management (UK)* 17, no. 7 (1985): 32–35.

5. Lynn Adkins, "Ralston Purina's Urban Commitment," *Dun's Business Month* 119, no. 1 (1982): 98–100.

6. David Clutterbuck, "The Renaissance of the Inner City," *International Management (UK),* February 1981, 12–16.

7. Susan Hocevar Page, "Slow Dancing in the Industrial Heartland," *New Management* 2, no. 2 (1984): 55–60.

8. John Herbers, "Starved Cities Hunger for Corporate Aid," *Business & Society Review,* no. 45 (1983): 8–11.

9. Christensen et al., "Xerox Corporation," pp. 458–484; Mary Tuthill, "Lending People in the Public Interest" *Nation's Business* 70, no. 5 (1982): 68–72.

10. "To the Rescue: Corporate Volunteers Aid Cities," *Business Week,* April 12, 1982, 126A, 126D.

11. Elisabeth Beattie, "The New Voluntarism," *Business & Economic Review* 31, no. 3 (1985): 22, 23, 28.

12. Melanie Lawrence, "Social Responsibility: How Companies Become Involved in Their Communities," *Personnel Journal* (1982): 502–510.

13. Gordon F. Shea, "Company Loyalty: Earning It, Keeping It," *AMA Management Briefing* (New York: AMA Membership Publication Division, 1987), pp. 49–51.

14. Christensen et al., "Dayton Hudson Corporation," pp. 528, 529.

11

Legal Aspects of Social Responsibility: Employer-Employee Responsibility and Relationships

BUSINESS EMPLOYER-EMPLOYEE RESPONSIBILITY AND RELATIONSHIPS

Sweeping human resources legislation enacted by local, state and federal governments during the 1960s, 1970s, and 1980s, combined with increased activity on the part of individuals and groups to improve "unfair" employment practices, has somewhat muted the power and need for unions while at the same time complicated the operation of many businesses.

Almost every facet of employment relations between employer and employee has been affected by new legislation that has been enacted by the various governments. Some of the major pieces of legislation are shown in Table 5. This chapter cannot cover all of the areas in depth; however, key areas of legislation and their impact on the worker, the employer, and society will be discussed.

It is not unreasonable for employees to expect such things as equal job opportunities, an equitable living wage, right to due process, right to privacy, workplace safety, freedom from harassment, vacation and health care, and other possible benefits from the employer. On the other hand, it is not unreasonable for employers to expect a fair day's work, unencumbered by drugs and alcohol, out of their employees in return for such benefits. How to accomplish this and get the employer and the employee to cooperate toward achieving these goals is not an easy task. The government, in its role of "benevolent benefactor" has stepped in with legislation in an attempt to "solve" many of these problems. In spite of this new legislation, many problems still exist in the employer-employee area.

EMPLOYER-EMPLOYEE INTERACTION AND RESPONSIBILITY

Many of the benefits for which employees have been working toward for years have now become a part of federal legislation. This does not mean that all is well in the plant or office between management and labor. Each piece of newly enacted legislation costs the company money. In order to pay for this, remedial action must be taken by the business. In many instances management has tightened its belt and cut back on employment levels; devised programs to divest themselves of older, more costly workers through early retirement programs; stripped pension funds; hired part-time people for whom they need pay no insurance or retirement benefits; implemented plant closedowns; have forced concessions out of union; and have in some cases even cut back on executive bonuses. These tactics have been applied by top management equally against factory workers and middle management white-collar workers. In the meantime the workers have not sat idly by. The unions are becoming more watchful and more reluctant to give large concessions to business; unions have initiated slowdowns while remaining inside the law; employees have changed jobs; some people have left the company and started their own business; and in some cases employees have bought out the company and made it successful rather than losing their jobs. As a result of all this help from the government and the noncooperation between the employer and employee, a recent *Business Week*–Harris poll showed that 65 percent of the salaried employees now feel less loyal to their company than they did only 10 years ago.[1]

Is top management being unfair and noncooperative or are the employees being unfair and noncooperative? The answer is possibly a little bit of both. One example that might help clarify this is the case where several years ago General Motors spun off its Clark, New Jersey, roller-bearing plant. Many concessions had been made by General Motors to the unions. This buildup of concessions to the unions by General Motors over numerous years caused the cost of operating the plant to rise considerably. In fact, General Motors could purchase quality parts from outside suppliers less expensively than they could manufacture them internally. General Motors decided to sell the plant; the employees wanted to purchase the plant. After considerable negotiations, General Motors helped its former employees purchase the plant.

The question might not be asked: "How can the employees profitably run the plant when the great General Motors could not?" The answer seems to be quite simple when it is explained. The new employee-owners plan to make the plant profitable by taking a 25 percent cut in salary and fringe benefits and reducing the labor force from 1,200 employees to 800 employees. But that means that the workers will now have to be 50 percent more productive to get the same amount of work processed. According to Jim Zarrello, chairman of the Clark UAW local, this will be accomplished by the employees now doing a day's work for a day's pay. " 'It's no secret,' Zarrello says, 'that the union helped create an atmosphere where people who were in the plant eight hours did four hours of work. That's appropriate when GM is making billions in profits—you make more jobs, and you make work easier for your men.' "[2]

Under this new arrangement, both the ex-employees and General Motors will benefit. The employees of the new company will receive bonus incentives and will be able to earn more than they did under GM's previous pay scale. GM, on the other hand, will quit losing an estimated $5 million per year on the plant and have a new source from which to purchase roller bearings and help keep the other competitors' prices in line.

Lincoln Electric Company of Euclid, Ohio, has successfully operated along similar lines for many years. They have no unions, high wages, guaranteed employment, piecework compensation, and a bonus system. In good times, workers have earned as much as $45,000 a year; and, despite some employee complaints about pressure, turnover at Lincoln Electric is only 0.3 percent per month.[3]

First quarter 1988 earnings at Ford set a record and surpassed GM for the industry lead.[4] Ford executives give much of the credit to the blue-collar worker and management and union leadership willingness to listen to them and to work with them in increasing productivity.[5] Productivity is not putting out more goods and services with more inputs but is defined as producing more goods and services with the same amount of inputs, or an improvement in operational efficiency.

From 1973 to 1979, U.S. manufacturing productivity increase averaged 1.4 percent per year, while Japan's rose at a 5.5 percent rate, West Germany by 4.3 percent, Canada by 2.1 percent, and Italy by 3.3 percent. U.S. productivity continued to lag into the 1980s when in 1986 it increased to 3.7 percent with an additional gain of 3.3 percent in 1987. In 1986 Japan's productivity rate increased by only 2.8 percent, so the United States has once again gained the initiative.[6]

In this area, as at Ford, the employer and employee can either work together positively for a common cause of beating out foreign competition or they can continue to fight one another as they have in the past with everyone losing. Increased productivity is a two-way street, however, and for it to continue working, both management and the worker must share in its fruits similar to what is being done at Ford, Lincoln Electric, and some other companies. If the gains are properly and fairly distributed between all those involved then the employer, employee, and society as a whole will all be better off. To show that this is not just someone's "opium-pipe dream," the next section will show how this can work.

IMPROVED PRODUCTIVITY

To continue living, a person must have an adequate income. Since most people obtain this income through working, they must produce a product that is competitive in both quality and price. This can be accomplished by continuously improving quality and productivity at a rate greater than that of the competition. If properly administered, this can be accomplished with increased income and profits to the employer, improved real wages and benefits to the employee, increased employment levels, and relatively stable prices and inflation rates.

Figure 4 shows in simple diagram form what productivity improvement is all about. Prior to explaining how the chart works, a few terms must be explained. N is the level of labor employment; W/P is the real wage of the employee, with W representing the take-home pay and benefits and P representing the price that must be paid by the employee for goods and services. If W increases relative to P or P decreases relative to W then employee real wage or purchasing power will increase. MPL is the productivity of labor (the amount of output per a given unit of input), while MPL_1 is the increased level of productivity (the increased amount of output with the original equivalent unit of input). S of L is the supply of labor N available and willing to work at a given real wage W/P.

Putting the plan into operation and increasing productivity can make everyone better off and happier. At time zero (now) the level of labor employment is N_0 and the employees real wage is W_0/P_0. This is point A on the chart. Increasing worker productivity from MPL to MPL_1 can have several favorable outputs. If real wages W_0/P_0 are kept constant then the business can hire more people to level N_1 without having to increase employee wages W_0 or product price P_0; this is point B on the chart. This has often been a goal of the unions in an attempt to increase membership; it would, however, give all gains to labor in the form of increased employment and none to management. If labor is held constant at N_0 then real wages can be increased to W_1/P_1 as depicted by point C on the chart. This does not increase employment but it does permit an increase in real wages. The key here is that real wage W_1/P_1 is higher than real wage W_0/P_0, which means that the spread has increased between take-home pay W and prices P charged or paid for items; a person can now improve his standard of living because he has more purchasing power. P_1 can be higher, the same as, or lower than P_0 and W_1/P_1 will still increase as long as P_1 does not increase as much as W_1. At point C, then, the employee is better off because of increased real wages, the business is better off because it can hold prices fairly stable, and society will be better off because of low inflation. An even more desirable point on the chart, brought about by the increase in productivity, is point D. At this point, all of the advantages listed for point C exist but the ability to hire more people to level N_2 also exists. Under this condition, labor, management, and society as a whole all benefit because the company can make more money, the employee can make more money, and more people can be employed. If productivity rates can be kept abreast or ahead of inflation, then even the customer will come out ahead because prices can be held stable or increased only a small

Figure 4
The Effect of Increasing the Marginal Rate of Productivity of Labor on Employment and Real Wages

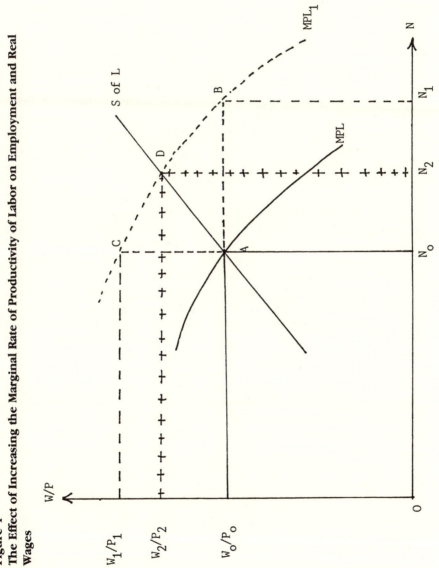

LEVEL OF LABOR EMPLOYMENT

amount while both management and labor also improve their positions. This then is the best of all worlds. It does, however, require absolute trust, co-operation, dedication, and restraint between labor, management, and government. There are some steps being made in this direction through the changing nature of work and the workplace.

THE CHANGING NATURE OF WORK AND THE WORKER

Over time, the nature of the work and the worker have changed, at least in the United States. There are still some menial tasks in existence, but on the whole many of the more tedious and cumbersome tasks have been lightened with the assistance of modern machines and equipment. In most instances the new machines and equipment have been beneficial to labor; however, in some instances they have created new work hazards and dangers, some of which have had to be corrected through new local, state, and federal legislation.

The attitudes of the worker has also changed over time. Most of this worker attitude change has been discussed throughout the earlier portions of the book so it will only be briefly summarized here. In the very beginning work was looked on as something undesirable and only for slaves. The Jewish people, however, looked upon it as noble and as an atonement for sins and a means of charity. During the late medieval times and up into the 1950s the Protestant work ethic predominated with work being a right and duty and a means of salvation. With the Hawthorne studies of the 1930s, changing life styles, increased education, the departure from Christian teachings and work ethics, and younger native born and raised people entering the work force, work started being looked at not only as a means of support and a means of salvation but also as a source where one could affirm his or her dignity and worth as an employee. In most recent times some have carried this to extremes with wanting to "start at the top" and be a "chief" rather than "climb the ladder," be "number one," establish their own morals and ethics, and promote the attitude that the world "owes them a living" just for being here.

All of this work and worker attitude change has resulted in many new laws being passed to help and/or placate the worker in his or her new-found environment.

FEDERAL HUMAN RESOURCES LAWS AND REGULATIONS

Because of the large number of laws put into place in the human resources area, the major emphasis will be placed on federal legislation with comment made on related local, state, and international law when it is of significance to the discussion.

Much of the legislation in this area has its foundation in the Fifth, Thirteenth, and Fourteenth Amendments to the Constitution. The Fifth Amendment states in part, "No person shall...be deprived of life, liberty, or property, without due process of law...." This is a prohibition upon the federal government. The Thirteenth Amendment states in part that "...neither slavery nor involuntary servitude, except as for punishment for crime whereof the party shall have been duly convicted, shall exist within the United States, or any place subject to their jurisdiction." This was aimed primarily at the states. The Fourteenth Amendment, which prohibited certain actions by state governments, was enacted primarily to provide equal protection for all under the law; it requires that all people similarly situated be treated on the same basis, both in the area of privileges and imposed liabilities.

Although not a perfect arrangement, most of the legislation in the human resources areas can be lumped into three relatively broad categories: civil rights legislation, fair labor legislation, and occupational safety and health legislation.

Civil Rights Legislation

Initially, civil rights acts were passed in 1866 and 1871. The Civil Rights Act of 1866 grants all citizens the right to make and enforce contracts for employment; the Civil Rights Act of 1871 grants all citizens the right to sue in federal court if they feel they have been deprived of any rights or privileges guaranteed by the Constitution and laws. Basically these two laws lay fairly dormant for about 90 years when Title VII of the Civil Rights Act of 1964 was passed. Title VII prohibits discrimination on the basis of sex, race, color, religion, or national origin in any employment conditions, including hiring, firing, promotion, transfer, compensation, and training programs. In 1972 and again in 1978, Title VII was amended. The 1972 amendment strengthened enforcement and expanded coverage to include employees of government and educational institutions, as well as private employees of more than 15 persons. The 1978 pregnancy amendment made it illegal to discriminate because of pregnancy, childbirth, or related conditions. In 1980 the Equal Employment Opportunity Commission issued expansion and clarification of sexual discrimination and harassment under Title VII. In 1984, the Supreme Court ruled that federal funds could be cut off from only the "programs or activity" receiving federal aid if they employed illegal discrimination practices; it narrowly interpreted discrimination. The Civil Rights Restoration Act of 1988 clarified and broadened the scope of the 1964 Civil Rights Act in this area. Although President Reagan vetoed this act as being too all encompassing and unwarranted expansion of federal authority, the veto was overruled in both the House and the Senate.

Fair Labor Legislation

The Fair Labor Act of 1938, which has been amended numerous times, is the basic labor and wage act in the United States. It covers such areas as minimum wages, overtime pay, and child labor prohibitions. The Equal Pay Act of 1963, the Civil Rights Act of 1964, and the Age Discrimination Act of 1967, and their amendments, are written in such a manner as to assure people of similar ability, seniority, and qualifications receive the same pay; attempts are now being made to stretch this legislation to include jobs of "comparable worth." Also considered as a piece of Fair Labor Legislation is the Mandatory Retirement Act of 1978 and its 1985 amendment, which prohibits forced retirement.

Occupational Safety and Health Legislation

Employee safety and health in the workplace is of paramount importance. To make certain that employee safety and health does exist in the workplace, the Occupational Safety and Health Act of 1970 was passed. The purpose of the act is "to assure as far as possible every working man and woman in the nation safe and healthful working conditions and to preserve our human resources." It covers every business, regardless of size, that affects interstate commerce. Under present day rulings, almost every business affects interstate commerce. Only federal, state, and local government workers are exempt because the government cannot readily proceed against itself in the event of violations.

This same act established three government agencies to administer and enforce the act: (1) the Occupational Safety and Health Administration, to establish and enforce the necessary safety and health standards; (2) the Occupational Safety and Health Review Commission, to rule on the appropriateness of OSHA's enforcement of the act whenever the OSHA actions are contested by employers, employees, or unions; and (3) the National Institute for Occupational Safety and Health (NIOSH), to conduct research on the causes and prevention of occupational health, safety, injury, and illness, to recommend new standards to the secretary of labor, and to develop associated educational programs.

Detailed standards covering most environmental hazards have been issued by OSHA. They cover such areas as material handling and storage, compressed gas, power tools, and toxic substances such as asbestos, cotton dust, lead, coal dust, and carbon monoxide. While most standards were helpful and important, there were also a number of nuisance rules as well. Almost 1,000 of the silliest were abolished as a result of complaints and in compliance with a President Carter directive.[7]

OSHA inspectors administer health and safety standards primarily by priority level because of the limited number of agency inspectors. First priority inspection is assigned to workplaces where there is imminent danger to worker health and safety; second priority inspection is reserved to looking into employee complaints where safety and health standards have been violated. Special inspection attention is applied to hazardous types of business, such as meat and meat products, lumber and wood products, and roof and sheet metal. Finally, random inspection of OSHA health and safety standards compliance is conducted on all sizes of workplaces that do not fall into one of the preceding categories.

EMPLOYER–EMPLOYEE RIGHTS

Both the employer and the employee have legal, ethical, and moral rights and responsibilities in the workplace. The major emphasis in this section will be placed on the legal rights of the employee in the workplace, along with some of the moral and ethical implications attached.

Employer Rights

Much is said today about employee rights but very little is said or heard in the area of employer rights. Certainly, as long as a business obeys all laws and conducts business in a moral and ethical manner, it is entitled to make a reasonable profit and expect a full day's work for a full day's pay from its employees along with proper legal, ethical, and moral conduct from these same employees. When employees steal company property, loaf on the job, cause job slowdowns, have excessive absenteeism, accept "kickbacks" and bribes, sell trade secrets, become involved in computer theft and vandalism, and participate in other types and forms of misconduct, this is certainly a violation of company rights and a blatant disregard for employee responsibility.

A few examples of where companies did not get what they expected should emphasize the point. The earlier discussed GM roller-bearing plant case is certainly an example of employees not doing a fair day's work for a fair day's wage. The United Auto Workers union, finding strikes harder to win, used work slowdown tactics against McDonnell Douglas Corporation's Long Beach, California, plant.[8] Three General Electric employees were involved in industrial espionage and bribery and cost the company millions of dollars and were a factor in the layoffs of thousands of employees.[9] In a computer scam at the Wells Fargo Bank over $21 million was embezzled.[10] Electronic "viruses" have been introduced into university and NASA computers.[11] To help combat these negative attitudes and actions by employees more companies are starting to use attitude tests to ferret out thieves.[12] And finally there is the joke about the one unemployed man who told his unemployed friend that "Certainly I am seeking employment, but not necessarily work." On the other side of the ledger is the cooperative work going on by the employees at Ford, Lincoln Electric, and many other companies around the country.

Employee Rights

The vast majority of employee rights today are governed by legislation, a large portion of which is shown in Table 5. Some of the major rights areas covered are affirmative action and equal employment, discrimination, sexual harassment, equitable living wages and benefits, equal protection, right to privacy and due process, freedom of speech, job satisfaction, and workplace safety and health. Because of the depth and complexity of many of these subject areas, only some of the more pertinent aspects of each area will be discussed.

Affirmative Action and Equal Employment

Working to achieve equal employment opportunities in the workplace and overcome job discrimination through affirmative action programs is an important social responsibility of most companies in the United States. How to achieve these goals and objectives is detailed in the legislation listed in Table 5 and in three executive orders. The requirements in these orders parallel those in Title VII of the 1964 Civil Rights Act.

Executive Order 11246 was issued in 1965 and prohibited discrimination on the basis of race, color, religion, or national origin as a condition of employment by federal agencies and by contractors and subcontractors on government contracts of $100,000 or more and 100 or more employees. Written affirmative action programs were also required to assure equal opportunity in employment. Executive Order 11375 was issued in 1967 and prohibited discrimination in employment based on sex. Executive Order 11478 was issued in 1979 and has three major parts. Part one prescribes that federal government employment policies are to be based on merit and fitness and not on race, color, sex, religion, or national origin. It supersedes part one of the earlier orders and requires each federal agency head to establish and maintain an equal employment opportunity program; this in turn requires widespread notification of available jobs, evaluation of the applicants based on job-related qualifications, and fair and equal treatment of all employees on the job. Part two requires all federal contractors or subcontractors who do as little as $10,000 worth of government business to comply with the provisions of the order. Part three puts the responsibility of nondiscrimination in employment by the contractors and subcontractors on the government agency dealing with them.

To many people, "affirmative action" means more than just equal job opportunities; it also means increasing the representation of minority groups and women in job categories traditionally staffed by white men so that there will be "equal" or "proportional" employment in all these areas. It is the responsibility of the Department of Labor's Office of Federal Contract Compliance Programs (OFCCP) to require and enforce affirmative action programs under Executive Orders 11246 and 11375 for all companies doing business with the federal government. Executive Order 11478, Title VII of the 1964 Civil Rights Act, the Equal Pay Act of 1963, and the Age Discrimination Act of 1967 and its later amendments are enforced by the Equal Employment Opportunity Commission.

Precisely how to interpret these requirements is not always simple. In the case of *Steelworkers* vs. *Weber,* the Supreme Court in a five-to-two decision found that voluntary affirmative action programs that use quotas to eliminate racial imbalance in "traditionally segregated job categories" are permissible under Title VII in the 1964 Civil Rights Act.[13] A similar but not identical situation is the famous 1978 *Bakke* vs. *University of California* reverse discrimination case where the University of California at Davis Medical School used a system that set aside 16 of 100 places in its entering classes for "disadvantaged" applicants who were members of racial minority groups. Since competition for these 16 positions were evaluated in terms of lower than normal standards, Bakke (a white male) sued under the equal protection clause of the Fourteenth Amendment. The suit claimed that Bakke could compete for only 84 of the 100 places, while the minorities could compete for all 100 of the positions; as a result, all individuals were not treated equally. The Supreme Court agreed with Bakke, with Justice Lewis Powell in his writing of the key opinion stating that affirmative action programs in general are permissible, as long as they consider applicants on an individual basis and do not set aside a specific rigid number of positions.[14]

More will be said about affirmative action programs as different subject areas are discussed in the remainder of the chapter.

Discrimination (General Background)

Discrimination exists in every imaginable area of work. In broad terms, legislation to cover almost every area of discrimination is covered by the laws listed in Table 5 and the three Executive Orders just discussed. First, discrimination will be defined from a legal standpoint and then several specific areas of discrimination will be discussed.

In recent times the courts have defined discrimination in three major different ways. Prior to and during World War II, discrimination was defined as "prejudicial treatment"; that is, actions that were motivated by personal animosity toward the group of which the target person was a member. This definition, however, did not solve problems of economic inequality. The courts then redefined discrimination to mean "unequal treatment"; this meant application of different standards or different treatment to different groups of applicants or employees. This definition permitted the employer to impose any requirements on the job as long as they were imposed on all groups; however, by picking the right requirements it was possible to reject certain groups of people. Finally, the courts have redefined employment discrimination also to mean "unequal impact." For example, the Supreme Court struck down a Duke Power Company test and educational requirements program that screened out a larger proportion of blacks than it did whites.[15] This met the equal treatment requirement but failed the equal impact requirement. Today, failure to meet both equal treatment and equal impact requirements is considered discrimination.

Age Discrimination

The Age Discrimination in Employment Act of 1967, amended in 1978, makes it illegal for an employer to discriminate against individuals between the ages of 40 and 70 in the areas of compensation, terms, conditions, or privileges of employment. This law has had a major impact in three areas: (1) in the area of pensions, after age 65, pensions can be frozen at whatever level the employees would have cost at age 65; (2) employers are not permitted to reduce insurance coverage after age 65, unless the employer can demonstrate that continuing coverage at the pre–65 age level will result in higher costs after the employee reaches age 65; and (3) employers are not permitted to reduce total health benefits for its employees between the ages of 65 and 70, except by the amount of Medicare coverage provided when the employee reaches age 65.

To establish a case of age discrimination, an aggrieved person must show that: (1) he or she is within the protected age group; (2) he or she is doing satisfactory work; (3) he or she was discharged despite satisfactory work performance; and (4) the position was filled by a person younger than the person replaced. The act does not apply, however, if age is a bona fide occupational qualification. The employer must, however, be able to prove this claim. Two court cases will show how this works.

In a Western Electric Company case a decision was made to discharge an employee where 14 years of accumulated performance appraisal data showed that the employee, Cleverly, had been given satisfactory appraisals and steadily increasing salary during his 14 years of employment with the company.[16] Upon discharge he was told that one reason that he was let go was to make room for younger people in his department; this discharge took place six months prior to the time he was to receive his pension. The company was found guilty of age discrimination and Cleverly was awarded back pay. Although the appraisal system was correct, it was used improperly and no proof was supplied that either his work was below standard or that his position required a person of younger age.

In another case, Greyhound Lines was able to show to the satisfaction of the Supreme Court that age was related to the safe conduct of the business.[17] Greyhound refused to hire applicants over 40 years of age and was able to supply statistical evidence that the safest drivers were between ages of 50 to 55 with 16 to 20 years of driving experience. The Supreme Court found that the above evidence showed that an optimum blend of age and experience could not be obtained in hiring an applicant 40 years of age or over.

With care, workers can be laid off without getting into age discrimination or other problems; if employees must be fired for any reason, Condon and Wolf outline and discuss 10 procedures that can help safeguard a company's right to fire.[18] Many companies have, however, chosen what they consider the early retirement package or retraining-relocation route as the safer and more humane approach. For example, Exxon was able to demonstrate its high regard for its employees and reduce its number of employees without resorting to mandatory layoffs through an early retirement program. Exxon used a combination of five years added to age for pension purposes, four weeks cash separation payment for each year of service, bridge payments prior to social security age, standard retirement benefits, continuous health benefits, career counseling, and an office and secretary for job search purposes. The average early retirement package cost Exxon over $100,000 per retiring employee.[19]

In the case of IBM, they needed less scientists and engineers and more sales and service representatives, but not necessarily less total people. Rather than fire the excess scientists and engineers and hire additional sales and service people, IBM chose to retrain and relocate the people it already had. As a result of this concept, 500 employees moved and were retrained for other IBM jobs, 400 employees retired, and only 44 workers quit.[20]

Sex Discrimination

Women are discriminated against in the workplace in many ways. Except for special situations, again where a bona fide occupational qualification can be demonstrated, this is prohibited by law. A few areas where discrimination by sex takes place is in areas such as pay, reproductive hazards, pregnancy and maternity care, job position and promotion, and child care. Although sexual harassment is predominately perpetrated against women, it will be discussed as a separate item because of its special importance and because in actuality it is not just an issue of discrimination against women.

The pay, or wage, gap between men's and women's take-home pay has always been skewed in the direction of considerably higher wages for men. In 1955, in the aggregate, women earned only 63.9 percent of what men earned; in 1970 the percentage had dropped to 59.4 percent and by 1983, it was back up to 63.9 percent. If 1970 is considered the low point, it has been estimated that by the year 2000 women's wages, in the aggregate, will be 74 percent of men's. Department of Labor survey data show that this move to higher grounds is well under way; the survey shows that even today women under 20 years of age earn 92 percent of what men earn; those in the 21–24 age bracket earn 86 percent of men's wages; those in the 25–34 age bracket earn 78 percent of men's wages; and those in the 45 and over bracket earn

61 percent of men's wages.[21] Wage discrimination is prohibited by the Equal Pay Act of 1963.

Most employers will say that they do not discriminate against women in the area of wages and that the wage gap is due to other causes, such as (1) women work fewer hours than men; (2) on the whole, women have less seniority than men do; (3) women work more intermittently than men do; and (4) women have lower educational levels than men do. This may account for some of the difference, but sociological and educational studies seem to indicate that even after adjusting for educational and work experience differences, approximately one-half of the difference still remains.[22] The pay gap situation, along with these findings, have done much to fuel the "comparable worth" issue, which will be discussed later in this chapter.

Reproductive hazards is another method, if it is improperly implemented, that can and has been used to discriminate against women. To keep women from applying for a particular job, some companies have been known to bar women from competing for the job on the grounds that the job poses an occupational hazard to their reproductive system. Concerned about this situation, the EEOC and the Department of Labor issued interpretive guidelines concerning the subject of employment discrimination and reproductive hazards. The guidelines states: "An employer's policy of protecting female employees from reproductive hazards by depriving them of employment opportunities without any scientific data is a per-se violation of Title VII."[23]

In simple English then, employers may not discriminate against, or even attempt to protect, women on the basis of potential hazards to their reproductive systems unless they have sound verifiable data to demonstrate an actual danger.

Pregnancy and maternity care is an area where, prior to the Pregnancy Discrimination Act of 1978, women could be forced to resign or take a leave of absence without pay, disability, or medical coverage, even when coverage was provided for other disabilities and medical problems. This new act now prevents this form of discrimination against women. The act, and the EEOC 1979 interpretive guidelines, require that: (1) women affected by pregnancy and related conditions be treated the same as other applicants and employees on the basis of their ability or inability to work; (2) women are, therefore, protected from being fired, refused a job, or a promotion, because they are pregnant or have had an abortion; (3) women usually cannot be forced to go on leave as long as they are able to work and their physician agrees; and (4) if other employees who take disability leave are entitled to get their jobs back when they are again able to work, so are women who have been unable to work because of pregnancy.

Prior to the 1978 act, temporary disability benefits were most commonly paid, if paid at all, in the form of sick leave or disability insurance, usually for a period of about six weeks. This has been charged dramatically in recent years. One survey shows that over 95 of 300 companies surveyed permit women who have a physician's approval to continue working as long as they want.[24] Maternity leave and benefits typically last for six months but can be extended if a physician verifies that the employee is still disabled after this time period.

There is no U.S. national policy, law, or requirement on length of leave or payments. Other countries do, however, have such national laws established by the government; Sweden provides 52 weeks with 90 percent of pay for 38 weeks; Finland provides 39 weeks with 80 percent of pay for 39 weeks; and Canada provides 37 weeks with 60 percent of pay for 15 weeks. Italy, Austria, Chile, and West Germany have similar national policies. Bills have been presented in Congress to provide similar required care in the United States.

Those in favor of a national maternity leave policy in the United States give several reasons for their focus on this area, including (1) a minority of parents are protected by present legislation; (2) the United Stages lags far behind other countries in developing and supporting parental leave policies; (3) six months' leave is standard in Europe, and more than 100 countries guarantee women some paid leave and job protection; and (4) the U.S. focus is on disability rather than on the child.[25] Those who oppose such a national policy do so primarily on three counts: (1) it will be too costly (up to $75 billion); (2) it will hurt productivity; and (3) it will be disruptive, particularly in smaller companies.[26]

Job position and promotion will be the last area of sex discrimination that will be discussed in this area. At the turn of the century, less than 20 percent of women worked outside the home. Today, more than 65 percent of women work outside the home. Creative Research Associates found that almost one-half of the successful female managers now earning more than $50,000 per year started out in clerical jobs and struggled on up into management positions. Some of these started out 10 to 20 years ago in secretarial pools; however, of the younger managers, under 37 years old, only 23 percent of these started out in secretarial positions.[27]

Today, women fill nearly one-third of all management position—up from only 19 percent in 1972.[28] In spite of this, it is felt by many that women still do not move as fast or as far as their male colleagues.[29] Even though 13 years of field studies by a variety of researchers show few differences exist between men and women in their management effectiveness, the underlying cause for only a few women in high management positions is felt to be related to the traditional corporate roles and male comfort levels with woman managers.[30]

The most rapid progress financially, as well as with promotion for women, is being experienced today in those industries and businesses where women have always been employed. Based on 1985 data, 61 percent of the jobs at Federated are held by women, 32 percent of management jobs are held by women at AT&T, and 37 percent are held at American Express. On the other hand, in manufacturing-type industries only 8 percent of the management positions are held by women at General Motors, 6 percent at General Electric, and 6 percent at Goodyear Tire and Rubber.[31]

Women are continuing to fight their way to the top in established companies; however, many are having problems getting beyond middle management. As a result, many of the brightest women are leaving large corporations for small companies or to establish businesses of their own. Self-employed women are now increasing at a rate five times faster than self-employed men.[32] There are now 2.9 million small businesses in the United States owned by women, making up 25 percent of the small businesses in operation. This figure is a 43 percent leap from a decade ago; in the same period, the total of men starting their own business was up only 9.8 percent.[33]

Even though women still lag behind men, much progress has been made in their climb up the ladder in both salary and promotion. It will still take some time for total equality to be achieved in both areas.

Although child care is not strictly a woman's problem, most of its responsibility still falls upon the woman. Companies' efforts to deal with child care take four main forms: (1) providing support where the community supply is lacking, (2) offering information about parenting or on how to select quality care, (3) giving financial assistance for purchasing community service, and (4) freeing up time to help employees balance the responsibility of family and work.

Companies are becoming more aware and sensitive to their employees child care concerns as they realize the importance of this issue. Stride Rite Corporation, Wang Laboratories, Corning Glass Works, and Merck Pharmaceuticals, just to name a few, all provide on-site child care centers, either operated by the companies themselves or by a professional organization such as Kinder Care. In the area of financial assistance, companies such as Procter & Gamble and American Can offer as an option in their cafeteria-style benefit package the choice of financial assistance for dependent care. With this concept in mind, the dual-career family with children can now evaluate the importance of dental care or numerous other options versus an allowance for child care costs. Most companies and surveys indicate that company-sponsored or supported child care centers help their ability to recruit new employees, improve employee moral, lower absenteeism, and result in lower employee turnover.

U.S. Department of Labor statistics show that over 50 percent of children in two-parent homes have both the mother and father working; in single parent homes over 60 percent of the parents work. Since this is a growing area of concern and one that exists, whether a person agrees or does not agree with dual working parents, more companies and communities are going to have to become concerned and involved with the issue. It is even of more importance and concern where the child has only one parent to carry the load of taking care of the child.

At present there is no federal legislation in this area; when attempts have been made to pass legislation it has been repeatedly defeated or vetoed since the late 1960s. Where state programs or local programs do exist, they vary from area to area. There are several varieties of assistance offered: subsidies are available for low income families; lunches are provided at some group care facilities; and centers to house group facilities are available at no cost in some communities. Working families are provided tax deductions on a sliding scale up to a maximum of twenty percent of the cost of care.

Pay (Wage) Issues

The government directly and indirectly affects compensation through various controls and guidelines. At certain times they have established wage freezes and guidelines. Wage freezes are government orders which permit no wage increases; wage guidelines, on the other hand, are suggested wage levels and are voluntary rather than legally required restrictions.

The Fair Labor Standards Act of 1938 and its many amendments are the basic labor legislation of the land. It has many provisions, of which three are most prominent: Minimum wages, overtime pay, and child labor prohibition, all of which will be discussed in more detail shortly.

The Davis-Bacon Act of 1931 and the Walsh-Healey Act of 1936 mandate that workers on projects covered by these laws be paid at least a government-defined prevailing wage rate in that area. Government-financed construction costing over $2,000 and production and supply contracts for purchases over $10,000 are projects covered by the Davis-Bacon Act and the Walsh-Healey Act, respectively.

The Equal Pay Act of 1963, the Civil Rights Act of 1964, the Age Discrimination Act of 1967, and their associated amendments are designed to assure that all people of similar abilities, seniority, and qualifications receive the same pay for the same work regardless of race, color, religion, sex, or national origin.

Minimum Wage

The Fair Labor Standards Act of 1938 established a minimum wage of 25 cents per hour; the present minimum wage rate is $3.35 per hour, with legislation now being debated in Congress to increase this to $3.85 in 1989, $4.25 in 1990, and to $4.60 in 1991. A number of people question the desirability of minimum wages on the basis that the law may price the marginal workers out of a job. Everyone does not agree, while still others want to compromise and are proposing a lower minimum wage for trainees and teenagers to help reduce the unemployment problem.[34]

The advocates of minimum wage legislation have adopted the reduction or elimination of poverty as their most important consideration. As arguments to support the achievement of this goal through increased minimum wages, they say: (1) increase in wage-earner income will lead to increased consumption expenditure, which in turn will increase the gross national product and employment; (2) the lowest paid workers are exploited by powerful employers who are protected from competition of other employers for the services of low-wage labor; and (3) labor income will increase because employers will adopt productivity-increasing methods to offset the mandated minimum wages, thus minimum wage increases would pay for themselves through increased efficiencies.

Those who oppose an increase in the minimum wage rate base it on the benefits of costs of minimum wage rates in alleviating poverty. Some negative factors that they list include: (1) reduced employment opportunities for low-wage workers in covered employment and the accompanying loss of efficiency; (2) lower wage rates will occur in jobs not covered by minimum wage legislation if the displaced workers seek employment in noncovered businesses; (3) fewer fringe benefits and nonwage amenities will be used by the employers to help offset the increased costs; (4) there will be less formal and informal training on the first jobs, which will make higher level jobs harder to find because of limited experience; and (5) it may have an adverse effect on inflation.[35]

What does the data show? One study suggests that employment of full time female workers increases when the minimum wage is raised as does those who are better skilled and schooled.[36] Since teenagers and blacks are typically located at the lower end of the wage scale, it appears that they are the ones most likely to be displaced. Another study shows that only 29 percent of wage earners at or below the minimum wage level were members of families with incomes below the poverty level.[37] Finally, the minimum wage was 40 cents per hour in 1948 and the unemployment rate among black teenagers and white teenagers was 10 percent; in 1970, when the minimum wage was $1.60 per hour, the unemployment rate among black teenagers was 35 percent; now the minimum wage is $3.35 per hour and the unemployment rate among black teenagers is 52 percent. [38] Since there has been no dramatic upsurge in racial discrimination since 1948, nor has there been any dramatic decline in black educational accomplishments, why has the unemployment rate among those whom it is supposed to help continued to worsen with each increase in minimum wage. It is very difficult for many people logically to see how if someone cannot get a job at $3.35 per hour that their chances will be improve by increasing the minimum wage to $4.60 an hour.

Overtime Pay

Any employee covered by the Fair Labor Standards Act of 1938 and its amendments who works more than 40 hours per week must be paid one and one-half times the base wage for all hours over 40 worked. If, in addition, a bonus is paid on a monthly or quarterly basis, the overtime pay must equal one and one-half times the combined base pay and bonuses. This requirement has a strong tendency to reduce the unnecessary need for and scheduling of overtime hours of work.

Child Labor Prohibition

A person under the age of 16 cannot be employed in jobs involved in interstate commerce except in nonhazardous types of work for a parent or guardian; even this type of work requires a permit. A person between the ages of 16 and 18 cannot be hired for work in dangerous jobs such as coal mining, logging and sawmilling, excavation operations, and manufacturing or storing explosives. To make certain of a child's age when they are being hired, many employers ask for age certificates that have been issued by a representative of a labor department, an education department, or by a local school.

Equal Pay and Comparable Worth

The Equal Pay Act of 1963 requires equal pay for equal work for men and for women and defines equal work as requiring equal skills, effort, and responsibility under similar working conditions. As pointed out in the earlier discussion on wage discrimination, American women working on a full time basis earn only about 64 percent of what men earn. There has been a growing movement in recent years to close this gap through the concept of equal pay for comparable work—or what has become known as the "comparable worth" issue. It is based on the concept that jobs that require comparable skills, educational levels, effort, and responsibility should be paid the same wages, irrespective of economic conditions or the market conditions of the job.

Comparable worth is not an issue of the 1980s but has been around for a long time. In 1915, the Commission of Industrial Relations was one of the first groups to advocate a "comparable worth" standard. During World War II, the National War Labor Board applied this principle to women working in defense-related industries; employers during World War II were required to pay women employees the same wages as men, "if women replaced men in jobs or if women performed work of comparable quantity and quality as men."[39] "In 1962, the Kennedy administration's proposal for equal pay legislation was submitted to Congress."[40] In 1963, the Equal Pay Act was passed and clearly rejected the "comparable worth" standard. The issuance of Title VII of the Civil Rights Act of 1964 did not resolve the issue either.

In spite of these setbacks, the proponents of comparable worth continued their fight through the court system. In 1981, the city of San Jose, California, and local 101 of the American Federation of State, Country, and Municipal Employees ended the country's first municipal strike over the issue of equal pay for comparable worth.[41] In the same year, in a five-to-four decision the Supreme Court ruled that a sex discrimination suit can be brought under the 1964 Civil Rights Act on a basis other than discrimination based on "equal or substantially equal work."[42] In this case, *Gunther* vs. *Washington,* a group of Washington Country, Oregon, prison matrons brought suit claiming sex discrimination because the male prison guards' job content has been evaluated as having 5 percent more job content than did their jobs, yet the male prison guards received 35 percent higher pay.

Some of the most effective arguments supporting the issue appear to be pleas or threats to management that if they do not take appropriate action, then the federal government will step in and do it for them through some form of a new legislation. They also argue that business can either pay women an adequate wage or pay instead through welfare programs.[43]

Some of the most effective arguments against "comparable worth" have been introduced into the Congressional Record by Congressman Willis D. Gradison, Jr.[44] He points out that (1) prices-economic values are determined by the interaction of supply and demand so that if more qualified people seek a particular job, the wage for that job will tend to be lower than it would be with fewer applicants, regardless of how useful or valuable the job is perceived from the standpoint of nonmarket criteria; (2) pay raises would tend to promote female job segregation by providing an incentive to remain in traditional female occupations; (3) pay raises would attract males to these areas and create more sex discrimination problems; and (4) raising the wages of lower paying female-dominated jobs would result in more problems for both men and women as firms shifted from labor to capital equipment (people being replaced by more machines) as costs climbed.

This is an issue that is far from over and one that will continue to remain in the news as long as it is not resolved to everyone's satisfaction. Both sides of the issue received considerable coverage during the 1984 presidential campaign, and it will certainly be an issue again in the 1988 presidential campaign.

Sexual Harassment

In 1980, the EEOC issued guidelines designed to curtail sexual harassment. Under the guidelines, all employers are expected to have specific polices that prohibit sexual harassment, establish a grievance procedure, and lay down procedures to discipline the offenders. This is simple to say, but because of its complexity, sexual harassment may be hard to define in some instances; all people cannot and do not agree on what constitutes sexual harassment under all situations.[45]

A little background history to the sexual harassment issue might help explain why defining it under all conditions has at times been difficult and how the definition is being more clearly defined each day. Back in the 1930s, one male supervisor's attitude and comments about female employees with respect to sex was, "There's no harm in asking!" At that time period courts found that for a man to be charged and convicted of sexual harassment a woman had to be physically assaulted or battered.[46]

In 1980 with the issuance of the guidelines on sexual harassment it became clear that any sexual advances, requests for sexual favors, and other verbal or physical conduct of a sexual nature constituted sexual harassment when: (1) submission to such conduct was tied to an individual's employment; (2) submission or rejection of such conduct is used as a basis for employment decisions affecting the employee; and (3) such conduct has the purpose or effect of substantially interfering with an individual's work performance or creating an intimidating, hostile, or offensive working environment. Items (1) and (2) are fairly straightforward, but item (3) has been difficult to tie down. If proper data, records, and witnesses are kept then the employee has in most instances won the case against sexual harassment under item (1) and (2) situations.

To improve chances of discouraging sexual harassment or winning a court case against sexual harassment, Moore and White list eight steps to follow if being sexually harassed:

1. Do not quit your job.
2. Act quickly.
3. Get support from your coworkers.
4. Ridicule the harasser.
5. If a union member, use the union grievance procedure.
6. Notify the company.
7. Keep a diary.
8. Find other victims to corroborate your charges if possible.[47]

Keeping records and dates of harassment is absolutely essential, as is notifying the company if harassment persists. Not doing these things may keep a person from winning a sexual harassment case if it is taken to court, as indicated by the recent *Neville* vs. *Taft Broadcasting Co.* case that took place in Buffalo, New York.[48] Miss Neville claimed that her immediate supervisor, the local sales manager, kissed her when they were returning from a sales trip. He then told her, that "if you do everything right with this company, you'll go a long way." She told her supervisor's boss but asked him to do nothing about it. She did not tell the general manager even though a written policy published to all employers about sexual harassment required this. Miss Neville said that her supervisor continued to harass her and always entered her office and pressed his body up against her chair and back and additionally made her sales goals impossible to meet. Eventually her supervisor wanted to fire her when she consistently underperformed her sales goals and those of other employees. Her supervisor's boss asked the supervisor to try one more time to get her to reach her sales goal. He did talk to her, and Neville promised to do better, but a few days later she was gone from work without explanation. At a later meeting with her supervisor, his boss, and the general manager, she told the story of sexual harassment. The general manager appointed a well-respected female department head to investigate and give him a report. She did and said that Neville was not sexually harassed but only invented the story because of her poor job performance. On the basis of this report, Neville was fired. Neville in turn took her case to court and lost. In January 1987, the court found that although she had been kissed as claimed, her work performance was so poor that the company had the right to terminate her on this count. If what Miss Neville said was true she would have had a much better chance to win the case if she had followed the eight points outlined by Moore and White. Based on an evaluation of this case by Stewart, he also points out four steps to be taken by companies to help them in sexual harassment cases. (1) have a written policy published to all employees about sexual harassment; (2) appoint an impartial investigator to decide what happened; (3) take all claims seriously; and (4) to get all evidence while it is available.[49]

The part of the earlier discussed description of sexual harassment that deals with "interfering with an individual's work performance or creating an intimidating, hostile or offensive working environment" also has been somewhat clarified by a 1986 Supreme Court decision that ruled that "creating a hostile environment through sexual harassment, even if the job status is not affected, also violates Title VII of the 1964 Civil Rights Act."[50]

Finally, not controlling sexual harassment in the workplace can be expensive for companies. The average size jury decisions and settlements are mostly in the $60,000 to $75,000 range, with some going as high as $500,000.[51]

Whistle Blowing

Blowing the so-called whistle occurs when someone inside the company reports real or imagined company misconduct to the public. The cost of whistle blowing can and quite often is costly to both the company and the whistle blower. It can seriously discredit a company or badly tarnish its image and will undoubtedly cost the company considerable money in lost business or lawsuits. The whistle blower often loses even when he wins his point. If it goes to the courts, lengthy lawsuits and mental anguish can take their toll; just as importantly, his career at the company where he works and even in the industry may be destroyed.

Why and under what conditions then would a person blow the whistle? Research indicates that those who observe alleged wrongdoing were more apt to participate in whistle blowing if (1) they had convincing evidence that wrongdoing had taken place, (2) the wrongdoing was serious, and (3) if it directly affected them. Miceli and Near in an evaluation and analysis of over 8,500 people arrived at distinct profiles of whistle blowers, observers of wrongdoing who do not act, and nonobservers.[52] In another article, a flow diagram and predictions for determining who might be a whistle blower and under what conditions they might emerge is discussed.[53] Finally, a recent *Harvard Business Review* article presents and evaluates a case study on whistle blowers that involves many of the points discussed.[54]

In the case of illegal activities within the company, (fraud, embezzlement, and so on) there is usually public support as well as legal support for the whistle blower. If the employee is fired for blowing the whistle, he may have recourse in the courts; in some states, whistle blowers are protected from discharge. On purely ethical and moral issues the public may side with the company.

Right to Privacy and Due Process

Rights to privacy and due process usually refer to invasion of a person's private life and/or unauthorized release of the confidential information about the person. Job applicants, employees, customers and many others, in most instances believe that their political, religious, social and private life and beliefs should not be exposed or subject to snooping analysis. Some areas people consider as threats to their rights of privacy involve lie detectors, disease and genetic testing, medical examinations, testing for and control of alcoholism and drug abuse, junk mail and unsolicited telephone calls, revelation of confidential records, surveillance devices, and computer data banks. Only lie detectors, drug abuse and drug testing, medical examinations, alcoholism and alcohol treatment, and AIDS will be examined at this time.

Prior to examining these areas, several helpful policy guidelines for dealing with privacy might be helpful. These guidelines include: (1) only relative, necessary, and useful information should be recorded and retained in the files; (2) the employee or person should have access to examine the records and be able to challenge their accuracy, all under the Freedom of Information Act; (3) there should be no secret or unknown files or records kept of the person; (4) the information keeper is responsible for its accuracy; and (5) information should be released only to those who have a need to know, and any information that is released outside of the organization should be done only with the person's knowledge and permission.

Polygraphs

The lie detector, or polygraph, is one instrument whose validity is often questioned. Employees and unions have often objected to being subjected to polygraph tests on the grounds that they are unreliable (they give incorrect conclusions in 5 to 10 percent of the cases), are an invasion of an individual's privacy, and may cause job loss to qualified employees; many businesses, on the other hand, vigorously support their use as a means of helping catch some of the 350,000 workers who internally steal as much as $50 billion a year from businesses.[55] Arguments for and against their use abound.[56]

Regardless of how employers and employees feel about polygraphs, their usage is probably going to be severely restricted in the future. A recent California case and congressional action will see to that. Thomas Kirtly was required to take a lie detector test as a prerequisite to employment at a Color Tile home improvement store in Milpitas, California. After taking the test he was asked to sign a form saying he did it voluntarily; instead he went to a lawyer and claimed the company had violated the California state law on polygraph testing. Kirtly won his case and $150,000, while Color Tile agreed to also pay damages of $750 to $28,000 to each of as many as 3,000 other employees and job applicants.[57]

Both the Senate and Congress are working on bills that will severely restrict the use of polygraph exams by private employers. Both proposed bills would ban all preemployment testing. From that point on, both bills diverge, with many exceptions and loopholes.[58] No matter how the bill turns out it would be wise for companies to consider new ways to avoid hiring new employees who might steal and to catch those who might already have stolen. Some companies are already doing this. They are looking at more vigorous job interviews, paper and pencil honesty tests, and tighter surveillance.

Medical Examinations

Medical examinations may invade the privacy of the individual, however, the relationship between the patient and the physician is usually such that medical tests of employees are usually permitted. The health and safety of both the patient and those with whom the patient will be working are at stake. Also involved may be cost of insurance, accidents, and other liability.

In addition, after a medical examination is made, the employer has an obligation to keep the medical findings completely confidential in order to protect the individual's privacy. Only if there is suitable medical or job-related reason can the data be released to others who have an absolute need to know. Finally, if there is any significant medical illness revealed, the employer has an obligation to advise the employee of this situation.[59]

Substance Abuse

Drug and alcohol abuse are the nation's number one health problem and the biggest detriment to productivity levels. A newspaper headline tells of 30 percent to 40 percent of the Armco Middletown Works steelworkers being drug and/or alcohol abusers.[60] Another newspaper article reports of teenagers from a high school of high scholastic rating disrupting the drug message of Ohio's Attorney General Anthony Celebrezze and yelling, "Free samples? Got any free samples?"[61] And on January 4, 1987, a Conrail locomotive, traveling near Baltimore, ran through several warning lights and crashed into a 12-car

Amtrak train killing 16 people and injuring another 175. Drug tests performed by the National Transportation Safety Board and the Center for Human Toxicology at the University of Utah showed that Conrail engineer, Ricky Gates, and brakeman, Edward Cromwell, had both ingested marijuana and one of the men (unnamed) also had PCP, an illegal hallucinogenic chemical.

Substance abuse is detrimental to both the employer and the employee. The cost of employees' substance abuse to business has been well documented. Drug and alcohol abuse is costing American business $39.1 billion annually in lost productivity; the human economic cost may well exceed $100 billion a year.[62] The employer pays with lowered productivity, increased health care costs, increased accidents and absenteeism, and in many instances eventual loss of a valuable employee. The employee pays with the loss of his or her health, increased financial and family problems, loss of respect, and often his or her job.

Industry has responded to much of this by implementing various testing policies. In 1982 only three percent of the country's largest companies used some form of drug screening.[63] At the same time period, 10 percent of the *Fortune 500* companies were testing. By 1985, the *Fortune 500* group had jumped to 25 percent;[64] by 1986 one-third of the companies were testing.[65] Other studies indicate that more than one-half of all companies are testing or are considering it.

Several areas of controversy have emerged regarding drug testing in the workplace. One area of conflict involves the employer's right to investigate and enforce rules in the workplace and the employee's obligation to cooperate in this endeavor. The controversy arises when the rights of the employer and the obligation of the employee come into conflict with the individual's rights to privacy and due process (Fourth Amendment protection against unreasonable search and seizure), which includes the right not to incriminate himself or herself (Fifth Amendment). Another area of conflict arises on precisely what to do when an employee tests positive for drug use. Finally, there is the question of the reliability of the test itself.

The most popular form of screening current and potential employees for substance abuse is by means of urinalysis. This test cannot determine whether a person is a chronic abuser or might just have been exposed to it. Traces of THC (tetrahydrocannabinol) will show up in urine if a person is exposed in a closed room with marijuana smokers (you might ask why a nonuser would be in a closed room with heavy users), and certain prescription drugs and varieties of herbal teas sold in the United States will result in positive findings for cocaine urinalysis.[66] Even consumption of poppy seed bagels and cough medicines can produce false positive results. Gas chromatography (GC) and mass spectrometry (MS) are highly sophisticated chemical analysis techniques that are 99 percent accurate in drug identification.[67] However, as a result of all of the other variables involved research indicates that urinalysis testing can be scientifically inaccurate as much as 20 percent to 50 percent of the time in trying to determine whether an employee is a true substance abuser.

Another problem with urinalysis testing is that those who want to "beat the system" have a good chance of doing so. The sophisticated drug-using crowd can learn to fool the tests; certain drug-oriented magazines have written articles on how to beat the tests.[68] In addition, the free-enterprise system has gotten in on the act and certain companies are selling and shipping "toxin-free urine" to those who are subjected to urine tests. During tests, the toxin-free urine is substituted for the person's possibly contaminated urine.[69]

Assistance programs for alcoholism have been established in many companies for a number of years. Usually it follows several steps, such as (1) the supervisor documents the effects, at work, from the employee's use of alcohol; (2) the supervisor discusses this with the employee and offers help; (3) the supervisor recommends, and may even require, the employee to participate in a rehabilitation program (such as Alcoholics Anonymous); and (4) if step (3) is not taken by the employee, the supervisor advises the employee that the consequence of not participating in a rehabilitation program may be the loss of his or her job.

The use of alcohol is not illegal, while the use of drugs in any amount is illegal. As a result, the same four steps listed above for alcohol abuse and assistance also can be used for drug use and assistance; however, additional steps are also recommended. Based on an in-depth study and evaluation of the available literature on drug use, abuse, testing, and rehabilitation assistance, the following ten areas of additional or modified control are recommended:

1. At the very least, the company should have a policy that addresses the use, possession, and sale of drugs and alcohol on company property. The policy should also include remedial action that will be taken with the employees if they fail to adhere to and abide in the policy.

2. Prominently display the drug and alcohol policy and require employees to read the policy periodically and sign that they have read it and will abide by it.

3. Advise the employees, through drug and alcohol training programs, of the dangers and consequences of use and abuse of alcohol and drugs. Present it in a medical and safety context.

4. Include a drug testing requirement in any employment contract, after first advising the employee that drug testing will be part of the contract.

5. Develop a policy on rehabilitation and employee assistance.

6. If random testing is done, have strong justification for doing it, such as safety.

7. Confirm a positive screen test with one of the accurate gas chromatography or mass spectrometry methods, especially if the data might be needed in court at a later date. Do not fire a person after only one positive test.

8. Deal only with test laboratories that are known and certified for doing the types of testing the company needs.

9. Establish a "chain of custody" in taking and handling samples since people's lives and careers are at stake. Careful records must be kept, including who took the sample, anyone that handled the sample, where it was stored, and how it was tested.

10. Practice good employee relation techniques.

Neither drug nor alcohol problems will go away overnight; however, every attempt possible must be made to control them. Continued education is needed as is continued help.

AIDS

AIDS is the acronym for acquired immune deficiency syndrome. People with AIDS suffer from life-threatening infections and other fatal diseases. There is presently no known cure or preventive medicine available for the disease. Studies conducted in New York, Miami, and California indicate that once diagnosed as having AIDS, women survived an average of 6.6 months after diagnosis, while men with AIDS survived an average of 12 to 14 months.[70] A person may, however, be exposed to the virus from 5 to 10 years prior to developing the disease.[71] The disease is transmitted primarily by sexually active homosexual or bisexual men, intravenous drug abusers, recipients of contaminated blood transfusions or blood products, and people who have had heterosexual contact with persons carrying the AIDS virus. Although this last group only accounts for about 4 percent of the AIDS cases, some 57,000 people have become infected through heterosexual intercourse.[72] As of the end of 1987, the AIDS epidemic had claimed approximately 28,000 lives.[73]

Researchers do not agree on the total seriousness of the epidemic. Dr. Robert Gould, writing in *Cosmopolitan,* claimed that there is so little risk of heterosexual transmission of AIDS that women can have healthy intercourse even with men who are carrying the AIDS virus. A report on AIDS, published in the *Journal of the American Medical Association,* contradicts Gould and says that the odds are 1 in 500 in contracting AIDS if the partner is infected. Masters and Johnson have just published a book stating that the virus is spreading like wildfire among heterosexuals. Each of them used different sources of base data to arrive at their conclusion. The truth is possibly somewhere in between all the claims. The key issue to the entire story, however, is that there a number of ways that one can acquire AIDS, and it is deadly no matter how a person acquires it. Medical doctors are well aware of this, but in spite of the fact that as many as 25 percent of surveyed medical surgeons have said that they would refuse to operate on AIDS patients, an ethics panel of the American Medical Association (AMA) informed the nation's doctors that they cannot refuse to treat people infected with the AIDS virus.

The AMA has made its decision on what to do about AIDS patients; what is and should the government and business do about employees who have AIDS and about the entire AIDS issue? The Reagan administration has called for mandatory testing of certain people, including hospital patients, immigrants, marriage license applicants, and prisoners.[74] In the meantime, courts are making a whole series of decisions that are establishing guidelines for what business and individuals might be permitted to do. In Los Angeles, attempted murder charges were dropped against a man who sold his AIDS-infected blood; the judge said the prosecutor failed to show as required by law that the defendant intended to kill.[75] In Orlando, Florida, a judge dismissed attempted manslaughter charges against a prostitute who continued soliciting sex after she contracted AIDS, because the prosecutors failed to prove she actually intended to kill any of her customers. In a far reaching seven-to-two Supreme Court decision, the Court ruled that people with contagious diseases are covered by a federal law that prohibits discrimination in federally aided programs.[76] The decision did not directly involve AIDS victims; however, they viewed it as a victory for them in protecting them from discrimination in housing, insurance, and health care.

What does a restaurant do if the chef comes down with AIDS, the word gets out, coworkers refuse to work with him, customers eat someplace else, and business goes on the skids? What happens if one of the secretaries in the secretarial pool comes down with AIDS and the other secretaries and some of the office managers refuse to work with her? In many cases discrimination lawsuits have resulted.[77] If the greater Cincinnati, Ohio, area is representative of the nation as a whole, as of mid-October 1987, the five largest nongovernmental employers in Cincinnati (GE Aircraft Engines, the Procter & Gamble Co., the Kroger Co., Armco Inc., and Cincinnati Milacron, Inc.) had no specific AIDS policy.[78] This may be partially because corporations are trying to adopt humane policies for AIDS victims. Humane policies and compassion are fine for the AIDS victim but so are compassion, humane treatment and policies required to protect the non-AIDS workers. As one medical doctor has put it,

There is no question that the diagnosis of AIDS carries with it considerable social damnation with possible loss of job and ability to support one's self. This is indeed unfortunate. But is it sufficiently justifiable to continue the contamination of unsuspecting people such as yourself? Is it justifiable to permit exposure to the personnel in the operating room to infection themselves and the spread of infection to others without doing something more basic to prevent the spread of infection?[79]

Dr. Heidt believes that the problem he has presented above is created because the politician has placed himself in direct conflict with the world of medicine, which tries to protect people from infection and to isolate a problem that it cannot cure. Is it not a very similar situation that faces business concerns today? What is business going to do to protect itself and its employees? Sooner or later every corporation in this country will have an AIDS problem. It might well be a hidden time bomb just waiting to explode. What are the politicians going to do to bring the epidemic under control? It is here and growing!

In the meantime, costs to cover the fallout from AIDS keeps increasing. Companies are already being hit with increasing costs for medical insurance and disability pay. Federal officials and health economists are saying that the AIDS epidemic will cost the nation $10 billion a year by 1991. *Money* magazine says that "AIDS has made stunning increases in the cost of health, life and disability insurance inevitable"; as an example to support this claim, they show that the expense of treating an AIDS patient from the time of diagnosis to death is considerably higher than the cost of medical care for people with most other serious illnesses. As a result, health premiums could rise up to 32 percent a year.[80]

Workplace Safety and Health

Every employee can expect workplace safety and healthy working conditions. If these conditions do not exist, then OSHA is the agency that will look into the situation and rectify any deviation from acceptable standards. Fines are mandatory where serious violations are found. First time willful offenses can be assessed a civil penalty of up to $10,000 for each violation; there is a $1,000 per day penalty for each day it is not corrected beyond the OSHA-designated deadline date. If the first willful offense results in death of a worker, a criminal penalty of $10,000 and six months in jail can be mandated. A second such conviction can mean a $20,000 fine and a one-year jail term. Employers can appeal citations, proposed penalties, and corrections they have been ordered to make. OSHA must prove the case when an employee appeals. If a state has a program at least as effective as the federal program then the Occupational Safety and Health Act permits the state to develop and administer such a program.

The value and effectiveness of OSHA continues to be debated; however, in 1982, relative to 1980, there were 530,000 fewer occupational injuries and illnesses and 4.7 million fewer lost work days in the United States. In 1983, serious injuries dropped another 8 percent and deaths in the workplace dropped 6 percent.[81]

SCENARIO

Ralph has periodic nose bleeds at home and at work. Fred, a coworker, suggests that he have the blood vessels in his nose cauterized to prevent the bleeding. Ralph refuses and says that if he lets his nose bleed for a few minutes it reduces his head pressure and he feels better. Ralph comes down with AIDS and his coworkers tell their boss that since fresh splattered blood has been recorded as causing AIDS infections if it gets on you, that either

Ralph leaves or they leave. As the boss, what would you do? As the company owner, what would you do?

NOTES

1. "The End of Corporate Loyalty," *Business Week,* August 4, 1986, 49.

2. Alan Sloan, "Go Forth and Compete," *Forbes* 128, no. 11. (1981): 41.

3. Maryann Mrowca, "Ohio Firm Relies on Incentive-Pay System to Motivate Workers and Maintain Profits," *Wall Street Journal,* August 12, 1983, p. 15; William Serrin, "The Way That Works at Lincoln," *New York Times,* January 15, 1984, p. F–4.

4. Janet Braunstein, "Ford Sets Record in Earnings," *Cincinnati Enquirer,* April 19, 1988, p. D–1.

5. "America's Blue Collars Get Down to Business," *U.S. News and World Report,* February 29, 1988, 52–53.

6. Ibid., p. 52.

7. "Gobbledygook Out," *Miami Herald,* December 6, 1977, p. A–17.

8. Alex Kotlowitz, "Finding Strikes Harder to Win, More Unions Turn to Slowdowns," *Wall Street Journal,* May 22, 1987, p. 1.

9. Darsen Dopps, "Industrial Espionage Costs Jobs at G.E.," *Cincinnati Enquirer,* November 16, 1986, p. F–1.

10. Hal Lancaster, "Fraud at Wells Fargo Depended on Avoiding Computer's Red Flags," *Wall Street Journal,* February 26, 1981, p. 1.

11. Walt Schaefer, "Grim Computer Message: Electronic Virus Chews Up Student's Notes, Projects," *Cincinnati Enquirer,* April 23, 1988, p. A–1. "Electronic Worms Infect NASA Apples," *Cincinnati Enquirer,* April 14, 1988, p. A–12.

12. Ed Bean, "More Firms Use 'Attitude Test' to Keep Thieves off the Payroll," *Wall Street Journal,* February 27, 1987, p. 33.

13. Gregory J. Mounts, "Significant Decisions in Labor Cases—*Steelworkers* vs. *Weber,*" *Monthly Labor Review* 102, no. 8. (1979): 56–57.

14. "The Bakke Ruling," *Wall Street Journal,* June 29, 1978, pp. 1, 17, 18.

15. Alfred Blumrosen, "Strangers in Paradise: *Griggs* vs. *Duke Power Co.* and the Concept of Employment Discrimination," *Michigan Law Review* 70, no. 1 (1972): 59–110.

16. *Cleverlv* vs. *Western Electric Company,* 594 F. 20 638 (8th Cir., 1979).

17. *Hodgson* vs. *Greyhound Lines, Inc.,* 419 U.S. 1122 (1975).

18. T. J. Condon and R. A. Wolff, "Procedures to Safeguard Your Right to Fire," *Harvard Business Review* 63, no. 6. (1985): 16–18.

19. Bruce Nussbaum, "Bracing Yourself for 'the Golden Boat,'" *Business Week* November 3, 1960, p. 152.

20. Dennis Kneale, "Cutting Output, IBM Tells Some Workers: Move, Retire or Quit," *Wall Street Journal,* April 17, 1987, p. 18.

21. "Women's Wages," *Wall Street Journal,* February 20, 1987, p. 19.

22. G. T. Milkovich and J. M. Newman, *Compensation* (Plano, Tex.: Business Publications, 1984).

23. H. M. Finneran, "Title VII and Restrictions on Employment of Fertile Women," *Labor Law Journal* 31, no. 4 (1980): 224.

24. M. Meyer, *Women and Employee Benefits* (New York: Conference Board, 1978).

25. *Maternity Benefits in the Eighties* (Geneva: International Labor Office, 1985), pp. 4–5.

26. "Require Firms to Give 'Family Leave' "? *U.S. News & World Report* 101, no. 4 (1986): 63.

27. "Following the Leaders," *Wall Street Journal,* March 24, 1986, 10D.

28. "Glass Ceiling," *Wall Street Journal,* March 24, 1986, special edition, 1D.

29. "Why Women Execs Stop before the Top," *U.S. News & World Report* 101, no. 26 (1986).

30. "Men versus Women," *Wall Street Journal,* May 27, 1986, p. 1.

31. "Room at the Top," *Wall Street Journal,* March 24, 1986, special edition, 7D.

32. "Glass Ceiling."

33. "Venturing Out on Their Own," *Wall Street Journal,* March 24, 1986, special edition, 4D.

34. Albert R. Karr, "Reagan May Ease Minimum Wage Stand if Legislation Is Diluted, Brock Indicates," *Wall Street Journal,* June 12, 1987, p. 3.

35. Masonori Haskimoto, "Minimum Wage Effects on Training on the Job," *American Economic Review* 72, no. 5 (1982): 1085.

36. Jere R. Behrman, Robin C. Sickles, and Paul Taubman, "The Impact of Minimum Wages on the Distribution of Earnings for Major Race-Sex Groups: A Dynamic Analysis," *American Economic Review,* 72, no. 4 (1982): 775.

37. Finis Welch, "The Trouble with the Minimum Wage," *Across the Board* 16, no. 8 (1979): 39.

38. George S. Handel, "Minimum Wage Hurts the Blacks Most of All," *Cincinnati Enquirer,* March 8, 1988, p. A–13.

39. Sandra Hurd, Paula Murray, and Bill Shaw, "Comparable Worth: A Legal and Ethical Analysis," *American Business Law Journal* 21, no. 3 (1984): 409.

40. Ibid., p. 410.

41. John H. Bunzel, "To Each According to Her Worth?" Public Interest 38, no. 67 (1982): 77.

42. Michael F. Carter, "Comparable Worth: An Idea Whose Time Has Come?" *Personnel Journal* 60, no. 10 (1981): 792–794.

43. Hurd, Murray, and Shaw, "Comparable Worth," p. 425.

44. Willis D. Gradison, Jr., *U.S. Congressional Record,* 99th Cong., 1st sess., January 3, 1985, pp. 1–3.

45. Eliza G. C. Collins and Timothy B. Blodgett, "Sexual Harassment . . . Some See It . . . Some Won't," *Harvard Business Review* 59, no. 2 (1981): 76–95; Mary P. Rowe, "Dealing with Sexual Harassment," *Harvard Business Review* 59, no. 3 (1981): 42–58.

46. P. Linenberger and T. J. Keaveny, "Sexual Harassment: The Employer's Legal Obligation," *Personnel* 58, no. 6 (1981): 60–68.

47. Marat Moore and Connie White, *Sexual Harassment in the Mines* (Oak Ridge, Tenn.: Coal Employment Project, n.d.).

48. *Neville* vs. *Taft Broadcasting Co., WGR-TV,* CIV—82–622C, Buffalo, N.Y.

49. Frank H. Stewart, "Policy, Action Important to Harassment Cases," *Cincinnati Business Courier,* February 23–March 1, 1987, pp. 27–33.

50. S. Wermiel and C. Trost, "Justices Say Hostile Job Environment Due to Sex Harassment Violates Rights," *Wall Street Journal,* June 20, 1986, p. 2.

51. "Sexual Dilemmas of the Modern Office," *U.S. News & World Report* 101, no. 22 (1986): 55–58.

52. Marcia Parmerlee Miceli and Janet P. Near, "The Relationships among Beliefs, Organizational Position, and Whistle-Blowing Status: A Discrimination Analysis," *Academy of Management Journal,* 27, no. 4 (1984): 687–705.

53. Janellie Brinker Dozier and Marcia P. Miceli, "Potential Predictors of Whistle Blowing: A Behavior Perceptive," *Academy of Management Review,* 10, no. 4 (1985): 823–836.

54. Sally Seymour, "The Case of the Willful Whistle Blower," *Harvard Business Review* 66, no. 1 (1988): 103–109.

55. Richard J. Tersiane and Robert S. Russell, "Internal Theft: The Multi-Billion-Dollar Disappearing Act," *Business Horizons* 24, no. 6 (1981): 11–20; "Bankruptcies Are Linked to Thieving Employees," *Arizona Republic,* November 15, 1981, p. C–10.

56. Gordon H. Borland, "The Case for the Polygraph in Employment Screening," and David T. Lykken, "The Case against the Polygraph in Employment Screening," *Personnel Administration* 30, no. 9 (1985): 58–65; "The Debate: Lie Detectors at Work," *USA Today,* December 15, 1987, p. A–10.

57. Keith Bradshaw, "With Lie Detectors on the Way Out, Employers Seek New Tests," *Cincinnati Enquirer,* March 13, 1988, p. I–3.

58. Ibid.

59. Mitchell S. Novit, "Physical Examinations and Company Liability: A Legal Update," *Personnel Journal* 61, no. 1 (1982): 47–53.

60. Irene Wright, "Armco Fights Drugs, Alcohol," Cincinnati Enquirer, December 5, 1986, p. A–1.

61. Kimberly Crockett, "Cheers Drown Anti-Drug Message," *Cincinnati Enquirer,* October 29, 1986, p. A–1.

62. Denis R. Zegar, "Substance Abuse in the Workplace—Issues and Answers," *Institutional Distribution* 22, (1986): 81.

63. J. Hoerr, "The Drug Wars Will Be Won with Treatment Not Tests," *Business Week*, October 13, 1986, 52.

64. Fern Schumer Chapman, "The Ruckus over Medical Testing," *Fortune* 112, no. 57 (1985): 57–63.

65. Jeff Block, "So What? Everybody's Doing It," *Forbes* 137, no. 3 (1986).

66. "To Test or Not to Test: Drugs Are an Increasing Cancer," *United States Tobacco & Candy Journal* 213 (1986): 45.

67. David J. Hanson, "Drug Abuse Testing Program Gaining Acceptance in the Workplace," *Chemical Engineering News* 64, no. 22 (1986): 8.

68. "To Test or Not to Test," p. 45.

69. "Drug-Test Fakery: Free Enterprise Rushes to Fill a Delicate Need," *U.S. News & World Report* 102, no. 11 (1987): 10.

70. Gina Kolata, "AIDS Differs in Women, Researchers Say," *Cincinnati Enquirer,* October 19, 1987, p. A–3.

71. "AIDS Risk Rises 5 Years after Infection," *Cincinnati Enquirer,* February 2, 1987, p. A–3.

72. "AIDS and 'Straits': Unsettling Questions," *U.S. News & World Report* 103, no. 7 (1987): 34.

73. "AIDS and the Innocents," *U.S. News & World Report* 100, no. 4 (1988): 49.

74. Joe Davidson, "Mandatory Testing of Certain People for AIDS Is Called by Reagan Aide," *Wall Street Journal,* May 1, 1987, p. 5.

75. "AIDS Murder Charge Is Dismissed," *Cincinnati Enquirer,* December 2, 1987, p. D–7.

76. Stephen Wermiel, "High Court Ruling on Victims of Disease Could Bolster Rights of AIDS Sufferers," *Wall Street Journal,* March 4, 1987, p. 3.

77. Roger Ricklefs, "AIDS Cases Prompt a Host of Lawsuits," *Wall Street Journal,* October 7, 1987, p. 31.

78. Rob Jaumeyer, "Local Companies Slow in Setting AIDS Policies", *Cincinnati Business Courier,* October 5–11, 1987, pp. 1, 39.

79. Robert S. Heidt, Sr., "Political Roadblocks Prevent AIDS Solution," *Cincinnati Enquirer,* February 6, 1988, p. A–7.

80. Diane Harris, "We'll All Pay," *Money* 16, no. 12 (1987): 107–134.

81. "OSHA Chief Leaves Agency in Limbo," *NFIB Mandate*, April-May, 1984, 6.

12

Ethical-Moral Considerations

ETHICS AND MORALS DEFINED

In discussing ethics and morals as it applies to individuals, business, and society, three words (ethics, morals, and ethical) will be frequently used. Therefore, a good starting point might be to give a quick dictionary definition of each word and then progress from there.

Ethics: The system or code of human conduct, with the emphasis on the determination of what is right and wrong.

Moral: Relating to, dealing with, or capable of making the distinction between right and wrong in conduct, good or right in conduct or character.

Ethical: Conforming to right principles of conduct as generally accepted by a specific profession or group, a given system of ethics, and so on.

With these three definitions in mind, the next step is to apply them to defining ethical conduct. Since so many of today's actions are based on legal concepts, this area must also be entered into the picture. First of all, legal behavior includes ethical behavior; Chief Justice Warren once said "law presupposes ethical norms and commitment."[1] Ethical conduct, however, goes beyond legality and is more comprehensive. For instance, it may be legal but it is ethical to take more time to do a job than is necessary to do the job? Or, is it ethical to call in sick when you are well and take a day of leisure? To believe that any action that is not illegal is acceptable is totally naive at the least and an invitation to complete chaos and disaster at the worst. If individuals, business, and society subscribed to this concept the only solution would be to codify all activities in which one is engaged.

If it can be agreed on that ethical behavior is legal behavior plus some other element, then it is important that this additional element be identified, if possible. At first blush, many people will probably agree that this additional element is the collection of moral principles and values of what is right and what is wrong and what is good and what is bad, as determined by group behavior or by some member of the group. At this point of definition, it appears that one's behavior is ethical if it is legal and in accordance with group norms. Based on discussions and some recent philosophies covered earlier in the book, this is what many would have everyone believe. This definition is, however, short sighted and flawed in that it does not clearly define "group" or the standards and values upon which the "group ethical norms" are based. For proper business and social conduct, these ethical standards and values must be shared by not only individuals but by the total business community and society as a whole. Without agreement by all parties involved, only legality exists to control the actions of everyone.

ETHICAL THEORIES

Ethical theories abound; however, only a few of the prominent ones will be explained here. Wherever possible these theories will also be tied in and associated with some of the theories and philosophies of the thinkers, writers, and leaders discussed in the earlier historical background section of this book.

The Judeo-Christian Ethic

The Judeo-Christian ethic is generally considered to be the foundation of Western ethical and moral standards. The Ten Commandments and the Golden Rule listed in Table 3 are firmly ingrained in this ethic as is the Protestant work ethic and faith, love, charity, fairness, and justice. The problem today, however, is that much of this basic truth has either been distorted, corrupted or applied only under certain circumstances or to the other person. It is not difficult to get most people to agree with the Ten Commandments, or at least on Commandments 5 through 10; that is, to agree with them in general or as they might apply to someone else. They will agree that no one, including themselves, should steal someone else's automobile; but, what about a pencil or pad of paper from work, making personal long-distance telephone calls on the company phone, padding the expense account, or taking home a company computer for their own use and "forgetting" to take it back—where is the cutoff point?

Studies indicate that most business managers and people believe in the Golden Rule and use it as their most important guide to ethical behavior. In simple terms it basically mandates people to treat others as they themselves would like to be treated. If you want to be told the truth then you tell the truth; if you want to be treated fairly, then treat others fairly. Since most countries and religions of the world have some form of belief that comes close to the part of the Golden Rule that relates to treating others as you want them to treat you, then in theory if properly adhered to it can personalize business relations as well as bring fairness into business. The only problems with this is that unless all parties involved also believe in and adhere to the Ten Commandments there may be marked difference in what constitutes fairness, love, charity, and justice between the parties whenever any exchange situation exists. Without a common foundation upon which to build, there are bound to be many differences and many problems.

Relativism

Ethical relativism is the view that says there are no absolutes, there are no "blacks" or "whites," things are always changing, and everything is relative. This is the philosophy expressed by Hegel, Marx, Spencer, and Dewey and to a certain extent by Bentham and Jevons in their pain-happiness and pain-pleasure concepts. This concept is very weak in many areas. There is no common standard in time or position; what is fair to one person may be unfair to another, what is fair in one situation may be considered unfair in another situation, and what might be accepted in one country might be unacceptable in another country. The final determinant of right and wrong and the worth of any belief is one's own belief and justification that supports it. It puts major emphasis on what is popular (and this is continuously changing) instead of what is necessarily right or wrong. Rather than offer a moral judgment that is binding on all people, at all times, everywhere, it is flexible and changeable in every situation.

Utilitarianism

This theory is referred to by some as the consequentialist ethical theory. It is expressed in the form that asserts that people should always act so as to produce the greatest ratio of good to evil for everyone. This has great appeal in the area of welfare economics and does not differ dramatically from the philosophies and beliefs of Keynes, Pareto, and Pigou; some might even include Marx in this category. As with Pigou, the utilitarians believe that when choosing between two actions, the one that produces the greatest net happiness should be the one chosen. Where most of them disagree with one another is in the area of how this principle should be applied. There are also several stated weaknesses in this concept. It ignores actions that appear to be wrong in themselves; it espouses the concept that the end justifies the means; the principles may come into conflict with that of justice (utilitarianism seems to associate justice with efficiency rather than fair play); and it is extremely difficult to formulate and establish satisfactory rules of application.

Egoism

Whereas utilitarianism places the emphasis on the best interest of everyone concerned, egoism emphasizes that an act is moral when it promotes the individual's best long-term interests. To a certain extent, this is what the Maslow model predicts is the epitome of everyone's dream in achieving self-actualization. It is riddled with errors and weaknesses. All of the stress is on the individual ("If it feels good, do it," "I am number one,"); it ignores blatant wrongs that exist in society; it is totally incompatible and on a collision course with the nature and the role of business and society as a whole; it cannot resolve conflicts of egoistic interest; it introduces and produces inconsistency in moral practices; and, finally, it undermines the moral point of view.

Legalistic Ethics

Legalistic ethics is based on the premise that moral rules are absolute laws that must always be obeyed. To a great extent this is the concept behind much of the social responsibility legislation discussed in the last five chapters. If people and business cannot and will not act in an ethical and moral manner on their own, then the local, state, and federal government will step in and through new laws force them to behave and act in the government's concept of what comprises an ethical and moral way.

Existentialism

Existentialism contends that no guidelines exist ("everyone is to do their own thing") and that each situation is unique and requires a new decision. The negative and dismal aspects of this philosophy have been discussed in more detail under Jean-Paul Sartre in Chapter 6.

Situational Ethics

Rather than acting like the utilitarians and producing the greatest happiness for the greatest number, the situational ethics concept advocates acting in a manner that produces the greatest amount of love, fulfillment, and benevolence. That is, it contends that moral action is the one that produces the greatest amount of Christian love of all the alternatives available. Christian love as used here refers to the Greek "agape" love; agape love is totally unselfish love, epitomized by Jesus, who made the ultimate sacrifice for all mankind. In part, this is the concept that Kenny was trying to portray in his concept of self-donation.

On the positive side, situational ethics humanizes business decisions and forces people to accept moral responsibility. In the area of weaknesses, it overemphasizes the concept of "love your fellow man, no matter what," without clearly spelling out on what basis this love should be founded. Certainly if it is true Christian "agape" love, it should be based on the Ten Commandments and all of the teachings of Jesus Christ; in most instances this is not what is done.

Kant's Categorical Imperative

Kant believed that in itself there was nothing good except a good will, and only when a person acted from duty did the person's actions have moral worth. He also believed that every rational creature has inherent worth; therefore, a rational person will always act to treat himself and other individuals as ends in himself. For example, intentionally injuring others would always be wrong because a rational person would never intentionally injure himself.

Kant's ethics add a humanistic dimension to making business decisions and implies the moral obligation to act from a respect for rights and a recognition of responsibility. They do not, however, show any clear way in which to resolve conflicts of duties, and they do not present any overwhelming reason why the prohibition against certain actions should hold without exception.

Ethical Theories Conclusions

These are only a few of the ethical concepts that exist; however, they are representative of those that do exist. All of the ethics theories presented, except the Judeo-Christian ethic, are based on humanistic philosophies and have no uniform foundations of what is right and what is wrong or what is just and what is unjust; it is all based on what one believes in one's own mind.

WHERE BUSINESS ETHICS STAND TODAY

Hardly a day goes by without picking up the newspaper and reading of someone or some business involved in fraud, price gouging, kick backs, negligence, pollution violations, or any number of other illegal or unethical practices. What is being done about this and what should be done about this by business, the government, and the academic community will be briefly examined after first looking at what the public thinks of the ethical and moral climate of the nation and its major professions.

Public Evaluation

Examination of studies conducted on how the public feels and evaluates its leaders, public officials, and leading business professions in the areas of honesty and ethical standards shows that even the best receive ratings well below what should be expected. Specific cases and examples of why the public may feel the way they do in giving these low ratings of public trust will be discussed later in this chapter.

Just how then does the public rate the status of management honesty and ethical standards? In 1981, the Gallup polling organization found that "business executives" ranked fifteenth in a field of 24 professions evaluated.[2] In a way, however, this is misleading since the public felt that 63 percent of the clergymen had very high levels of honesty and ethical standards, while only 19 percent of the business executives fell into this category. In the overall rankings, business executives and building contractors ended up in a tie; business executives were outranked by clergymen, druggists, dentists, doctors, engineers, college teachers, policemen, bankers, TV reporters and commentators, newspaper reporters, funeral directors, lawyers, stockbrokers, and senators. The only groups that ranked lower than business executives were congressmen, local political officeholders, realtors, labor union leaders, state political officeholders, insurance salesmen, advertising practitioners, and, bringing up the bottom of the list with a 6 percent vote, were car salesmen. In a recent *U.S. News*/CNN poll, 71 percent of the people polled said that they are dissatisfied with honesty and behavior today; this is almost equal to the 72 percent who were dissatisfied in 1973 at the time of the Watergate scandal; 54 percent of the people said that people are less honest today than 10 years ago.[3]

The results of these polls do not speak very highly of the honesty and ethical standards of U.S. professional people. Another study conducted in 1979, shortly before the Gallup Poll, might shed some light on why the results were so low.[4] The major group of reasons given came in one category where 34 percent of those polled said the main factors causing lower standards were society's standards are lower, there is more social decay, today's society is more permissive, materialism and hedonism have grown, there is a loss of church and home influence, and there is less quality and more quantity desires. The next highest category of responses accounted for 13 percent of the votes and included such items as competition, the pace of life, stress to succeed, existing economic conditions, the cost of doing business, and more businesses competing for less.

Although the major category of reasons listed as causes for lower ethical standards are things that the average citizen is to a great extent responsible for and can and should do something about, these are not the areas that they voted for to provide an improvement in ethical standards. The same *Harvard Business Review* study reveals that the vast majority of those participating in the study want someone else to take the primary action. Some items covered in these areas include public disclosure, media coverage, a better informed public, government regulation and intervention, federal courts, and education of business managers.

Business

Are business ethics and honesty really as bad as the survey in the preceding section indicates or is it just a carryover from the old saying that "Business and ethics don't mix?" There are many honest, moral, highly ethical businesses and businessmen; however, when stories come out about illegal payments by Lockheed to Japan for business contracts, Ford's continuing to manufacture and battle with the federal government on regulations of the Pinto after many deaths in the car, Firestone's battle and reluctance to admit a problem of defective tires, Audi blaming its car problems on the public, and the graft and corruption in the federal government and the financial world, it is no wonder that the public perceives business and those who run it as amoral at best.

Two studies conducted by *Fortune* magazine, one conducted in 1955 and another in 1980, might supply some clues to why the ethical and moral character in business is now perceived to be so low. In 1955, the *Fortune* magazine staff interviewed a sampling of 115 25-year-old men.[5] They were called the "organization men" and "company men" at that time. These men were confident, ambitious, credible young men who expected security in their jobs and opportunities to go all the way to the top. They were concerned with and participated in community affairs, and organized religion played an important role in their life in both the area of church going and ethical precepts and conduct. It gave them roots for themselves and their families and it gave them serious moral and ethical precepts to guide them in their personal and ethical choices.

In 1980, 25 years later, a second study was made in this same area with 82 men and women from all over the United States being interviewed.[6] The results were markedly different. These people were hard driving, fast moving, and career-path oriented, for which they were given the name "fast trackers." They measured their self-worth according to the achievement of their professional goals. Their jobs and career came ahead of everything else, including family and children. The traditional basis of the work ethic of working now with success coming later holds little appeal for them. They want fast success. They reject company loyalty by preferring job hopping as the best way to climb the ladder of success and fulfill their potential of "self-actualization." Few devote time to public service or show concern for social problems. They have little concern or interest in religion and consider it "too proscriptive or irrelevant to today's secular twenty-fives."[7] The major portion of those interviewed stated that they were agnostic or privately spiritual, except in the South where church participation is still active.

Government action and intervention, public concern and outcry, and stakeholder pressure are forcing business to take another look at its honest and ethical policies and attitudes. Most companies are responding to this pressure by generating internal codes of ethics. Table 1 presented a study that shows how companies are participating in such programs.

The single most important factor in improving the climate of ethical behavior in a company is the action and behavior taken by top-level management. Total support by top management cannot be overemphasized. In addition to setting examples by their behavior and conduct, they should also as a minimum:

1. Establish clear policies that encourage moral and ethical behavior. Establish minimum permissible and nonpermissible acts. Set realistic goals and objectives for employees so that they are not pressured into using unethical tactics to meet these goals and objectives.

2. Put the code of ethics in writing and make certain that all are aware of its contents. Make certain new potential employees read it prior to being hired, with the knowledge that noncompliance with the code is ground for dismissal. Make all employees read the code and sign that they have read it and will comply. This should be done at least once each year.

3. Be willing to assume responsibility for immediately disciplining wrongdoers. Inaction on the part of management will set bad examples and only encourage others to try and get away with the same or worse things. Cooperate 100 percent with all plant, local, state, and national enforcement officers in all cases where their services are required. This will not guarantee 100 percent compliance with all ethical and moral standards, but it will certainly go a long way in improving them.

4. Give serious consideration to establishing a specific organizational position where people who feel that ethical and moral practices have been violated can go to report it and have it discussed. A few companies have ombudsmen who hear such cases and act as the ears for top management. If handled properly, this could eliminate, or at least minimize, the potential for "whistle blowing."

If the study that the *Wall Street Journal* did of 220 Pittsburgh-area managers is any indication of how the managers in the rest of the country feel, then the above program is definitely needed.[8] The top five areas of values listed by these managers were self-respect, family, security, freedom, accomplishment, and happiness; the top five attributes were honesty, responsibility, capability, ambition, and independence. In this same study, a review of 202 codes of conduct found that 75 percent or more of the codes stressed relations with the U.S. government, customer-supplier relations, political contributions, conflicts of interest and honest books or records; 75 percent or more did not include references to personal character matters, product safety, environmental affairs, product quality, or civic and community affairs.

Finally, business is also trying to self-police itself and educate itself on how to be a better ethical corporate citizen. On February 4, 1988, the Business Roundtable (an association in which chief executive officers from 200 major corporations focus and act on public issues) released a landmark study of business ethics.[9] The study gathered information from 100 Roundtable companies and examined the philosophies, policies, and procedures of 10 of those companies in depth. They were Boeing, Champion International, Chemical Bank, General Mills, GTE, Hewlett-Packard, Johnson & Johnson, McDonnell Douglas, Norton, and Xerox. Among other things, the report points out that there is no conflict between ethical practices and acceptable profits. The purpose of the study is to improve ethics in corporate actions.

Government

Government action is a "mixed bag." There is, of course, Watergate. More recently there are cases of former top White House aides Michael Deaver and Lyn Nofzinger who were not only found guilty of unethical practices but were also convicted in court cases involving their lobbying activities. Senator Joseph H. Biden, Jr. (D-Delaware) recently fell from grace for plagiarizing a speech and had to drop out of the Democratic presidential race. Add to this the Iran-Contra affair, insider stock trading schemes, and other scandals and one finds a government that certainly has to improve its ethical and moral image.

The federal government is, of course, trying to portray a very positive ethical and moral image by passing and policing all of the legislation discussed in Chapters 7 through 11. The house Ethics Committee periodically takes off after one of its less important members while letting most of the big ones escape.[10] And now, Vice President Bush is pledging he will create a special White House ethics panel if he is elected president.[11]

Universities

Universities and business schools are getting on the band wagon to help corporate America resolve its ethical and moral problems through increased educational programs in this area; however, the universities are not without their own problems.

In 1982, *Fortune* published a story on "Industrial Espionage at the Harvard Business School."[12] This is a situation where six teams participate in a business case to see who can do the best job of running the business. All teams share the same main computer. Team 2 comes into control of team 6's confidential code and has access to all of team 6's information. Team 2 uses this information and passes it out to the other teams. Team 6 finds out about the breaking of the code and complains about it. Team 2 is assessed a penalty and loses the competition, but nothing further is done about it. Harvard has been criticized many times about its lax stand on teaching ethics and morals to its students. More recently, a panel convened by the National Institute of Mental Health found that Stephen Breuning, an influential psychologist at the University of Pittsburgh, "did not carry out the described research."[13] He was banned from receiving any further grants for 10 years. The School of Medicine at the University of California, San Diego, announced that a young scientist-physician had committed "extensive research fraud" in heart research; Harvard, Cornell, and other universities have had similar ethical problems.[14]

All is not bad or negative at the universities, however. Many of them are setting up courses in ethics, and corporations are rushing to schools, hiring consultants, and setting up codes of ethics. Even Harvard is getting on the bandwagon. The Harvard Business School has issued an ethical module of cases in which the 15 articles and discussions cover various areas of ethical problems.[15] Martin A. Siegel, former Kidder Peabody & Co. managing director, has made a personal gift of $20 million to Harvard, with another $10 million to be contributed by Harvard alumni, for the purpose of teaching students that "ethics pays."[16] Many universities are working and cooperating with business in establishing university campus centers for economic education. Much of the centers' activities are funded by donations from business. What these centers do is that instead of trying to find and teach each of the hundreds of thousands of elementary and secondary students the "truths" about business, the centers teach the teachers who in turn teach the students. This is basically using the same technique and method that was used by Dewey at Columbia to promote his philosophies throughout all the school systems of the world.

On the surface this sounds very encouraging; however, is it as great as it sounds? Review the first part of this chapter on the different theories on ethics and ask yourself which of these forms of ethics is being taught in the universities? Peter Drucker, for one, is concerned about this.[17] Drucker asserts that courses being offered in business ethics tend to focus on the social effects of the business decision; the courses teach the students how to justify most acts if it can be shown that good, or benefit, from it will cover a large number of people. He uses the Lockheed bribery case to speculate that a person schooled in consequential ethical theory (also called "utilitarian ethical theory" by some) could be used to justify the bribe. After all, the millions of dollars paid by a Lockheed executive to keep 25,000 people employed at Lockheed making L–1011 Lockheed passenger jets certainly justified a bribe. The ethical theory used here teaches that the end justifies the means. Drucker questions whether these courses are not teaching students "a set of ethics for those in power" that is different from "the ordinary demands of ethics which apply to them as individuals."[18]

Industry, universities, and others must be watchful of the kinds of ethics being taught to them and their employees. When they hire consultants and experts to come into the company to help them with their ethics problems, they might ask questions about where all the ethics experts came from all at once, what their credentials are for teaching ethics, and what type of ethics theory or theories they teach? If these questions are not asked and answered, possibly the article written by Oliver Williams will come true; this article discusses whether business ethics taught in the school system today might not be a modern day's "Trojan Horse."[19]

SPECIAL SITUATIONS AND PROBLEMS

The special situations presented here are not the only situations that could be presented but are representative of some of the thought process and techniques that present day businesses use in making their decisions.

Rely and Tylenol

Rely tampons, as well as other brands of tampons, were reportedly the cause of large number of cases of toxic shock syndrome, which had led to the death of numbers of people. Rely came under the brunt of the attack and it moved very quickly.

In mid-June 1980, Procter & Gamble became aware, at a meeting at the Center for Disease Control (CDC) in Atlanta, that the CDC was looking into the possible statistical link between tampons and toxic shock syndrome. At that time no specific brand of tampons had been singled out, although studies conducted in Wisconsin and Minnesota did indicate a statistical link between Rely and toxic shock syndrome.[20] Procter & Gamble began its defense of Rely and conducted tests on Rely and toxic shock syndrome during the months of July and August 1980 and into September.

After a meeting with the FDA and CDC in September 1980, and a report from the state of Utah that statistically linked Rely and toxic shock syndrome, Procter & Gamble announced its voluntary suspension and sale of Rely.[21] Under a consent agreement with the FDA, Procter & Gamble denied any violation of any federal law or product defect, agreed to buy back any unused Rely tampons, pledged their research expertise to the CDC to investigate toxic shock syndrome, and agreed to finance and direct an educational program about toxic shock syndrome.

This entire procedure from initial awareness through reaction, defense, and corrective action took approximately four months. Initial consumer reaction to the Rely tampon case showed an unfavorable attitude toward Procter & Gamble in a poll taken by Leo Shapiro and Associates right after Procter & Gamble withdrew Rely from the market; in a second survey, conducted in mid-October by the same company, after the quick action of Procter & Gamble, the customer attitude had now turned to one of admiration for Procter & Gamble.[22]

Tylenol was faced with a not too dissimilar situation when bottles of Tylenol medication showed up contaminated with cyanide poison. The manufacturer did not even try to put up a defense in this situation but ordered all Tylenol pulled from store shelves and requested all Tylenol in customer's possession be returned. They then followed this up with an investigation and found the contamination occurred after the product had been shipped. Again, this quick positive action in the removal of Tylenol from the market resulted in Johnson & Johnson receiving praise for its conduct, with eventual market recovery.

This quick, positive action by Procter & Gamble on Rely and by Johnson & Johnson on Tylenol showed ethical concern for the customer. This concern for the customer paid off in the form of respect, admiration and continued business from the customer.

Audi and Firestone

More than two years ago there were charges of sudden, unintended acceleration by the Audi 5000 sedan. Audi initially blamed the drivers for the sudden acceleration problem when the National Highway Traffic Safety Administration, in late 1986, said had resulted in reports of 513 accidents, 271 injuries, and five deaths.[23] Within two years this had grown to 1,757 complaints, 1,273 accidents, and five deaths.[24] Audi argued that drivers were unintentionally pressing the accelerator instead of the brake, and to correct the situation Audi would recall the cars and reposition the brake pedals.[25] Basically they were telling the drivers that they did not know how to drive the car rather than taking full ethical and moral responsibility for their product.

Passing the buck as Audi did totally backfired on it. In March 1986, New York's attorney general demanded the Audi 5000 be recalled; this was followed shortly thereafter by the Illinois attorney general issuing a similar demand and an airing of the problem in November 1986 by CBS's "60 Minutes."[26]

Audi sold 74,061 cars in the United States in 1985 (its best year), with a slip of 44.2 percent (to 41,332 cars) two years later, and a possible further projected slippage to 20,000 cars in 1988. It is quite possible some Audi franchises might fail.[27] In fact, about one-fourth of the 409 U.S. Audi dealers have threatened to quit unless something dramatically is done quickly.[28] In spite of all these problems with U.S. Audi sales, Audi A. G. Chairman Ferdinand Piech recently told Wards Automotive International that world sales were setting records, so that the 10 percent of total world Audi sales that occurred in the United States was a minor concern to them; to this he added, "And of course, we must teach Americans how to drive."[29]

This "fight to the death" attitude of Audi has now gone on for about four years and may actually cause the death of the Audi automobile in the United States. They certainly have an image problem that requires correcting, and even then it is a long way back.

The Firestone 500 series of steel-belted radial tires were kept on the market long after consumer groups, government agencies, and lawsuits had attacked them for selling defective tires. According to federal authorities, these tires were prone to blowouts, tread separation, and other dangerous deformities. In addition, the tires' readjustment rate of 7.4 percent was more than twice as high as that of competitive steel-belted lines. All of these associated conditions were reportedly responsible for at least 34 deaths and hundreds of accidents.[30] The battle for information and to force a recall or not to force a recall went on between Firestone and the Traffic Safety Administration for years. In the meantime, the company lost millions of dollars in sales and much customer goodwill because of the adverse publicity that was generated. Even though none of the other seven Firestone radial lines being sold at that time were found defective, many Firestone customers defected to other brands.

In both of these cases the companies were well aware of serious technical problems with their products; however, both chose to fight it out rather than give in. In both instances this lost the company millions of dollars in sales and gave them an ethical and moral "black eye" as far as customers were concerned.

Pinto and Cost-Benefit Analysis

The social response to the Ford Pinto gas tank problem was similar to that of both Audi and Firestone—fight it all the way. In 1977, the magazine *Mother Jones* released a study by Mark Dowie, general manager of *Mother Jones'* business operations, that charged Ford with putting unsafe cars (Pintos) on the road. He charged in part that for more than eight years Ford successfully lobbied with vigor, and some blatant lies, against the Federal Motor Vehicle Safety Standard 301, which would have forced a redesign of the Pinto's dangerous fire-prone gas tank. According to Dowie, conservative estimates involving Pinto crashes indicated that the crashes had caused 500 burn deaths to people who would not have been seriously injured if the car had not burst into flames.[31] Dowie went on to say: "Ford waited eight years because its internal 'cost-benefit analysis' which places dollar value on human life, said it wasn't profitable to make the changes sooner."[32]

Rather than continue on with the detailed court battle that ensued as a result of this problem and show a similar pattern and result to that of Audi and Firestone, it is more important at this point to examine the "cost-benefit analysis" part of the case. Since many companies use this concept in determining whether to build something, it is interesting to see what was involved in the Ford Pinto case in this area and then consider that when human lives are involved whether this is a legitimate ethical, moral, and justifiable approach to solving the problem.

"Cost-benefit analysis" data, released by J. C. Echold, director of automotive safety for Ford, showed that a technological gas tank improvement that would have prevented gas tanks from rupturing would cost eleven dollars per car and would not be cost effective to society. The costs and benefits were broken down in the following way:[33]

Benefit (cost to Ford without gas tank fix)

Savings:	180 burn deaths, 180 serious burn injuries, 2,100 burned vehicles
Unit Cost:	$200,00 per death, $67,000 per injury, $700 per vehicle
Total Benefit:	180 × ($200,000) + 180 × ($67,000) + 2,100 × ($700) = *$49.5 million*

Cost (cost to Ford to add gas tank fix)

Sales:	11 million cars, 1.5 million light trucks
Unit Cost:	$11 per car, $11 per truck
Total Cost:	11,000,000 × ($11) + 1,500,000 × ($11) + *$137 million*

It is obvious from these figures that Ford could make an additional $87.5 million by not installing the improved gas tank. However, if other expert data that say the serious burn injuries to burn death ratio is 10:1 rather than the 1:1 ratio used by Ford, then the $49.5 million benefit becomes $158 million and Ford will actually lose $21 million by not installing the fuel tank improvement. It was also estimated that a rubber bladder could be placed inside the gas tank at a cost of only $5.08 to provide safety similar to the $11 gas tank improvement. Ford Pinto customers were not given an option on the Pinto to install either one of these "fixes," even at extra cost to the customer. In the meantime hundreds of people were burned to death or seriously burned.

What are the ethical and moral obligations here on the part of Ford, or any other company, to build a product as safe as possible to prevent the possibility of death and injury? In this case, Ford still would have made a profit with the new improved tank installed but possibly not quite as large a profit, if their cost-benefit analysis data are used. How much is a person's life worth or how much is a whole body, rather than a burned or maimed body, worth? Which ethical theory did Ford use in arriving at their decision?

Cost-benefit analysis is certainly a valid procedure to use in determining whether to make an item, purchase this or that piece of equipment, or how well to build a piece of equipment, as long as it does not involve human life. When it involves known life-and-death situations with people, it should not be considered as a valid decision making technique.

Takeovers and Green Mail

The current high rate of corporate takeovers has dominated much of the recent financial news. There are huge sums of money being bargained away and the lives and careers of many company managers are being altered by these takeovers. In some instances stockholders have benefited and in other cases they have been hurt.

The reduced value of the dollar, a drop in stock prices, and relatively low interest rates have continued to fuel takeovers. Takeovers in 1985 amounted to over $180 billion; the total of friendly and unfriendly takeovers announced by early March 1988 was in excess of 230 takeovers, worth $73 billion. If the pace keeps up it is estimated that the number of deals announced will reach $439 billion during 1988.[34]

The attempted acquisition of a company can take the form of a friendly or an unfriendly takeover. The takeover attempt can be successful or unsuccessful. The attractiveness of a company as a takeover target lies in the company having a high cash flow, an underevaluation of its stock assets, an excess of capital assets and pension fund assets, and being relatively free of debt.

Major Arguments for Company Takeovers

Some of the major reasons in favor of company takeovers are:

1. The most important influence on the terms of a corporate merger or takeover is a business consideration that will permit synergy to occur by the combination of the firms. By the combination, the profits can be greater than could be achieved by each one individually.

2. The combination may enable a firm that lacks general and technological management to obtain it from the other company.

3. Managerial benefits also may be produced by managers seeking to reduce cyclical risks through business diversification.

4. A firm may want to diversify into a new product or new market and starting from scratch may be prohibitive due to the start up costs.

5. From a corporate investment standpoint, the company performing the takeover may provide the best use of its own capital by being able to obtain a rate of return greater than its cost of capital.

A number of economists and investment executives feel that the current takeover wave is a healthy redistribution of assets that corporate managers have failed to deploy to their shareholders' benefit. The raiders identify inefficiencies, call management to account, and precipitate takeovers that return to shareholders the full value of their share. The outcome: reallocation of underused resources and a more efficient, stronger economy. It has been said that assets that change hands usually move into stronger ones.

Major Arguments against Company Takeovers

Takeovers are opposed by many. Some of the major reasons they give against takeovers include:

1. The corporation may at times have a low stock price because of general market conditions or a downturn in the particular industry in which it resides.
2. New capital is not created through corporate takeovers. Capital is merely being transferred from one owner to another. In the case when a corporation decides to build new plants and equipment, new capital is created and investment takes place that affects the country's gross national product in a positive manner.
3. The life of the company may be drastically altered. The takeover may put a heavy financial burden on the company, thereby reducing potential growth and possibly compromising the jobs and careers of employees. Also, by diverting management from their duties in running the company, the corporation may seriously compromise its market share.

There are numerous people who question the moral and ethical behavior of the raider. The motivation in some instances may be no more than greed. The resulting distress to the company, management, and employees may not be considered by the raider; his actions may be dictated by how much money he can take away. His argument is that it was the lack of efficiency of management that has caused the problem. While this may at times be the case, the issue is by no means clear-cut.

Unsuccessful Takeovers

Unsuccessful takeovers quite often hurt both the company and its stockholders, while making the person, group, or company attempting the takeover quite wealthy. This harm to the company and stockholders usually occurs as the result of the company acquiring more debt or siphoning off profits in order to repulse an outside raider. The debt might be taken on by the company in an attempt to make the company a less desirable takeover candidate, or the debt might be acquired by the company in order to pay off the raider in the form of "green mail." Green mail is defined as the purchase of a raider's stock for a premium price in order to end a takeover threat.

Many companies are frustrated with paying green mail, stockholders are furious, and a few raiders are becoming wealthy. Gillette paid $558 million to Ronald O. Perelman, chief executive officer of Revlon, Inc., in green mail to prevent Gillette's takeover; the Revlon group made a profit of $39 million on the exchange and Gillette's stock prices fell almost $11 the day following the green mail deal.[35] Other such green mail payments by Texaco, Goodyear Tire and Rubber, and Safeway netted raiders similar or larger net profits from their raiding activities.[36]

Green mail hurts companies and stockholders in that it usually increases company debt and possibly drives down its stock value because of this increased debt. In a few instances, however, the attempted takeovers have actually increased the value of company stock as new stockholders have realized the true value of the stock. Many stockholders and companies still want legislation to control green mail; although there is a lot of "noise" in Congress about doing something, it appears that nothing will be done in the near future.[37]

Even though most people feel that green mail is not a truly ethical practice when it is undertaken strictly to make a large profit for a few (the raiders) at the expense of many (the company, its employees, and its stockholders), there are those that support it on the basis that if the acquisition had been successful, the stockholders would also have reaped huge profits in the sale of their higher priced stocks.

Friendly Takeovers

Friendly takeovers primarily take the form of leveraged buyouts, buy-backs, and divestitures.

A leveraged buyout is an action by management or an independent to take the company private. The process involves leverage or heavy debt used to buy back the shares. The company arranges to borrow against company assets and cash flow to fund the purchase.

Buy-backs may or may not actually result in a shift of company ownership. The technique does, however, help the existing management retain control of the company and keep it out of the hands of raiders. High cash flow and low stock prices, which make a company attractive to a raider, also can be used to strengthen management control of the company. High cash flows and accumulated cash can be used to repurchase stock. The buy-back will support or increase the stocks' price by reducing the amount of stock outstanding and increasing earnings per share of the remaining reduced number of outstanding shares of stocks. It will also use up excess loose cash. All of these things tend to discourage potential raiders.

Spin-off and divestiture of different lines of business or divisions is another technique that allows companies to eliminate weak, low profit, or undesirable parts of the company. In the current economic situation, there has been a tendency for companies to go back to their basic business in which they have expertise in managing and growing. The popular approach of the 1970s of adding on businesses is taking a turn to getting back to the basics.

Unfriendly Takeovers

Unfriendly takeovers begin by a raider purchasing a significant amount of stock of the company to be taken over. The objective is to gain controlling interest in the target company. If the raider has only a relatively small amount of money, financing becomes the most important consideration. The raiders obtain their financing to purchase the target company's shares from large investment banking firms.

In order for the raider to determine what he can offer for the target company, he must do some calculations and raise the money. The procedure might go something like this: The target company's cash flow is $9 million per year. With this amount of cash flow the bank will loan a multiple of nine, or $90 million. After takeover, the raider can then liquidate the target company's excess assets in the pension plan, sell off unwanted plants and real estate, and cash in any CDs that show on the balance sheet; this may be worth another $30 million. If the raider puts in an additional $5 million of his own money in equity he can then put in a bid for $125 million.

Once an estimate is generated on what can be paid for the target company, a new company is created on paper. The investment banker then creates a package of junk bonds to be issued by the paper company once it gains control of the target company through a tender offer to the stockholders. The investment banker has investor contacts who wish to purchase the bonds; the banker gets their commitment to buy the bonds. Once the raider is in control of the target company, he can raise the cash by selling off parts of the company and through future profits.

It is through this network and the private market that seemingly small raiders pose a threat even to some of the largest corporations. The corporations, however, have not taken this all laying down and have taken a number of actions to block takeover attempts. Some of these antitakeover strategies are shown in Table 12.

Although all of the antitakeover measures have "pet names" they are all loosely considered to be "poison pills" and are referred to as such. A study conducted by the Securities and Exchange Commission has stated: "Overall, the evidence presented here is consistent with the view that poison pills are not in the best interest of shareholders."[38] Some large institutional pension funds apparently agree with this report because in the spring of 1987 four of them waged proxy fights at more than 30 shareholders' meetings in attempts to overturn antitakeover measures.[39] They are making it a shareholders rights issue. In the past, such pension fund referendum proposals were lucky to get 5 percent of the vote; in recent votes, however, many of the voting levels in favor of referendums ran in the 20 and 30 percent range, with some even hitting the 40 percent range.[40] Not all institutional investors agree with this approach or believe it is their responsibility to challenge management. They feel that their job is to manage money and not management.

This is an area where there is no simple legal solution, while at the same time it is an area fraught with ethical and moral concerns. Should the stockholders be protected from green mail? Should buyers be permitted to take over companies and then fire large numbers of employees? Should stockholders be permitted to take their chances in reaping huge benefits if a takeover attempt is successful while at the same time possibly suffering a reduction in stock value if the takeover attempt fails and green mail is paid? Should the small shareholder be protected from rapidly falling stock prices

Table 12

Actions Taken by Management to Block Takeover Attempts

Strategy Name	Strategy Description
Crown Jewel	A takeover target company often sells its most prized subsidary in order to discourage the raider.
Golden Parachute	This is a guarantee of a hefty payment to top executives who lose out in the takeover attempt. Such agreements, which are now a standard part of many top-level employment contracts, ensure corporate officers that they will be paid off if the company that buys their firm fires them or reduces their power.
Tin Parachute	This is a guarantee of substantial payments to the rank and file employees who might lose out in a company takeover.
Green Mail	Money is paid by the takeover target company to the corporate raider in an attempt to make the potential acquirer go away.
Pac-Man	A maneuver in which the takeover target firm "bites" back at the raider by turning the tables and trying to take it over.
Poison Pill	A new issue of prefered stock that gives the holders the right to redeem it at an enormous premium after a takeover. It raises the cost to the acquiring company and is meant to discourage them.
Porcupine Provisions or Shark Repellent	Corporate by-laws that are defensive measures meant to put obstacles in the way of an acquiring company.
Scorched-earth Policy	A means by which a company tries to turn itself into an undesirable acquisition and therefore appear unattractive to any buyer.
Staggered Boards	A shark repellent in which company by-laws permit staggered election of the board of directors so only a portion of the directors are elected each year.
Supermajority	Requires a supermajority of stockholders' approval for a takeover. The corporation determines what constitutes a supermajority which can be as high as 90 to 99%.
White Knight	A company that will block an unfriendly merger, often at the suggestion of the target company, by taking it over on more favorable terms.

if the takeover attempt fails, because professional traders and well-informed arbitragers who initially bid the price up will sell quickly and the stock price may drop dramatically? Should company employees be protected from layoffs when companies restructure in an attempt to ward off a takeover? These are but a few of the moral and ethical questions generated in this entire area.

SCENARIO

You and your boss, John, are working late one night. After work is completed John suggests that the two of you stop off for a bite to eat. You prefer to get home to your wife and children but you know John would be upset if you did this, so you reluctantly agree to get a quick bite to eat with him.

John orders food and an alcoholic beverage; you just order food since you do not drink. As time wears on John orders several more drinks for himself. Finally you suggest that you leave for home and that you will drive since you did not drink anything. This enrages John, and even though he is way too drunk to drive he insists upon doing the driving anyway. John is known for his fierce temper and you know that if you do not let him drive he may get angry with you and fire you on the spot.

You now have several moral and ethical problems to face. Do you let John drive and possibly let him involve you and someone else in a serious or fatal accident because of his drunken state? Do you insist on driving to safeguard him, yourself, and other innocent people from a possible serious accident, and risk losing your job? Do you call a cab or your wife to come pick you up and let John drive home alone and risk a serious or fatal accident, even though if he makes it safely home he may fire you for your decision? What other options do you have and what would you do? Which ethics theory did you use to arrive at your answer?

NOTES

1. S. L. Saki, "Implications for Decision Making," in C. Van Dam and L. M. Stallaent, eds., *Trends in Business Ethics* (Boston: Nijhoff Social Sciences, 1978).

2. George Gallup, "Poll Gives Clergy High Ethics Rating," *Norman (Oklahoma) Transcript,* September 19, 1981, p. 8.

3. "A Nation of Liars?" *U.S. News & World Report* 102, no. 7 (1987): 54–59.

4. Stephen N. Brenner and Earl A. Molander, "Is the Ethics of Business Changing?" *Harvard Business Review* 55, no. 1. (1977):

5. Daniel Seligman, "The Confident Twenty-five Year Olds," *Fortune* 67, no. 2 (1955): 100–102.

6. Gwen Kinkead, "On a Fast Track to the Good Life," *Fortune* 101, no. 7 (1980): 74–84.

7. Ibid., p. 84.

8. Rick Wartzman, "Nature or Nurture? Study Blames Ethical Lapses on Corporate Goals," *Wall Street Journal,* October 9, 1987, p. 21.

9. *Corporate Ethics: A Prime Business Asset* (New York: The Business Roundtable, February 1988).

10. Brooks Jackson and John E. Yong, "House Ethics Committee Suddenly Gets Tough to Quell Criticism of Leniency with Violators," *Wall Street Journal,* December 2, 1987, p. 58.

11. "Bush Calls for Panel on Ethics," *Cincinnati Enquirer,* March 11, 1988, p. A–8.

12. Thomas Moore, "Industrial Espionage at the Harvard Business School," *Fortune* 106, no. 5 (1982): 70.

13. Daniel Greenberg, "Publish or Perish—Or Fake It," *U.S. News & World Report* 102, no. 22 (1987): 72.

14. Ibid.

15. Kenneth E. Goodpaster, "Ethics in Management," *Harvard Business School Course Module* (Boston: Harvard Business School, 1984).

16. "Harvard's $30 Million Windfall for Ethics 101," *Business Week,* April 13, 1987, 40.

17. Peter F. Drucker, "What is Business Ethics?" *The Public Interest* 138, no. 63 (1981); a similar article was published in *Forbes* 128, no. 6 (1981).

18. Drucker, "What is Business Ethics?" p. 22.

19. Oliver F. Williams, "Business Ethics: A Trojan Horse?" *California Management Review* 24, no. 4 (1982): 14–24.

20. Richard Severo, "Rely Tampon Recalled by Maker: Linked to Toxic Shock Syndrome," *New York Times,* September 23, 1980, p. 1.

21. Dean Rotbart and John A. Prestbo, "Killing a Product," *Wall Street Journal,* November 3, 1980, p. 21.

22. Ibid.

23. Douglas R. Sease, "Audi Problems with Sudden Acceleration May Not be Over, Despite Recent Recall," *Wall Street Journal,* January 20, 1987, p. 31.

24. James R. Healy, "Audi Drives to Polish Its Image," *USA Today*, March 23, 1988, p. B–2.

25. Sease, "Audi Problems," p. 31.

26. Healy, "Audi Drives," p. B–2.

27. Ibid., p. B–1.

28. Ibid., p. B–2.

29. Ibid.

30. Arthur M. Louis, "Lessons from the Firestone Fracas," *Fortune* 98, no. 4 (1978): 45.

31. Mark Dowie, "Pinto Madness" *Mother Jones* 12, no. 8. (1977): 18–32.

32. Ibid., p. 20.

33. W. Michael Hoffman, "Case Study–The Ford Pinto," in *Case Studies in Business Ethics*, ed. Thomas Donaldson (Englewood Cliffs, N.J.: Prentice-Hall, 1984), pp. 151, 152.

34. Daniel Kadlec, "Merger Wave Might Drown Our Economy," *USA Today,* March 10, 1988, p. B–1.

35. "A Flurry of Green Mail Has Stockholders Cursing," *Business Week,* December 8, 1986, 32–34; "What to Do About Green Mail," *U.S. News & World Report,* December 15, 1986, 55.

36. "What to Do about Green Mail," p. 55.

37. Linda Sandler, "Green Mail Infuriating Many Stockholders, but Fighting It Still Offers Little Satisfaction," *Wall Street Journal,* December 11, 1986, p. 63.

38. Gregg Fields, "Poison Pills May be Costly to Shareholders," *Cincinnati Enquirer,* November 11, 1986, p. B–6.

39. Mike Boyer, "Shareholders Stand Up: Pension Funds Battle Antitakeover Provisions," *Cincinnati Enquirer,* June 21, 1987, p. D–1.

40. Ibid.

13

Philanthropy

The dictionary defines philanthropy as the disposition or effort to promote the happiness or social elevation of mankind, by acts or charity, making donations, and so on; love or benevolence toward mankind in general. Ireland and Johnson define corporate philanthropy as a transfer of a charitable nature of corporate resources to recipients at below marked prices.[1]

Various forms of philanthropy and charity have existed since the early days of mankind. It started taking its most visible forms as we know it today back in the 1910s and 1920s with the success of the YMCA, Community Chest, welfare federations, hospitals, colleges, and universities; these groups all provide the foundation and format for today's charitable giving.

CONFLICTING VIEWS ON PHILANTHROPY

As in most other subject areas, there are also conflicting viewpoints about charitable giving by business concerns. The book's two opening quotations are representative of the two sides of the issue. Chapter 2 also points out several different conflicting viewpoints on philanthropy.

John D. Rockefeller III, a well-known philanthropist, presents another argument in favor of philanthropy. He feels that philanthropy is necessary in order to support the nonprofit sector of the market; this includes such groups and organizations as churches, museums, libraries, hospitals, private colleges and universities, the Salvation Army, the Red Cross, and other private health and welfare groups; it offers these institutions the freedom and independence they need to operate properly and efficiently.[2]

American Express, IBM, and other companies are also using charitable giving as a marketing tool so that both the charity and the company come out ahead. For example, at the end of 1983, American Express launched its first nationwide "cause-related" marketing program and ran it for three months. Every time an American Express card was used during this three-month period a penny was donated to the restoration of the Statue of Liberty. The program raised $1.7 million. American Express has run similar programs on a regional area basis in over 50 areas and donated over $4.5 million to charitable causes.[3] IBM and Apple Computer are donating computers to colleges and selling them to students at extremely low prices in order to establish a user base among these people.[4] Chapter 10 covers several other areas in which corporate charitable giving is discussed.

Most of the negative positions held on philanthropic giving hinge on the concept so eloquently voiced by Friedman in the opening quotation of Chapter 1. Unless the company is making money for the stockholders the company is not doing the correct thing. Evelyn Davis, a frequent presenter of resolutions to limit charitable contributions, once remarked to the Great Atlantic & Pacific Tea Co. Chairman Melvin W. Alldredge, "Don't make any charitable contributions, Mel. Give us higher cash dividends so we can make more charitable contributions to whoever we want."[5]

Proving to the satisfaction of the stockholders that various philanthropic endeavors participated in by companies result in a profit favorable position for the company is what generates much of the pro and con arguments in this area. Over the years, numerous studies have been conducted in an attempt to determine if charitable giving, properly handled, improves company profits and increases stock prices and dividends, or if it just appears to do so. Depending on which study is reviewed and examined, what time period is taken, and all the many other variables taken into consideration, the results are sometimes conflicting, confusing, and difficult to prove valid or invalid. Each company and its individual shareholders must determine how deeply and in what type of philanthropy the company should become involved. If the company is to be a good corporate citizen in today's world of expanded social responsibility it most certainly must have some positive involvement in this area.

RECENT AND PRESENT STATUS OF PHILANTHROPY

From 1935 up to 1982, companies were permitted by federal tax law to allocate up to 5 percent of taxable income to philanthropic causes. Numerous companies, in Louisville, Minneapolis, and Baltimore did give 5 percent, with Dayton-Hudson probably being the most outspoken enthusiast of this concept.[6] Under changes in the 1982 tax code, the amount was increased from 5 percent to 10 percent. In 1982, while corporate profits decreased by 23 percent, corporate donations rose 13 percent; and in 1983 corporate philanthropy rose another 7 percent.[7] In 1982, donations amounted to an estimated 1.1 percent of pretax income for the largest industrial companies and 1.7 percent for firms in the $25 million to $49 million sales range.[8] According to a United Way of America report, philanthropic giving was supposed to increase from $48.2 billion in 1980 to $90.4 billion in 1988[9]; in 1986 donations were already at $87.22 billion dollars.[10] In spite of these hefty donations, only 9.1 percent of all U.S. companies give more than 2 percent of their net income to charity.[11] Additionally, of all the taxpaying businesses in the United States, only 6 percent give more than $500 to charity a year.[12]

These figures do not, however present the entire picture. Corporate donations are only the direct donations that can be accounted for; however, financial donations from company executives and employees, or executives' and employees' time, or use of company facilities, are difficult to calculate and are not included in any of these numbers. To help coordinate all of this and to understand better what is going on, overall corporate philanthropy is now being directed and more closely linked to overall corporate objectives.[13]

THE DIRECTION IN WHICH PHILANTHROPY IS HEADED

Now that the debate on whether business should give money away and support philanthropic causes has been discussed, here and in Chapter 2, and what the present status of philanthropy is, it is not unreasonable to ask where philanthropy is headed.

The evidence that now exists shows that corporate philanthropy is here to stay; however, it is being more carefully considered. In many instances corporate contributions are now viewed not as a charity but as a corporate investment in society made on behalf of corporate shareholders.[14]

Should corporate philanthropy become more professional? Joseph James believes that corporate philanthropy should become more professional and selective through objectively assessing priorities, better understanding the multitude of issues and groups competing for the limited funds, and developing more systematic procedures for program planning and decision making.[15] Due to the large number of soliciting agencies, some corporations have started to become more selective about the agencies they support; they also tend to expect more from the agencies they support and require from them: (1) more earned income, (2) better management, (3) cooperation among groups, and (4) consistent quality.[16]

CHARITABLE CONTRIBUTION RECIPIENTS

Where does charitable money come from and to whom does it go? Using 1985 data, Americans gave about $80 billion to charities; this was an increase of almost 82 percent from 1980 contributions.[17] The breakdown or giving shows 84 percent comes from individuals, 6 percent from bequests, and 5 percent each from foundations and corporations; on the receiving side, 48 percent goes to religion, 14 percent each to health and education, 11 percent to social services, 6 percent to the arts and humanities, 2 percent to civic and public programs, and the remaining 5 percent to other charities.[18]

An examination of the above data shows that better than four out of every five dollars of charitable giving comes from individuals. With continued federal cuts proposed through 1989 there is considerable concern among charities about where the additional funds will come from to make up the deficit.

President Reagan's Task Force on Private Sector Initiatives (possibly better known as the Verity Commission for its chairman, C. William Verity, Jr.), at a quarterly meeting in February 1982, recommended that by 1986 every company in the United States, large or small, give 2 percent of its net profit to "nonprofit organizations engaged in public service."[19] Needless to say, this did not happen, although many additional companies did increase their giving to this level. Since in 1958 only 5 percent or $4 billion, in donations came from corporations, it is impossible to imagine how corporate giving will make up for the estimated loss of $70 billion cut from both government-run and private nonprofit services.[20] The answer from the Reagan administration is basically, "cut bureaucratic fat."[21] It appears from the data given above that, if the deficit is made up, that it will come mostly from a "cut in bureaucratic fat" and an increase in monetary and free time contributions from individuals, and not from corporations or foundations.

FOUNDATIONS

Prior to 1938, there were only 19 corporate-based foundations. During World War II and the Korean War, when excess profit taxes were in effect and corporate tax rates were raised to as high as 82 percent, foundations grew rapidly and by 1965 there were nearly 1,500 corporate-based foundations.[22] In 1987 there were 25,639 grant-making foundations.[23]

The main purpose of corporate foundations was not to dodge taxes but to give them greater flexibility in the timing of gifts. The structure of foundations is such that in years when business is good, the corporate foundation can take in extra payments, while in years when business is lean, the corporate foundation can continue to disburse the same amount of money to the needy social demands.

Requests for grants are large but the number awarded is few. The Ford Foundation gets 2,000 grant requests per week but only makes 1,500 grants a year; this is a ratio of 1 grant awarded for every 16 submitted. Carnegie Corporation finances 1 out of every 25 grant requests.[24]

Both foundation assets and money put out for grants has continued to increase. Between 1976 and 1986 assets grew from $30.1 billion to $103.1 billion, while grants awarded grew from $1.9 billion to $6 billion during the same time frame.

Different foundations grant their money in different areas. The Ford Foundation confines its grants to areas of poverty, human rights and social justice, public policy, education and culture, population, and international affairs.[25] The Lilly Endowments, Inc., focus primarily on education and religious studies.[26] Carnegie Corporation founded 2,508 libraries and continues to fund educational programs, children's programs (they conceived, financed, and gave birth to Sesame Street), avoiding nuclear war, and strengthening human resources in developing countries.[27]

WHAT TO LOOK FOR IN CHARITABLE GIVING

One way of examining how well the charitable institutions are doing is to look at what percentage of their total budget is spent on fund raising and other expenses and what percentage is spent for actual services. Some charities, such as the American Red Cross, spend as much as 86 percent of their funds for services, while others spend less than 45 percent of their funds on service, with the larger percentage of the funds being spent on fund raising, fund management, and other activities. The National Charities Information Bureau rating service like to see at least 60 percent of revenue go directly to the program and no more than 30 percent into fund raising.[28]

HOW TO CHOOSE THE MONEY RECIPIENT

As soon as there is any indication that you either have money to give away or you are considering giving money away, there will be thousands of "worthy causes" at your door asking for it. You must then answer a number of questions, such as: (1) do you really want to give any money away and if so how much, (2) to what types of charities do you want to award the money and how do you determine how much to give and which ones to support, and (3) after deciding on a charity to support, what type of control and feedback are you going to require?

One procedure, used by the Dayton-Hudson Corporation, is outlined in Chapter 10. Another procedure, presented by Morris and Biederman in the *Harvard Business Review,* recommends that the following steps be taken in managing corporate contributions:

1. Align your gifts with your products and goals.
2. Put some distance between your corporate contributions effort and the CEO.
3. Choose the right organizational structure for your needs.
4. Pick a manager to give company money away.
5. Treat grant seekers like customers.
6. Set long-term budgets for contributions.
7. Expect to prepare for opposition.[29]

Once the above steps have been taken, then the Dayton-Hudson Corporation procedure can be followed to determine to whom the money should be given or the six rules given by Morris and Biederman can be followed. These six rules are:

1. Don't run your contributions program as a public relations experience.
2. Don't automatically renew grants to programs.
3. Don't get too involved in your grantees' day-to-day operations once you have written their checks.
4. Don't try to please everyone.
5. Take a chance on an unconventional cause.
6. Don't work in isolation.[30]

SCENARIO

Anderson Industries, Incorporated, has contributed 5 percent of its net earnings to charitable causes every year since it was first permitted to do so in 1935. This past year has been an excellent year, and net earnings are higher than ever before; in fact, net earnings are at $100 million, which is at twice the level of last year. At the 5 percent level of giving, this means that they have $5 million to allocate this year versus the $2.5 million they had available last year.

You are director of the group that is responsible for determining and presenting management policy on charitable contributions. Next week you have to appear before a committee of the board of directors and make a recommendation on how to distribute the company's charitable funds for the year. What would you recommend? Should you distribute the entire $5 million? Should you double all contributions to last year's charities or should you add some new ones? Should you reduce your 5 percent level of giving? What other options do you have? How will the committee of the board of directors, the stockholders, your in-house managers who want more money for expansion, Mr. Anderson, and your competitors respond to your recommendations? Is this the best recommendation for Anderson Industries and society as a whole?

NOTES

1. T. Ireland and D. Johnson, *The Economics of Charity* (Blacksburg, Va.: Center for Study of Public Choice, 1970).

2. John D. Rockefeller III, "In Defense of Philanthropy," *Business and Society Review,* Spring 1978, 26–29.

3. Philip Maher, "What Corporations Get by Giving," *Business Marketing* 69, no. 12 (1984): 80–89.

4. Ibid., p. 86.

5. Norman Kurt Barnes, "Rethinking Corporate Charity," *Fortune,* October 1974, 169.

6. Thomas Murray, "Corporate Philanthropy: What to Expect," *Dun's Business Month* 120, no. 1 (1982): 55–57.

7. Maher, "What Corporations Get by Giving," pp. 80–89.

8. Roberta Reyves, "Gift Horses and Hobbyhorses: The Pros and Cons of Corporate Charity," *Barron's,* March 28, 1983, pp. 38–40.

9. Stephen Delfin, "Philanthropy: Beyond Good Intentions," *Public Relations Journal* 41, no. 9 (1985): 7–10.

10. Janice C. Simpson, "Charitable Donations Surged to Record $87.22 Billion in 1986, Survey Shows," *Wall Street Journal,* May 12, 1987, p. 32.

11. Delfin, "Philanthropy," pp. 7–10.

12. Louis Williams, "Who's Serious about Corporate Responsibility? (Or 187 Ways to Amuse a Bored Cat)," *Journal of Communications Management* 11, no. 4 (1982): 3–6.

13. Martin A. Paley, "The Uses of Philanthropy," *Cornell Executive* 9, no. 3 (1983): 42–44.

14. Hayden Smith, "Corporate Philanthropy Poised for Takeoff," *Fund Raising Management* 14, no. 5 (1983): 18–24; Baine P. Kerr, "Responsible Corporate Giving from the Donors Viewpoint," *Fund Raising Management* 14, no. 7 (1983): 62–65.

15. James A. Joseph, "Directing the Flow of Corporate Largesse," *Business and Society Review* 42, no. 2 (1982): 40–42.

16. Marian Stein, " 'Shape Up' or Lose Corporate Backing," *Fund Raising Management* 14, no. 2 (1983): 46–77.

17. "Taxing Time for America's Charities," *U.S. News & World Report* 101, no. 25 (1988): 56–57.

18. Ibid., p. 56.

19. Marvin N. Olasky, "Reagan's Second Thoughts on Corporate Giving," *Fortune* 106, no. 6 (1982): 130–134.

20. " 'Tis the Season for Charity to Worry," *Business Week,* December 1, 1986, 70.

21. Ibid.

22. Norman Kurt Barnes, "Rethinking Corporate Charity," *Fortune* 90, no. 4 (1974): 169–182.

23. Pat Ordovensky and Wendell Cochran, "The Good Far Outweighs the Problems," *USA Today,* December 15, 1987, p. A–1.

24. Ibid.

25. Pat Ordovensky, "Ford Foundation Has Its Own Ideas," *USA Today,* December 16, 1987, p. B–4.

26. Wendell Cochran, "Lilly Drug Cash Cures Home City," *USA Today,* December 16, 1987, p. B–4.

27. Pat Ordovensky, "Carnegie Not Afraid of Risk," *USA Today,* December 16, 1987, p. B–4.

28. " 'Feeling Charitable? Find Out Where the Money Goes," *Business Week,* November 17, 1986, 212–213.

29. Richard I. Morris and Daniel A. Biederman, "How to Give Away Money Intelligently," *Harvard Business Review* 63, no. 6 (1985): 151–157.

30. Ibid., p. 158.

PART IV

Social Responsibility Audit and the Future of Social Responsibility

14

The Social Responsibility Audit

For many years there have been "financial audits" performed by most companies. In recent years there has been more pressure placed on business management to perform what has become known as the "social audit." The mere fact that a company should conduct a social audit carries with it the implication that business does have an obligation to society. This book has tried to describe some of the areas in which business does have an obligation and commitment to society. In many instances, federal legislation dictates what the minimum obligation of business is: however, how a company determines how well they are meeting these obligations is to a great extent the responsibility of the company itself. This can be accomplished through a social audit. Keith Davis and Robert Blomstrom define the social audit in this manner: "A social audit is a systematic study and evaluation of an organization's social performance, as distinguished from its economic performance. It is concerned with possible influences on the social quality of life instead of the economic quality of life. The social audit leads to social performance."[1]

SOCIAL AUDIT HISTORY

External expression of the concept of social audit appeared as early as 1940 with Theodore J. Kreps' presentation of a monograph on the "Measurement of the Social Performance of Business."[2] Kreps' monograph, however, measured what today would be classed primarily as economic factors: employment, production, payroll, and dividends and interest.

Many consider the true founder of the present day social audit as Howard R. Bowen. In his book, *Social Responsibilities of the Businessman,* he proposed the social audit of a company be conducted every five years by a high level independent group of disinterested auditors. The auditor's report would evaluate the company and make recommendations. Although it covered many of the same areas as Kreps' earlier works, it also included a number of socially oriented activities.[3]

With the passage of all the social legislation in the 1960s, the 1970s, and into the 1980s, today's social audit attempts to focus on such social responsibility areas as pollution-environment, community relations, employee relations, corporation philanthropy, consumer issues, minority employment, and ethical-moral standards.

Most audits have been internal to the company, with some companies issuing external reports on how well the company is doing in this area. A number of firms include a section in their annual report devoted exclusively to social responsibility activities. Some firms publish a separate detailed periodic or annual report on their social responsiveness. Some of the firms fitting into this last category include General Motors, Bank of America, Atlantic-Richfield, Control Data, and Aetna Life and Casualty Company. Although reporting in this area has been slow in growing in the United States, it has been doing quite well in Europe, especially in Germany where many of the reports not only include positive effects of corporate activity but negative ones as well. In the United States, Atlantic-Richfield is one company that uses this same positive-negative effects format in their special report on social responsibility areas.

SOCIAL AUDIT PURPOSE

A well-managed company of today will make every effort to meet its obligations to society. To help them with this, some companies have written objectives and policies in this area. In spite of this, social objectives and goals exist in an area that is not always easy to assess and objectively appraise. Just because it is not easy is no excuse for not trying to do something constructive about it. To gain some semblance of control in this area and to make certain that social objectives are actually being met, more companies have started using a social audit to measure, monitor, and evaluate the contributions that the company is making to society.

Referring again to the Keith Davis and Robert Blomstrom article, they have listed several positive purposes and benefits to be obtained from a social audit:

1. It gives management the information it needs to evaluate the effectiveness of programs related to affirmative action, ecology, community development, and the like.

2. Since managers tend to direct attention to those activities for which reports and evaluations are required, the existence of a social audit tends to promote active concern for meeting social performance goals.

3. It provides information that enables management to compare the relative effectiveness of different social programs.

4. It enables management to provide information to external groups that make demands on the firm for social performance.[4]

As helpful as an information and social responsibility status report might be to both the company and the stockholders, care must be taken in generating this data and the resulting report. The company must determine the best medium for disclosing the information to the public. The disclosure medium, whether a specific section of an annual report or a separate document, must be devoted to social responsibility activities in order to show in a meaningful and effective manner the interrelationship of company resources and company commitments. A well-presented report system will reinforce the corporate social conscience and demonstrate the balance between the corporate objective of profitability and the company's obligation to society. According to an Ernst & Whinney survey, developing a good social reporting system is an evolutionary process which goes through stages: (1) establishing a foundation, (2) improving reporting quality, and (3) refining the system.[5]

THE SOCIAL AUDIT

The social audit is a systematic attempt to assess and evaluate the performance of the company in the area of social responsibility. The basic steps taken in performing a social audit are monitoring, measuring, and appraising all aspects of the company's social responsibility performance. This social audit can be performed by company personnel or by outside auditors.

Table 2 is a social audit form for performing a macrosocial audit on the company of concern. As a first level evaluation of how a company is doing in the areas of legal compliance, ethical-moral compliance, and philanthropic giving, Table 2 defines strengths and weaknesses for which an evaluation scale from seven to one can be used. The scale value of seven will mean outstanding and will be next to the "strengths" listing of planning, organizing, directing, and controlling; this scale will be followed from left to right in descending value, by six (excellent), five (above average), four (good or average), three (fair), two (poor), and one (does not exist), which will be adjacent to the "weaknesses" column. If desired, Table 2 can also be reassembled into three separate tables: one for legal compliance, one for ethical-moral compliance, and one for philanthropic compliance. If the 7-to-1 scale is also inserted into these three new tables, the areas can be separately evaluated; if the evaluation (7-to-1 scale) rating marks on any of the tables are connected with a vertical line that connects the rating marks from the top of the chart to the bottom of the chart, a clear picture can be quickly seen on where the company stands in the area of social responsibility.

The application and use of Table 2 need not stop here; it can be further slightly modified and used for monitoring, measuring, and appraising specific areas of social responsibility compliance. For example, Table 2 can be simply modified to examine any specific area of social responsibility. If the company is in any way involved in a product that might result in air pollution, then Table 2 can be modified as shown in Table 13. Table 13 is just a sample to show that a similar table can be generated for any areas of social concern. It can remain as simple as Table 13 or it can be developed into a much more complex check list with several subsections or categories under the major areas of planning, organizing, directing, and controlling.

SOCIAL AUDIT APPRAISAL AND EVALUATION

Once the social audit is completed it must be appraised and evaluated. The depth, the detail, and the completeness of the audit that is desired must be reflected in the makeup of the initial audit measuring and monitoring procedure that is used. A detailed appraisal and evaluation cannot be obtained from a simple measuring and monitoring program.

The literature describes numerous approaches that show how to appraise and evaluate the social audit and determine the company's true involvement in the social responsibility arena. The major contributions in this area will be combined and condensed into four representative approaches. The first three approaches emphasize use of quantitative methods, whereas the fourth approach simply lists what the company has done in this area.

Cost of, or Outlay Approach, of Social Programs

Not only are the responsibility activities of the company listed, but expenditure data are shown for each social responsibility area. Under this method, the company can show outside sources how much money the company has committed to each specific social responsibility area.

One weakness with this approach is that while it may show how much money has been spent on the program, it does not show how effective it has been.

Program Management Approach, or Value Approach, of Social Programs

This approach also lists the social responsibility activities of the company and takes a look at their costs, but it goes one step beyond this by attempting to evaluate the social programs in terms of the value they are to the company

Table 13
Typical Strengths and Weaknesses in Planning, Organizing, Directing, and Controlling Air Pollution

	Strengths	Rating Scale 7 6 5 4 3 2 1	Weaknesses
PLANNING	A committee or organization studies, evaluates and prepares legal interpretations, practices and codes on air pollution to be adhered to by the company.	— — — — — — —	No formal committee or organization studies, evaluates, and prepares legal interpretations, practices and codes on air pollution to be adhered to by the company.
ORGANIZING	There is a clearly defined written policy on air pollution controls and standards.	— — — — — — —	There is no clearly written policy on air pollution control and standards.
DIRECTING	The president and all management levels firmly support direct adherence to all air pollution requirements.	— — — — — — —	Little or no direction or support is given with respect to conduct, penalties, or punishments to be taken by management and/or employees in the area of air pollution compliance.
CONTROLLING	All key company personnel are required to know, measure and record in the authorized record book (on an hourly basis) the level of specified pollutants.	— — — — — — —	There is little or nothing known about air pollution level requirements, the need to record air pollution levels and compare against standard levels, or how to take remedial action if it becomes necessary to take such action.
	All deviations above standard levels must be reported immediately to proper authorities and proper remedial action taken.	— — — — — — —	
	All standards and controls are in place.	— — — — — — —	

in the areas of goodwill, loyalty, and trust that is engendered throughout the community, the customers, the suppliers, and the employees.

Although the first part of the concept is quantifiably measured, the goodwill, trust, and so forth part of the program involves much value judgment.

Cost-Benefit Analysis

This is a fairly ambitious quantitative approach. It involves sophisticated quantitative measures and techniques of each of the social responsibility areas in determining the costs and the total benefits of the program relative to the investments made in the programs.

This is the most detailed approach yet discussed, but again it has its problems associated with it. The major problem areas revolve around the area of quantifying the benefits derived from a specific program.

Inventory, or Descriptive Approach, of Social Programs

This is the simplest approach and the only one that has no quantitative analysis associated with it. All that is required in this approach is to list and describe the programs in which the company is involved. This list can then be used to inform the public of the various programs in which the company participates.

The major weakness with this approach is that it does not inform either the company or the public of the extent to which the company is involved in social programs or the effectiveness of the programs.

SCENARIO

You are a May MBA graduate. You are the first MBA student hired by a small conservative manufacturing company. The management of the company is not quite certain what to do with their first MBA.

One of the vice presidents has a brilliant idea. The company has no formal social responsibility or social audit program and the local minister on the board of directors has been pushing for such a program for the company. Since MBAs learn all about social responsibility and ethics in school (don't they?) why not put our new MBA to work in this area. The vice president's suggestion carries and you are assigned the task to come up with a social responsibility and social audit program for the board of directors meeting in mid-September.

How would you approach the problem? What social areas would you include in this program and why? Who would you talk to in preparing the program and to what depth of analysis would you go? How would you present your suggested program at the meeting (you have one-half hour in which to present it)? How will you handle the rebuffs and negative responses to all or parts of the program?

NOTES

1. Keith Davis and Robert L. Blomstrom, "Implementing the Social Audit in an Organization," *Business and Society Review* 16 (1975):13.

2. Theodore J. Kreps, "Measurement of the Social Performance of Business," Monograph no. 7, *An Investigation of Concentration of Economic Power for the Temporary National Economic Committee* (Washington, D.C.: U.S. Government Printing Office, 1940).

3. Howard R. Bowen, *Social Responsibility of the Business* (New York: Harper and Row, 1953).

4. Davis and Blomstrom, "Implementing the Social Audit," pp. 13–18.

5. Scott S. Cowen and Mitchell G. Segal, "Corporate Responsibility: Part I—In the Public Eye: Reporting Social Performance," *Financial Executive* 49, no. 1 (1981): 10–16.

15

The Future of Social Responsibility

Agree with it, disagree with it, like it, or dislike it, social responsibility and social responsiveness are here to stay and everyone must live with them. This does not mean that if there are parts of them with which one is not in full agreement that one should not try to do something to correct or modify them.

Government, business, and society are going to have to work together more closely in the future if reasonable standards and progress are to be made in this area. To amplify and clarify what is meant here, a standard four-quadrant box and grid network can be constructed. Call the base axis "concern for society" and the vertical axis "concern for profits and economics." If the crossover point of the two axes is called "no concern, or zero concern," and the extreme right end of the base axis and the extreme top of the vertical axis are labeled "high concern, or maximum concern," then the basic box and grid is assembled. As in the Blake-Mouton grid discussed in Chapter 6, the ideal point on this social responsiveness grid would be the upper right-hand quadrant, where both social concern and economic and profit concern would be maximized. Overemphasis would be placed on social welfare in the lower right quadrant of the grid, overemphasis would be placed on business in the upper left quadrant of the grid, and little concern or emphasis would be placed on either business or society in the quadrant touching on the crossover axis. What all parties involved must work for is a meeting of the minds so that all programs end up in the upper right quadrant of the grid. This is, of course, easier said than done. It should, however, be a goal toward which to work.

CHANGING VALUES

Values in the areas of government, business, education, religion, work force, and society have been changing with time. If these changes are in undesirable directions to those who read this book, then they still have an opportunity to help change them in the direction they wish to see them go.

Government

If government continues in the direction in which it has trended over the past 50 years, it will only get more powerful, more oppressive, and more righteous than it already is. There is no argument that there were many social ills that needed to be rectified and still do need to be improved upon. Business certainly has some responsibility to society in helping resolve these problems, but as Jerry McAfee, chairman of the board and chief executive officer of the Gulf Oil Corporation, implies, society also has some responsibilities to business. If government and society will work with business then everyone can fulfill their commitments and obligations. He lists five responsibilities government and society have to business: (1) setting rules that are clear and consistent; (2) keeping the rules technically feasible; (3) making sure the rules are economically feasible; (4) making the rules proactive not retroactive; and (5) making the rules goal setting, not procedure prescribing.[1]

If the above five recommendations are honestly implemented and adhered to by government and business, they can go a long way toward reducing the adversary relationship that still persists between government and business in many areas. There also continues to be considerable talk and lip service about business and government working together more closely and being more cooperative with one another like that found in Germany and Japan; however, unless there is a big change in government attitude in this country, it does not appear that this level of cooperation will take place in the near future.

Business

Foreign and domestic takeovers are continuing. Businesses are growing larger and controlling larger segments of the market, and foreign business takeovers in the United States are growing at a much more rapid rate than is the growth of U.S. companies in foreign lands.

Up until recently, productivity increases of companies in foreign countries far outpaced productivity gains in this country. Only in the past year have productivity gains in the United States exceeded those in other countries.

Imports continue to exceed exports due to the still relatively high value of the dollar and the restricted performance of United States industry. Increased inflation is knocking on the U.S. door.

Many of these problems can be minimized, but not eliminated, by increased worker-business involvement and cooperations with one another in helping increase productivity and sharing the fruits between business, workers, and society. This is not, and has not, been strictly a business-generated problem but is one shared by all sectors of the economy; however, business must do much of the leading in this area.

Education

Education is one of the areas of biggest change. Knowledge of history, geography, the classics, ethics, morals, government, social concepts and values, and how business works has reached an all-time low. Allan Bloom charges that students ignore history and that universities lack moral purpose.[2] On a nationwide test of history and literature given to 7,800 high school juniors, not one in three knew in what half century the Civil War took place, and only 31 percent could identify the Magna Carta.[3] Only 55 percent of the students answered the history questions correctly and 52 percent answered the literature questions correctly. In another set of tests where the students ranged in age from 18 to 54 and had completed at least one quarter of college work, large numbers of students said Dwight D. Eisenhower was a 17th-century president, Ralph Nader was a baseball player, Charles Darwin invented gravity, *The Great Gatsby* was a magician in the 1930s, Sid Caesar was an early Roman emperor, and Pablo Picasso painted masterpieces in the 12th century.[4]

In the area of teaching morality and values in the classroom there are also problems. A nationwide poll showed one-third of young adults felt that it was okay to steal from an employer.[5] A Gallup poll showed Americans overwhelmingly want schools to help their children develop the right moral guidelines.[6] This is not easy, however. The "Ten Commandments" and prayer have been removed from the school system; John Dewey's teaching of humanism and relativism still permeates the school system as does Jean-Paul Sartre's existentialism. On top of this, in recent years, psychologists challenged and replaced previous moral education and standards of restraint and control with values that said " . . . sexual restraint was not necessarily the best option for children, that moderate drug use could be salutary, that some forms of destructive behavior seemed a therapeutic function, or at least constituted self-expression."[7]

Even more recently, a new system of value education has been introduced into the school system and has gained great influence in teacher training schools. It is called "values clarification" and rather than being taught as a separate course in most schools, it is a methodology of learning that is promoted in courses that prospective teachers take. Although it claims to be a theory of moral education, it has the reverse affect; it focuses on procedures and is indifferent to outcome—this is part of its appeal. In this system "Teachers should try to 'flush out' or clarify students' own value systems; they should 'be concerned with the process of valuing and not particularly with the product.' "[8]

As an example of what happened in one values clarification class, students concluded amongst themselves that a fellow student would be foolish to return $1,000 dollars she found in a purse at school.[9] What does the teacher do here? The teachers are taught that if they come from a position of what is right or wrong then they are not truly a counselor but are setting themselves up as judges. Go one step further. Suppose this same class or an individual therein decides that as a result of their values clarification that it is all right to bring "crib" notes to a test and to use them if needed. If the teacher says that this is dishonest and he or she will not tolerate this, then is the teacher imposing his or her value clarification on the student because the teacher is in a position of power to do so or is it an attempt on the part of the teacher to teach a minimal level of morals and ethics. How far can the student or the teacher go under this system without "infringing" on the rights of the others? Is the teacher a "bully" if he or she insists on honesty? Is there to be no right or wrong or ethics or moral principles taught or upheld in the present day school systems? Without being taught adequate moral and ethical standards upon what does a student base his or her value? How can business expect honesty, integrity, and moral and ethical behavior out of employees in the future if they are not exposed to right and wrong in everyday life? The result of this technique is the same as earlier versions of "everything is relative," "there are no absolutes," 'think whatever you want," "do your own thing," and "history and experience, and teachings of the elders, is mean- ingless." Perhaps, as a minimum, it would be a good idea to get the "Ten Commandments" put back up again in all school classrooms.

Another point to ponder is, why were 5 of the 10 winners of the latest Westinghouse Science Talent Search students who were born in foreign countries or children of parents who were born in foreign countries? Perhaps it can be partially explained by an announcement that was made in Washington by the National Science Foundation on the same day the Westinghouse an- nouncement was made in Washington. The National Science Foundation, in measuring educational achievements around the world, found that in knowl- edge of chemistry, American twelfth graders placed eleventh on a 13-country list and in biology they finished in last place.[10] Most high school students in the United States get only one or two years of science at most; in Romania they are expected to take six or seven years of science. Deficiencies in science start prior to high school; science interest is usually stimulated at an early age. Yet according to a recent study conducted by North Carolina's Research Triangle Institute, only one in three grade-school science teachers has taken a college chemistry course, and only one in five has had college physics.[11]

As sad and depressing as all of the above sounds, William J. Bennett, Secretary of Education, believes that the children can get a better education than they now get if parents and taxpayers demand greater results from teachers and school administrators.[12] In addition to teaching the three basic "R's" he feels that much improvement also can be achieved in ethics, morals, and other areas through merit pay, teacher recognition, and contracts awarded on the basis of teacher performance. When asked if teachers complaints about being underpaid were justified and if increased pay would help, his comments were:

I'll say again what I have been saying for years. I think our very best teachers are underpaid. I also think a large number of mid-level teachers who are quite adequate to the task are being paid adequately. . . . But that 10 percent, 15 percent or 20 percent of the teachers who are not doing a good job with their students are overpaid by the entire amounts of their salaries.[13]

Bennett's solution to the problem is to pay the first-rate teachers more, pay the middle-level teachers what they are now getting, and get rid of the incompetents.

For a teacher's point of view on the same subject, a recent survey conducted on 13,500 public school teachers by the Carnegie Foundation for the Advancement of Teaching found that the majority of the teachers feel that student achievement is up, educational goals are more clearly defined, more is expected of students, and school leadership has improved. In spite of these positive achievements, the majority of teachers surveyed feel that they have been bypassed, their workloads have not improved, regulations have increased, and overall working conditions have declined. Fifty percent of the surveyed teachers gave education reform at "C," 13 percent a "D," and 6 percent a failing grade.[14]

In examining both sides of the issue, it appears that all is not yet well in schools, although some progress is being made and there is still a long way to go. Now that things are starting to move in the correct direction it is time for business, government, and society to work together more closely and keep the improvements moving in the correct direction.

Business is not entirely off the hook in the area of education. American Assembly of Collegiate Schools of Business (AACSB) very heavily pushes the teaching of "organizational behavior" courses in management even at the expense of "principles of management" and other structural foundation management courses. It does very little good to have an employee or student know how to behave or treat an employee if they do not even know what an organization structure is, what difference there is between a formal and an informal organization, how how staff and line positions differ. Yet many behavioral management courses do not discuss these subjects and many behavioral management textbooks devote only a few or no pages on these very fundamental management operational concepts. In a survey conducted in 1983–1984 amongst employers and graduate students, they both listed courses in "organizational behavior" well down on their list of most important areas of knowledge.[15] Employers ranked "organizational behavior" eleventh and "management principles" fourth, while graduates ranked "organizational behavior" tenth and "management principles" eighth.[16]

If employers would prefer colleges to teach subjects in certain areas, why do they not then express their views more forcibly? This subject area was debated in two articles that appeared in the July-August issue of *Harvard Business Review*. Milton Friedman commented "Businessmen support their enemies. They support people who are undermining the basis of the free enterprise system on which their future depends."[17] This quote is based on the fact that many corporations are providing support to universities who are hostile to and/or lack basic knowledge in the competitive enterprise system. In most colleges the professors who are classified as "liberals" far outnumber the "conservatives."[18] The major thrust of the article on why business should continue to support universities that are in many instances hostile to the competitive enterprise system is that if business attempts to dictate to educators what they should do it will drive a wedge between them and industry.[19]

Business can combat this by either being more forceful with universities in what is being taught, withdrawing their support from universities, or working with them to make certain that the true story is taught. Many businesses today are working with and helping universities set up special "centers for economic education." These centers bring in public and private school teachers and teach them the basic facts about what is going on in the business world; these teachers then go back into their school system and dispense the updated information to their students. Since most of these centers are supported from contributions from industry, universities are happy to get the extra money they generate.

Much of business also has been lax in the area of communicating social responsiveness on their part and educating the employees and the outside world on what is going on in this area. This can be improved through the use of house organs, annual reports and shareholders reports, special social responsiveness reports, speakers bureaus, and advertising and public relations firms.

Religion

The Judeo-Christian work ethic and ethical-moral standards upon which this country was founded and under which it operated and prospered for most of its existence have been and are being beaten down and removed from the American culture in case after case through judicial decisions and rulings. Prayer and teaching of Judeo-Christian principles, as well as the Ten Commandments have been removed from the school system; it has been replaced by philosophies of relativism, humanism, existentialism, and values clarification. The general details of how all this came about and its negative impact on U.S. business and society have been outlined and discussed throughout the book.

Possibly a look at union history and development can offer some clues as to what might be done in this area. Unions were consistently thwarted from achieving their goals and objectives through repeated defeats at the hands of judicial interpretations of the courts. It was not until favorable legislative laws were passed that the unions were able to make many of their social gains. It seems like there might be a lesson to be learned here from the unions for those fighting for corrections in the education system and the return of Judeo-Christian rights in the school system, the churches, and society as a whole.

Work Force

As discussed in earlier chapters, the work force is becoming younger and more highly educated. The trends in population growth over the next few years, by age groups, as depicted by the Bureau of the Census, U.S. Department of Commerce, are as follows. Ages 1–19 show slow growth; 20–44 show rapid increase; 45–59 show slow increase, as does the age group over 60. A larger percentage of the work force is now also being made up of native-born Americans and by women.

Without a large influx of foreign labor, the increased education levels and the younger age levels means that labor will be more demanding upon management in the future. It also means that with the rapid growth of population in the 20-to 44-year-old age groups that there will be a larger and more intense demand for existing middle and higher management positions. Unless industry is able to expand rapidly, this could create some serious management problems in the next 10 to 20 years. Even further down the road, with the small growth in population in the 1- to 19-year-old bracket, there could be a shortage of capable people if management does not start preparing for that situation now.

Society

"Society" as discussed in this section will refer to the stakeholders. Great steps forward have been taken by business in bringing the stakeholder into its confidence and attempting to grant them many of their desires. Much has been done and more needs to be done; however, care must be taken that the stakeholders do not go overboard and demand from industry more than they truly need or deserve. Society must also exhibit some restraint and patience in their demands on business. Unless it is a life-and-death situation, it will do little good to force a company out of business by demanding immediate changes when corrections over a limited reasonable time would accomplish the same thing, keep the company in business, and save many jobs. This is not to say that where stakeholders have a legitimate problem or complaint that they should not take appropriate action to rectify the situation.

Society's demands on industry have been extensive and industry has tried in most instances to respond favorably to this initiative. In some instances these demands have caused the stakeholders new problems, for which they blame industry. One instance is the case of home fast food preparation and the extensive use of plastic containers. On the one hand, it has helped working people to have good meals on short notice, but has caused trash and garbage landfill problems as a result. As in all other situations, it is again emphasized that all parties involved must cooperate and work together to solve the problems—not just yell at each other.

EPILOGUE

This book has tried to present a little bit of the history and background as well as the present day status of what the area of social responsibility is all about. From time to time it also presents some of the author's and other people's views on what steps might be taken to improve existing situations.

In some areas, vast improvements have been made; in other areas it appears that the remedy has been worse, or at least created more or worse problems than it fixed. Only by continued and improved effort and cooperation on the part of government, business, and society can meaningful progress be made.

Those companies who have been able to do so have been going to the step beyond social responsibility to what they call social responsiveness. This is where the company makes itself aware of social problems and responds to them in a constructive manner before the government or society forces them to do it. If a company can afford to do this, it also usually works out to be a useful, profitable, and competitive tool.

Finally, vast progress has been made in many areas of social responsibility; however, further progress is needed. In some cases a step backward may be more beneficial than two steps in the direction now headed. Also, in the areas of overlapping responsibilities and decision making, a good look at these areas is needed for an improved integrated operating mechanism.

NOTES

1. Jerry McAfee, "How Society Can Help Business," *Newsweek* 92, no. 1 (1987): 15.

2. "A Nation That Has Lost Its Intellectual Bearings," *U.S. News & World Report* 102, no. 18 (1987): 73.

3. "What Americans Should Know," *U.S. News & World Report* 103, no. 13 (1987); Robert Clerc, "Schools Fail the Humanities," *Cincinnati Enquirer,* September 15, 1987, p. A–10.

4. Jaime M. O'Neill, "No Allusions in the Classroom," *American Legion Magazine* 124, no. 5 (1987): 16.

5. Robert Webb, "Teaching Morality in Schools," *Cincinnati Enquirer,* November 6, 1988, p. A–16.

6. Ibid.

7. Gary Bauer, "Teaching Values in the Nation's Classroom," *American Legion Magazine,* April 1987, 32.

8. Ibid.

9. Ibid., pp. 32, 33.

10. Lew Lord, Nancy Linnon, et al., "What Puts the Whiz in Whiz Kids?" *U.S. News & World Report,* March 14, 1988, pp. 48–58.

11. Ibid., p. 55.

12. "Let's Get Back to Basics!" *American Legion Magazine,* November 1987, pp. 18, 19, 48, 50, 52.

13. Ibid., p. 19.

14. "Most Teachers Give Reform C or Worse," *Cincinnati Enquirer,* May 22, 1988, p. A–7.

15. Marjorie G. Prentice, "An Emperical Search for a Relevant Management Curriculum," *Collegiate News & Views* 37, no. 2 (1983–84): 25–29.

16. Ibid., p. 26.

17. Robert H. Malott, "Corporate Support of Education: Some Strings Attached," *Harvard Business Review,* 56, no. 4 (1978): 133–138.

18. Ibid., p. 136.

19. Louis W. Cabot, "Corporate Support of Education: No Strings Attached," *Harvard Business Review,* 56, no. 4 (1978): 139–144.

Name Index

Subject Index

About the Author

JERRY W. ANDERSON, JR., is Chairman of the Department of Management at Xavier University in Cincinnati. He has published numerous articles in publications such as *Business Horizons, Energy Management, Midwest Academy of Management, American Society for Training and Development, USA Today,* and *International Academy of Management and Marketing.*